THE *Millennium* CHAMPAGNE & SPARKLING WINE GUIDE

THE *Millennium* CHAMPAGNE & SPARKLING WINE GUIDE

DK PUBLISHING, INC.

A DK PUBLISHING BOOK

Project Editor Rosalyn Thiro
Art Editor Anthony Limerick
Senior Designer Tessa Bindloss
Editors Lesley McCave, Clare Pierotti
DTP Designer Lee Redmond
US Editor Mary Sutherland

Maps Chris Orr
Map of Reims Stephen Conlin
Additional Illustrations Sarah Young

Reproduced by Colourscan
Film outputting bureau Graphical Innovations
Printed and bound by Wing King Tong, Hong Kong

Visit us on the World Wide Web at http://www.dk.com

Published in Great Britain by Dorling Kindersley Ltd.

Library of Congress Cataloging-in-Publication Data
Stevenson, Tom.
The millennium champagne and sparkling wine guide / by Tom Stevenson.
p. cm.
ISBN 0-7894-3561-6
1. Champagne (Wine) 2. Sparkling wines. I. Title.
TP555.S74 1998
641.2'224--dc21 98-17158
CIP

To A. R. for suggesting SuperFizz, which evolved into this guide.

This first edition is also dedicated to the memory of the father of California sparkling wine: Jack Davies, who died after a short illness in 1998.

CONTENTS

REIMS 10 Km
CHAMPAGNE
VEUVE
CLICQUOT-PONSARDIN

PREFACE

So now we know: the *Titanic* was not launched with a bottle of Champagne, and the rest is history, as they say. What is it about sparkling wine that possessed the first person to crack a bottle on the bow of a ship? The bubbles! The same bubbles that spout a fountain over the winner of a Grand Prix. When a glass is raised, it is the incessant froth that makes sparkling wine such a wonderful *joie de vivre*, the ultimate drink with which to celebrate and toast.

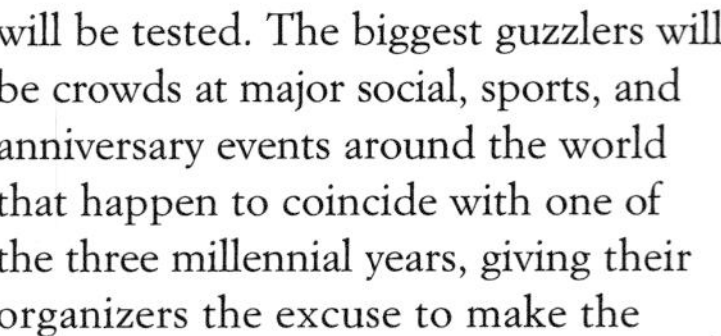

Yet, as we approach the millennium, which promises the mother of all parties, rumors are rife that real Champagne is about to run dry! In just five years, the industry has veered from an economic depression that created a crisis of mounting stocks to talk of a shortage.

More corks will fly at midnight on December 31, 1999, than at any other time, but the celebrations do not start or end there. The millennium effect will last for three years, with the end-of-century festivities in 1999, the inevitable celebrations in 2000, and a year later for those who recognize 2001 as the true Year One of the new millennium, just as AD 1 was.

However, it will not be from individuals cracking open a few bottles at midnight on three consecutive New Year Eves that stocks will be tested. The biggest guzzlers will be crowds at major social, sports, and anniversary events around the world that happen to coincide with one of the three millennial years, giving their organizers the excuse to make the events even bigger and more special than usual. More likely than not, it will be genuine Champagne that flows freely at such times. But fear not – this enormous demand will affect supply, but there is no real likelihood of Champagne disappearing from the shelves. After a few years of plummeting sales, stocks grew to one billion bottles, and production now averages over a quarter of a billion bottles each year. Furthermore, over the last decade production has exceeded demand, so that there are still about a billion bottles in stock.

Champagne *per se* will not run out. Moreover, sparkling wines from other parts of the world have never looked so exciting, with a new quality-minded generation in Germany, and South Africa about to join the ranks of established fizz industries in France, Italy, Spain, the US, and Australasia. However, special vintages and *cuvées* are always in high demand and will certainly be depleted over the next few years. Hence, *The Millennium Champagne & Sparkling Wine Guide* has been conceived to help you choose the very best fizz, whether you want to drink some now or lay some down for those once-in-a-lifetime occasions.

Tom Stevenson

Champagne Vilmart looks to the third millennium with its 1990 Cuvée Création.

INTRODUCTION

A brief history of sparkling wine, how it is made, how to store and serve it, and what style to choose.

A Brief History

Wines have accidentally effervesced since biblical times, as shown by "wine … when it moveth itself" (Proverbs) and "neither do men put new wine into old bottles, else the bottles break" (Matthew). But as a deliberate style, sparkling wine dates only from the 17th century.

The Champagne Riots of 1911 were all about protecting the quality of this frothy, frivolous wine *(see p20)*.

An English Invention

Until the end of the 17th century the wine made in the Champagne region of France was a murky *rosé* color, and it was still, not sparkling *(see p18)*. The first French document that mentions sparkling Champagne, dated 1718, refers to the emergence of this style "more than 20 years earlier." As French glass was too weak for fizzy wine before about 1695, and an efficient seal such as a cork was not available, sparkling Champagne's debut in France must have been between about 1695 and 1698.

The English, by contrast, already had the technology – their glass was coal-fired and strong, and they had cork – and there is proof that they used it to make still wines sparkle at least 30 years before the French. At the Royal Society in 1662, a Dr. Merret stated that "our wine-coopers of recent times use vast quantities of sugar and molasses to all sorts of wines to make them drink brisk and sparkling." There is also evidence that the English deliberately put a sparkle into the imported still wines of Champagne. In 1676 the dramatist Sir George Etherege wrote that "sparkling Champaign … makes us frolic and gay, and drowns all sorrow."

The Joy of Fizz

No other drink has develope[d] such a hedonistic image as Champagne. Winners, lovers and revelers of all kinds have been drenching themselves with it throughout the 20th century as well as imbibing it. And aficionados happily spen[d] small fortunes to savor a great *cuvée*.

Growth of an Industry

Even if the Champenois did not invent sparkling wine, they began to capitalize on their *terroir's* unique suitability *(see p16)* to the style in the 18th century. Markets were found across Europe, and Americans took to it soon after George Washington served it in 1790. In the 19th century sparkling Champagne was exported under the *marques* (names) of famous houses, and most of the civilized world began to drink it in quantity.

Champagne is so extraordinary a wine that its greatest role has become one in which it is not drunk at all, but dashed against the side of a ship about to be launched.

The secret of sparkling winemaking leaked out to other wine regions in France and Germany by the 1820s, as far as America by the 1840s, and all the way to Australia by the 1850s. At the turn of the 20th century Champagne was enjoying its Golden Era, turning over 30 million bottles a year compared to 600,000 a hundred years earlier. The technology to produce sparkling wine on a vast commercial scale was available to all wine-producing countries, and the world was awash with bubbles.

Sparkling wine's most powerful image has long been that it is a drink for the exuberant and extrovert.

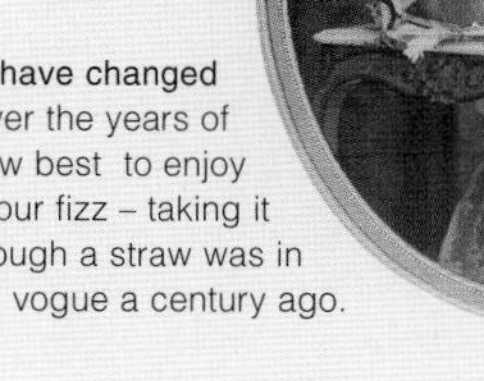

Ideas have changed over the years of how best to enjoy your fizz – taking it through a straw was in vogue a century ago.

Some brand names have become world famous.

Louis Roederer, whose monogram this is, was the favored *grande marque* of those famous hedonists, the Russian tsars. That some of their Communist usurpers also drank Champagne is not so well known.

How It Is Made

The theory behind sparkling wine is simple. Fermentation converts sugar into alcohol and carbonic gas – if the gas is set free the wine is still; if not, it is sparkling. To capture the gas, the wine undergoes a second fermentation in a sealed container. The gas gushes out in the form of tiny bubbles when the container is opened.

The Grapes

Various grapes are used, but Chardonnay and Pinot Noir are best for premium-quality sparkling wine – they are relatively neutral, with a good balance of sugar and acidity when ripe.

Cuve Close Method

Most cheap fizz is produced by *cuve close* ("Charmat" or "tank" method). Both fermentations take place in large vats, then the wine is bottled under pressure. As *cuve close* is a bulk-production method it attracts low-caliber base wines, but the speed and minimum yeast contact makes it perfect for sweet, aromatic fizz such as Asti *(see pp50–51)*.

Méthode Champenoise

The greatest *brut*-style (dry) sparkling wines are made by *méthode champenoise.* As in *cuve close*, the first fermentation takes place en masse, sometimes in oak *barriques*, but the second takes place in the actual bottle in which the wine is sold.

In the European Union the term *méthode champenoise* is reserved for Champagne. However, the terms below are all synonymous with *méthode champenoise*:

English-Language Countries

Traditional Method

France

Méthode Traditionnelle
Méthode Classique
"Crémant" appellations

Spain

The "Cava" appellation

Italy

Metodo Classico
Metodo Tradizionale
Talento

Germany

Flashengärung nach dem Traditionellen Verfahren
Klassische Flashengärung
Traditionnelle Flashengärung

South Africa

Cap Classique

There are 250 million bubbles waiting to gush out of the average bottle of sparkling wine.

Three winemakers capture the sparkle of twice-fermented grape juice.

Malolactic Conversion

Most fizz undergoes "malolactic," a natural process of fermentation that converts hard malic acid into soft lactic acid and adds creaminess to the wine. Of the few producers who prevent the malolactic, Bollinger, Alfred Gratien, Krug, and Lanson are the most famous. In the New World the malolactic is often overworked because grapes are picked early and have higher levels of malic acid.

Blending and the Prise de Mousse

The blending *(assemblage)* of the base wine is undertaken after the first fermentation. The Champenois are the masters of this and may create a nonvintage *cuvée* from as many as 70 base wines. Sugar, selected yeasts, yeast nutrients, and a clarifying agent are then added to induce the mousse. The second fermentation is often referred to as the *prise de mousse*, or "capturing the sparkle," and it can take months to complete. In contrast to the first fermentation, which should be relatively fast and warm, the second is slow and cool.

Autolysis

When the second fermentation is complete, the yeast cells undergo an enzymatic breakdown called autolysis, which is epitomized by an acacia-like flowery finesse. Good autolysis adds complexity.

Remuage and Disgorgement

In *méthode champenoise* only, the yeast deposit created during the second fermentation is encouraged down the neck of the inverted bottle into a small plastic pot held in place by a crown-cap. *Remuage* (or riddling), as this is called, takes eight weeks by hand, or eight days by machine. The sediment is removed (disgorged) by immersing the bottle in freezing brine and ejecting the semi-frozen pot without losing too much wine or gas.

The Dosage

Before corking, the *liqueur d'expédition* is added. In all cases except *extra brut* (very dry), this will include some sugar. The younger the wine, the greater the dosage of sugar required.

The Main Stages of Méthode Champenoise

First fermentation en masse in oak or stainless steel.

Bottled with sugar and yeast for second fermentation.

Sediment collected by the *remuage* method.

Disgorging the sediment for a crystal-clear wine.

The internal pressure in a bottle of sparkling wine is equivalent to the pressure of a double-decker bus tire.

STORING AND SERVING

Most fizz is best drunk within a year or so. Only a few *cuvées* are capable of developing truly complex aromas and flavors after disgorgement.

A wide, shallow glass is not the ideal vessel for drinking sparkling wine – the mousse goes flat too quickly. However, it is perfect for those special occasions when you want to stack them high and watch them froth.

WHY STORE?

Typically, Chardonnay turns "toasty" and Pinot Noir "biscuty," although the reverse is possible and even a whiff of clean sulfur can contribute to the toastiness of a wine. Some first-class Chardonnays develop specific, complex aromas such as flowery hazelnuts, creamy brazil nuts, and mellow walnuts. The greatest Champagnes can age gracefully for decades to create rich nuances of macaroons, coconut, cocoa, and coffee.

HOW TO STORE

Fizz is more sensitive to temperature and light than other wines, but there should be no problem keeping it for a year or two at any fairly constant temperature between 40 and 60°F (12–18°C). Higher temperatures increase the rate of oxidation; erratic temperatures can seriously damage the wine. If you do not have a cellar, keep it in a cool place inside a box. Very long-term storage should be at 48–52°F (9–11°C) in total darkness. There is no reason why bottles should be stored horizontally other than to save space: the CO_2 in the bottle neck keeps the cork moist and swollen even when upright. Some Champagnes have retained their sparkle for a century under ideal conditions.

Champagne *cuvées*, boxed up and ready for shipment.

Some Champagnes, such as Roederer Cristal, are shipped with a yellow, anti-UV wrapping, which you should leave on while storing. Brown-glass bottles offer better protection against ultraviolet than green-glass, and dead-leaf or dark green is better than light or bright green.

Chilling

Temperature determines the rate at which bubbles in a sparkling wine are released. Bubbly should not be opened at room temperature – the wine will quickly froth up and go flat. Chill it, ideally down to 40–45°F (4.5–7°C), the lower temperature for parties and receptions where the room temperature is likely to rise.

It is okay to chill wine in a refrigerator for a couple of hours, but try not to leave it longer than a day because the cork might stick or shrink. Emergency chilling of a sparkling wine by putting it in the coldest part of a freezer for 15 minutes is fine.

A bucket of ice and water (never just ice) is still one of the quickest ways to chill a bottle of fizz, but faster still are the gel-filled jackets that are kept in the freezer and slip over the bottle for about six minutes. Invert the bottle gently a couple of times before opening to help chill the wine in the neck.

Gel-filled jacket for efficient, fast chilling.

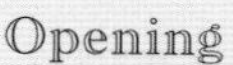

Opening

Remember that the secret of success is to try and prevent the cork from actually coming out.

Remove the foil to begin, or simply score around the base of the wire cage. Then gently untwist the wire and loosen the bottom of the cage, but don't remove it. Hold the bottle with a cloth if you are a novice, and completely enclose the cork and cage in one hand (the right, if you are right-handed). Holding the base of the bottle with your other hand, twist both ends in opposite directions, backward and forward.

As soon as you feel pressure forcing the cork out, try to push it back in, but continue the opening operation ever more gently until the cork is released from the bottle with a sigh, not a bang.

The "Champagne Star," made by Screwpull. Designed specially to open a bottle of fizz, it is the best bet for a stubborn cork.

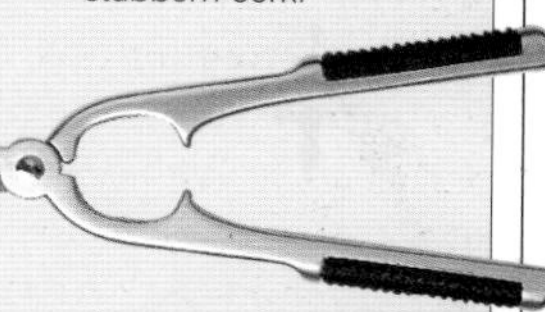

A steel wire cutter and grip for the cork – a more basic way of opening bottles.

Pouring

Pour a little into each glass first to allow for the foam, then go back and top up each one to between two-thirds and three-quarters of the glass. Do not tilt the glass and pour gently down the inside – it is not lager!

Untwist the wire and loosen the cage.

Twist cork and bottle in opposite directions.

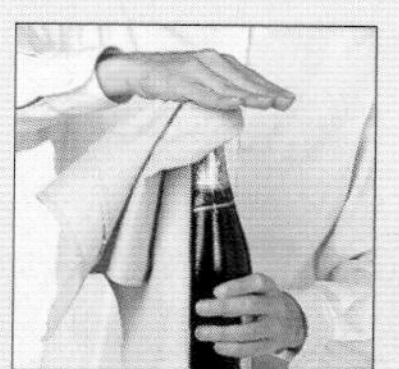

Allow the cork to be released with a sigh.

Styles

Dry *(brut)* is a classic style of bubbly, while *sec* and *doux* indicate a rising scale of sweetness. Other categories of style include the basic division of vintage and nonvintage, grape variety, color, and degree of mousse.

What's in a Vintage?

A Champagne vintage implies that the harvest was exceptional; for most other fizz "vintage" is best regarded as a statement of age, not quality. Vintage Champagne must be 100 percent from the year, but elsewhere it varies (95 percent in California; 85 in Australia). Store vintage Champagne for 8–10 years from the date of harvest. The term nonvintage (NV) sounds derogatory to many people, but wines from various years can be skillfully blended to create some of the finest *cuvées* available.

Color

Pure Chardonnay *blanc de blancs (*white wine made from white grapes) make good *brut*-style sparkling wines, and the best come from the Côte des Blancs in Champagne. In the New World, *blanc de noirs* (white wine made from black grapes) can be various shades, but in Champagne the skill is to produce as white a wine as possible from Pinot Noir or Meunier, and the most famous is Bollinger's Vielles Vignes Françaises. Champagne *rosé* can be made by blending white wine with a little red. Sparkling red wines are also available, such as Australian Sparkling Shiraz.

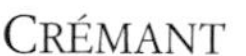

Crémant

The *crémant* style has a soft mousse, and few producers outside France have a reputation for it. Normal fizz has a pressure of 5–6 atmospheres, while *crémant* has 3.6. To be a true *crémant*, the mousse must unfold slowly, leaving a creamy cordon in the glass. Mumm de Cramant [*sic*] is the best known.

Prestige *cuvées* are particular wines that producers feel best epitomize their style. Examples are Dom Pérignon (made by Moët & Chandon), Cristal (by Louis Roederer), and

Belle Epoque (by Perrier-Jouët). They are produced in tiny quantities, and it is their rarity value that determines the high price. The selection of base wines is the most significant defining factor in any prestige *cuvée*.

The World's Best Producers

An overview of Champagne, other parts of France, and Spain, Germany, Italy, the US, Australia, New Zealand, and South Africa.

France
The Champagne Region

The world's finest *brut*-style sparkling wine is created from Chardonnay, Pinot Noir, and Meunier grapes grown on the pure chalk hillsides of the Champagne region in northern France. A fizz from anywhere else, including other parts of France – no matter how good – is simply not Champagne.

Chardonnay, whose acidity is well suited to Champagne, is cultivated across about a quarter of the AOC area.

A Unique Viticultural Region

Elsewhere in the world sparkling wine producers have to work hard to produce decent fizz, but the Champenois can make it almost without trying. The region is in a viticultural twilight zone where the vine struggles to ripen each year. Grapes eventually ripen at a relatively low alcoholic strength, ideal for a second fermentation, and have a very high level of ripe acidity, which is necessary for the wine to age well in bottle.

It is true that Chardonnay and Pinot Noir can be grown almost anywhere, and vines thrive on chalk hillsides in many places, but only in the Atlantic-influenced north of France (the country's northernmost winemaking region) do these and other factors come together, albeit precariously, with a climate that is barely on the right side of the knife-edge between success and failure. Yet the risks are deemed worth taking because, when all goes well, the result is undoubtedly the world's finest sparkling wine.

The harvest brings Champagne to life in the autumn. Even grapes from lesser years can make good Champagnes.

Veuve Clicquot *(see p34)* is one of the largest and best-loved houses, exporting its top-notch fizz to scores of countries.

OC DISTRICTS

e main Champagne districts, ompassing some)00 acres of eyards, lie within the C (Appellation d'Ori- e Contrôlée) delimited ion. Reims and Épernay the area's main towns.

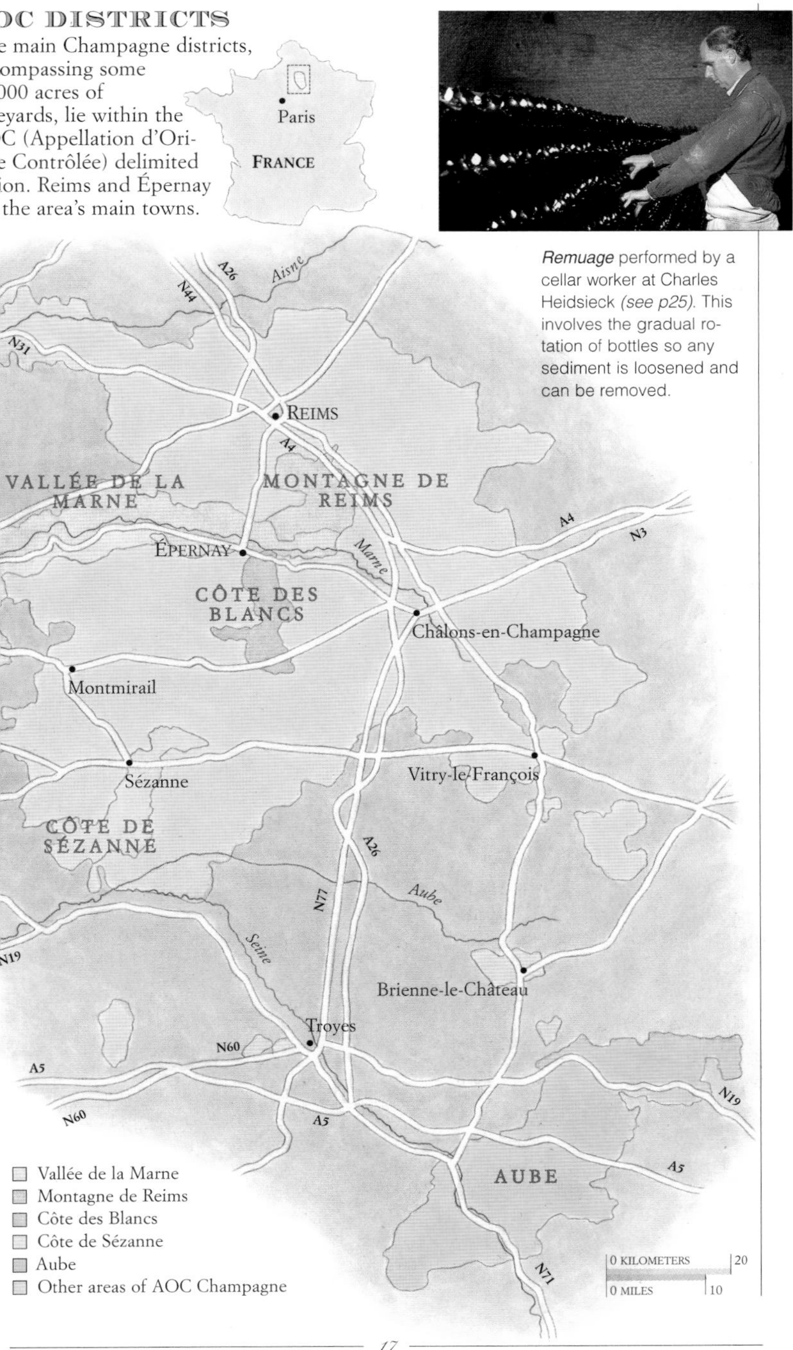

Remuage performed by a cellar worker at Charles Heidsieck *(see p25)*. This involves the gradual rotation of bottles so any sediment is loosened and can be removed.

CHAMPAGNE – A STILL WINE?

It may seem strange to us now, but the wine of Champagne was originally still, not sparkling. It was introduced in this form to the French Court – traditionally the domain of Burgundy – in the 15th century. Merchants from around Europe took this still wine to other parts of France, Spain, Italy, England, and the Low Countries.

Iron sign in Hautvillers, Vallée de la Marne.

The English are known to have put a sparkle into imported Champagnes in the 17th century *(see p8)*. Dom Pérignon (1639–1715), a monk at Hautvillers Abbey, near Reims, is widely thought to have invented sparkling Champagne, but there is little hard evidence to support this. Most French gourmands despised the idea of fizzy Champagne at the time. However, in the 18th century the habit of drinking sparkling as well as still Champagne spread across Europe and as far as Russia.

Ruinart, in Reims, was the first Champagne house.

THE FIRST CHAMPAGNE HOUSES

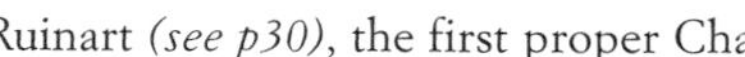

Ruinart *(see p30)*, the first proper Champagne house, was founded in 1729. Others soon followed, though the vast majority of Champagne produced was still, and this remained the situation up to the end of the 18th century. Several houses started out as textile firms, offering gifts of Champagne to customers, until demand for the gifts outstripped that for the textiles.

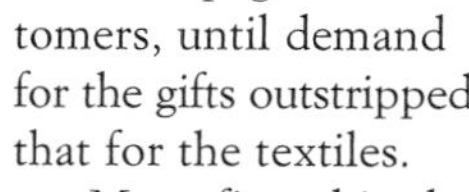

Many firms hired German salesmen, renowned for their linguistic and commercial skills, some of whom later set up their own firms in the Champagne region (such as Krug and Bollinger).

Heidsieck & Co Monopole was founded in 1834 by Henri-Louis Walbaum, a member of the famous Heidsieck family.

Best Houses

1. Billecart-Salmon p22 *Mareuil-sur-Aÿ*
2. Bollinger p23 *Aÿ-Champagne*
3. Gosset p24 *Aÿ-Champagne*
4. Charles Heidsieck p *Reims*
5. Jacquesson p26 *Dizy*
6. Krug p27 *Reims*
7. Laurent-Perrier p28 *Tours-sur-Marne*
8. Moët & Chandon p2 *Épernay*
9. Pol Roger p30 *Épernay*
10. Louis Roederer p31 *Reims*
11. Ruinart p32 *Reims*
12. Salon p33 *Le Mesnil-sur-Oger*
13. Veuve Clicquot p34 *Reims*
14. Vilmart p35 *Rilly-la-Montagne*

GRAND CRU AREA

The *crus* of Champagne are 300 or so villages whose vineyards are rated according to a percentile system called the Échelle des Crus. Of the villages surrounding Épernay and Reims, 17 have *grand cru* status – the quality of their grapes is rated 100 percent.

A decorative carving in Rilly-la-Montagne, in the Montagne de Reims district, acknowledges the village's long association with the vine.

Vallée de la Marne
Montagne de Reims
Côte des Blancs
Grand cru districts
Railroad line
• Important village

0 KILOMETERS 5
0 MILES 2

10 6 4 11 13 REIMS
14 Sillery Puisieulx Beaumont-sur-Vesle
Rilly-la-Montagne Mailly-Champagne Verzenay Verzy
MONTAGNE DE REIMS
Louvois Bouzy Ambonnay
VALLÉE DE LA MARNE
5 Dizy 2 3 Aÿ-Champagne 7 Tours-sur-Marne
Mareuil-sur-Aÿ ÉPERNAY 1 8 9 Chouilly Oiry
Cramant Avize Oger Le Mesnil-sur-Oger 12
CÔTE DES BLANCS

REIMS
Roederer Krug Heidsieck Ruinart Veuve Clicquot
BLVD LOUIS ROEDERER
BLVD GÉNÉRAL LECLERC
BLVD LUNDY
AVENUE JEAN JAURÈS
RUE DE CERNAY
RUE CÉRÈS
RUE DE VESLE
RUE VOLTAIRE
BLVD DE LA PAIX
BLVD PAUL DOUMER
RUE DU JARD
RUE DE VENISE
RUE DES MOULINS
BLVD DOCT. HENROT
RUE DE COURLANCY
RUE CLOVIS CHEZEL
0 METERS 500
0 YARDS 500

Moët & Chandon produces more than 13 percent of all *négociant-manipulant* (house) Champagne.

Champagne Takes on the World

It was not until the early 19th century, when the entrepreneurs of the most famous houses hawked their brands to all four corners of the globe, that the production and therefore name of the Champagne region became synonymous with sparkling wine. The English and Americans, especially, took to Champagne's natural appeal as a wine to celebrate with, and were drinking vast quantities by the mid-19th century. Surprisingly to us now, it was a sweet wine that they were imbibing. At the turn of the century one in ten bottles was as sweet as the dessert wine Sauternes.

In the early 20th century, as increasingly more land in the Champagne region was given over to viticulture, and the quality of the wine grew ever higher, the Champenois started to quarrel over the Champagne name. Not only were other nations calling their own sparklers "Champagne" but some houses were using grapes from other parts of France. The Champagne Riots of 1911 brought the issue to a head, with growers from the Marne and Aube fighting in the streets of Aÿ. Worse still, the vineyards were the scene of trench warfare a few years later as German forces swept into Champagne.

Exports suffered after World War I, as the Russian market collapsed and Prohibition took America *(see p54)* and parts of

Since the Americans christened Charles-Camille Heidsieck *(see p25)* "Champagne Charlie" and George Leybourne hit the boards with his celebrated song *(see p29)*, Champagne has been affectionately referred to by some nickname or other. In England, the Victorians were the first to call it fizz. The Edwardians knew it as bubbly, in the 1960s and 1970s it was champers, and in the 1980s it became known as shampoo.

The world's most prestigious wine has long been associated with celebration, romance, and general *joie de vivre.*

Théophile Roederer was once a separate company from Louis Roederer *(see p31)* but was purchased by the latter in 1907.

Scandinavia out of the equation. Domestic sales increased, however, and the Appellation d'Origine Contrôlée (AOC) rules for Champagne were drawn up in 1927. In World War II the cellars came under German control and only just escaped being blown up as the Germans retreated.

Many new markets have developed since the 1950s, but at the millennium France is drinking almost twice as much Champagne as the rest of the world put together.

There are over 9,000 brands of Champagne marketed by 2,500 houses, growers, and cooperatives. Also, there are 3,000 buyers'-own-brands, making a total of more than 12,000 seemingly different brands. With each offering an average of four *cuvées*, there are thus about 50,000 "different" Champagnes!

The Champagne Quality

The Champagne name is considered such a guarantee of quality that it is the only AOC wine not obliged to mention AOC on the label. The Champenois are not only blessed with perfect growing conditions for sparkling wine but they have also spent centuries perfecting their art. It is they who developed the *méthode champenoise* and who take the *assemblage* more seriously than other producers.

Who are the Producers?

A Champagne "house" is a *négociant-manipulant* (NM on labels) – it makes and sells Champagne using its own vineyards and buying extra grapes from small growers. There are over 250 houses, producing about 70 percent of the wines and nearly all exports. The biggest house is Moët & Chandon. Some small growers and cooperatives, collectively known as the *vignoble*, also make their own wines, mostly for the domestic market. On pages 22–35 we take a closer look at the best houses.

Gosset *(see p24)* started to make Champagne in the 16th century, though it was a still wine at the time.

BILLECART-SALMON

A SMALL, family-owned house that produces Champagne of great finesse, Billecart-Salmon is famous for its delicate *rosé*, which represents one-fifth of all it sells.

Founded in 1818, the firm says its wine "crosses the centuries..."

Nicolas-François Billecart established the house in 1818 with the help of his brother-in-law Louis Salmon, in Mareuil-sur-Aÿ, where his family has lived since the 1500s.

Billecart-Salmon's entire range will delight those who enjoy a purity and ripeness of fruit in their Champagnes, yet also want them to be able to age well. Billecart-Salmon was exceptional 20 years ago, but due to the acquisition of another 25 acres of vineyards and a constant upgrade in grapes, the wines are even better today.

Billecart-Salmon quickly gained a worldwide reputation but nearly went belly-up just 12 years after being founded, when an American agent lost the company a staggering 100,000 golden francs.

The essence of the Billecart-Salmon style has always been its meticulous production, from the double *débourbage,* or cleansing of the must, through the use of its own cultured yeast (from natural yeasts of Avize, Cramant, and Verzenay), to its long, slow, very cool fermentation. This regime was formulated by James Coffinet, the *chef de caves* under Jean Roland-Billecart until the mid-1980s. That Coffinet was headhunted by Pol Roger *(see p30)* is a testament to his winemaking skill and reputation. The fact that his successor, François Domi, has made even better wines under François Roland-Billecart should reassure aficionados of this house.

Building on its reputation for *rosé*, Billecart-Salmon introduced a superb new wine with its 1988 vintage Cuvée Elizabeth Salmon.

The Billecart house has an attractive English-style garden and the only Chasselas vine in Champagne.

BOLLINGER

The Bollinger house in the village of Aÿ was spared from destruction during the Champagne Riots of 1911. A growers' uprising had started when the government tried to bring in strict laws to control the Champagne name.

THE KEY TO "Bolly's" success is its 346 acres of top-rated vineyards, providing bout 70 percent of its needs compared with .2 percent for the average house. The keys to ts style are judicious selection of grape juice, he use of oak *barriques*, minimal malolactic *see p10)*, and extraordinary reserve wines.

Who drinks Bolly? Everyone does, among them James Bond, Prince Charles, and Joanna Lumley in the comedy series *Absolutely Fabulous*.

acques Bollinger first sold wines in 1822 or Müller-Ruinart (now Henri Abelé); even years later he formed a company vith Paul Renaudin, using the vineyards f the Comte de Villermont. The house vas called Renaudin Bollinger until 1984.

Bollinger's vintage Champagnes are ll 100 percent barrel-fermented, whereas ts nonvintage Special Cuvée is 50 ercent. Reserve wines are bottled in magnums vith a tiny dosage of sugar and yeast, which helps o keep them fresh, or *pétillant* (lightly sparkling). There are some amazing Bollinger reserves up to 80 years old, although 15 years is usually the limit set for commercial use.

Reserve wines are bottled in magnums, and some are left undisturbed literally for decades.

Lily Bollinger (1899–1977) was responsible for Champagne's most famous quote. When asked how she enjoyed a glass of Bolly she replied: "I drink it when I'm happy and when I'm sad. Sometimes I drink it when I'm alone. When I have company I consider it obligatory. I trifle with it when I'm not hungry and drink it when I am. Otherwise I never touch it – unless I'm thirsty of course."

GOSSET

JEAN GOSSET was Seigneur d'Aÿ in 1531, and his son Claude was a vigneron in 1555, but there is no proof that they traded wine. Therefore, the honor of founding the house goes to Pierre Gosset in 1584.

The temperature inside stainless-steel fermenting tanks is checked by Jean-Pierre Marson of Gosset.

As mayor of Aÿ between 1584 and 1592, Pierre had the privilege of receiving Henri IV, who in all probability drank Gosset's wine, although it was still, not sparkling, at the time. (Ruinart was the first Champagne house on record to produce sparkling wine.)

In 1992 Gosset became the first new *grande marque* (literally "famous name") for more than 30 years, although ironically the Syndicat des Grandes Marques de Champagne was disbanded in 1997.

In 1994, after 410 years of family ownership, Gosset was sold. While this was very sad, at least it was not taken over by one of the large groups. It is now owned by the Cointreau family, under the direct control of Béatrice Cointreau. The *chef de caves* and enologist remain the same at Gosset, as do the winemaking techniques, which involve the use of some wood and an avoidance of malolactic fermentation. The production level is also unchanged, at just over 500,000 bottles (similar in size to Krug). Small is indeed beautiful at Gosset, where the Grande Réserve, Grand Millésimé, Grand Millésimé Rosé, and Celebris consistently rank among the best Champagnes.

Béatrice Cointreau, who has breathed some fresh air into the Champagne trade, enjoying Gosset.

An extremely large bottle of Champagne was produced by Gosset in 1986 to celebrate the 100th anniversary of the Statue of Liberty. Made of pure crystal, the "Salomon" held the equivalent of 24 bottles of Champagne, and was 20 percent larger than a Nebuchadnezzar size of bottle.

CHARLES HEIDSIECK

THERE ARE THREE Heidsiecks in Champagne: Charles Heidsieck, Piper-Heidsieck, and Heidsieck & Co. Monopole. All three claim roots back to the Heidsieck firm established by Florens-Louis Heidsieck in 1785.

Daniel Thibault justly won the award of Sparkling Winemaker of the Year in 1994 for his contribution to nonvintage Champagne.

The first two belong to Rémy-Cointreau, a French family-owned group that includes Krug. The best of the three is Charles Heidsieck, established in 1851 by Charles-Camille Heidsieck, a grandnephew of Florens-Louis. He was known as "Champagne Charlie" in the US in the late 1850s through his flamboyant and daring lifestyle, which landed him in prison in 1861 for smuggling French company contracts through enemy lines to the Confederates.

Charles Heidsieck Reserve has been the most consistent and best-value nonvintage Champagne since the late 1980s, when Heidsieck's master blender Daniel Thibault transformed the brand. Its rich, complex flavor is tinged with oaklike vanilla, though the stainless-steel fermented *cuvée* has never seen so much as a stave of oak.

Much is made of Thibault's extensive use of reserve wines, but it is his philosophy of Champagne's *crus* (Champagne-producing villages) that has had the greatest influence. Thibault insists on emphasizing the individual characteristics of each village by allowing the fermentation to progress as naturally as possible. He wants a palate of the purest colors when he paints his blend on the canvas of a *cuvée*. To his mind, he cannot possibly produce an expressive Champagne blend if each component part has not been allowed to express itself.

Charles-Camille Heidsieck inspired George Leybourne's famous

1860s music-hall song "Champagne Charlie." For a shilling, however, Leybourne would insert the name of any other Champagne firm in his song. The most quoted version is for Moet and Shandon [*sic*], so Moët must have had more shillings than anyone else, even then.

Jacquesson & Fils

The label of the 1985 Dégorgement Tardive ("late disgorgement") depicts the gold medal awarded by Napoleon after he visited the cellars in 1810.

On July 4, 1849, the *Niantic* dropped anchor in San Francisco Bay, and her crew deserted to join the gold rush. The abandoned, beached ship was used as a warehouse, then hotel, for a few years. When the hotel was demolished in the 1870s some 35 baskets of wine labeled *Jacquesson* were found. Newspaper clippings report this wine was "so completely covered as to be almost excluded from the air, and some of the wine effervesced slightly on uncorking, and was of a very fair flavor."

IT WAS NOT UNTIL 1974, when Jacquesson was purchased by the Chiquet family of Dizy, that the foundations of the superb quality we know today were laid down.

The firm was established in 1798 by Claude Jacquesson and his son Memmie. They built about six miles of magnificent cellars in Châlons-sur-Marne (now called Châlons-en-Champagne). The "richness and beauty" of these cellars prompted Napoleon to award the house a special medal.

In 1834 Jacquesson employed a young German by the name of Joseph Krug, who later left the company to set up his own house. By 1867 Jacquesson was selling in excess of one million bottles, but after Adolphe Jacquesson died in 1875, his family chose other careers and sales dwindled. In the 1920s Jacquesson was bought by a broker called Léon de Tassigny, who moved the firm to Reims. The Chiquet family, who have owned it since 1974, have been growers for generations (their cousins, in Dizy, sell under the *récoltant-manipulant* Champagne Gaston Chiquet label).

Some of Jacquesson's base wines are vinified in large oak *foudres* (large wooden casks or vats), which are also used to store the reserve wines. This factor contributes to the great complexity that these Champagnes can have.

The Chiquet family's vineyards in Aÿ, Dizy, Hautvillers, and Avize provide the heart and soul of the Jacquesson style.

KRUG

As far as wine investors are concerned, Krug is he only blue-chip Champagne on the market: it never fails to attract bidders at auction.

Ever since the house was founded in 1843 by the Mainz-born oseph Krug, the family has put quality first, regardless of popuar taste or production costs. No better example exists of the extraordinary lengths Krug goes to than Krug Grande Cuvée, which is fermented in small oak *barriques*, eceives 35 to 50 percent of reserve wines rom six to ten different vintages, and spends about five to seven years on its yeast. With he possible exception of the tiny house of salon *(see p33)*, this sort of quality is not equaled by any other producer, although it could be if others were willing to sell tiny quantities at extremely high prices.

Krug's house in Reims *(top)* was used as a hospital during World War I. Jeanne Krug was one of the last women to evacuate the heavily shelled city. The family has its own philosophy for making wine, such as using small oak *barriques (bottom)*.

Not everyone appreciates the Krug style, but that merely makes Krug drinkers more elitist. The problem is that it is the world's most famous yet least-consumed Champagne, so it gets deified on the one hand and vilified on the other.

Most regular wine drinkers have never drunk Krug, and even the wine trade and wine writers rarely have a chance to taste it. Happily, I have tasted Krug countless times and can honestly say that I have detected a drop in quality just twice in over 20 years: namely Clos du Mesnil 1980, and a very green Grande Cuvée that was circulating in 1988, and in the twilight zone of Champagne that is as close to perfection as you can get.

Krug is served at some of the most fashionable social events in England. Guests at the annual bash of novelist and politician Jeffrey Archer are greeted with a plate of shepherd's pie and a glass of the bubbly.

LAURENT-PERRIER

Bernard de Nonancourt's Château de Louvois was built in 1680 by Louis XIV's Secretary of State for War, on the site of a ruined castle. It is said to be haunted.

THE LAURENT FAMILY were coopers in the village of Chigny-les-Roses. When, in 1812, they tired of seeing other people's wines in their own casks, they set up a house in the remains of an abbey at Tours-sur-Marne.

Eugène Laurent married Mathilde Émile Perrier, but they died without heirs. Marie-Louise de Nonancourt, one of the Lanson family *(see A–Z listing)*, bought the firm in 1938, keeping the name Laurent-Perrier. It became very successful under her son Bernard and is now ranked in the top six houses. The Laurent-Perrier group also includes De Castellane, Delamotte, Lemoine, Joseph Perrier, and Salon *(see p33)*.

The general house style leans toward light and elegant, but the vintage is fuller, while the prestige *cuvée* Grand Siècle can be almost sumptuous in its richness, attaining great complexity and finesse with age. Laurent-Perrier is also famous for its *rosé*, and it is one of the few houses to make it by the *saignée* method, whereby surplus liquid is drawn off from the fermenting vat. The nonvintage *rosé* with the salmon pink label is the best known, but the vintaged Grand Siècle Cuvée Alexandre is a class apart. Bernard de Nonancourt named it after his daughter, and no doubt his winemaker, Alain Terrier, did not dare produce anything but the best.

In the 1980s there was a trend for nondosage (extremely dry) Champagnes, which died a quick death, to the relief of many. But few people knew that Laurent-Perrier had sold a "Grand Vin Sans Sucre" a century earlier. In 1893 the firm described it as: "The natural highest class Champagne of remarkably fine flavor, taste and bouquet, without any added sugar or alcohol, shipped by Laurent-Perrier & Co. A wine of marvelously clean taste, invigorating and exhilarating properties, superior to all Champagnes containing sugar."

MOËT & CHANDON

WHILE Napoleon's patronage laid the foundations for Moët's early success, what has sealed this firm's fortune is a marketing vision that keeps it several steps ahead of the rest of the pack.

Jean-Rémy (1758–1841), grandson of the founder, Claude Moët, had one great claim to fame: his friendship with Napoleon, which had begun when the young Bonaparte was still at military school in Brienne. The Emperor would stop off at his old friend's cellars on his way to war with Prussia.

After Jean-Rémy retired in 1832, control of the house went to his son-in-law Pierre Gabriel Chandon. Later, the firm started to associate itself with another historical figure, Dom Pérignon, the 17th-century Benedictine monk from the Abbey of Hautvillers, who is credited (wrongly) with inventing Champagne *(see p18)*. Moët had the foresight to purchase the Abbey back in 1823 and happily fostered the legend. The crowning glory of this association was the use of Dom Pérignon's name for the very first prestige *cuvée*. The name had already been registered by Mercier but had never been used. Moët purchased the name in 1930 and used it in 1936 to launch their 1921 vintage (a 15-year-old wine speaks volumes of the sort of maturity expected of Champagne in those days). So successful was it that Moët was able to return to Mercier in 1970 and purchase the entire company. Moët & Chandon is now part of the LVMH (Louis Vuitton-Moët Hennessy) group.

That Moët & Chandon is Champagne's largest and best-known producer is due to ceaseless marketing strategies. From making ephemera, such as this 1920s fan, to sponsoring international sports events, Moët has made itself a household name in the wine-drinking world (though few people realize they should pronounce the "t" of Moët!).

By 1900 Moët & Chandon's small army of workers was enjoying company rights and benefits, such as sick pay, that at the millennium are still denied in many industries around the world.

Pol Roger

Pol Roger's descendants needed a presidential decree to change the family name from Roger to Pol-Roger. On labels it is still written without the hyphen.

POL ROGER was only 19 when he founded the house in 1849. His son Maurice took control in 1899 and built up the firm's reputation, particularly between the two wars in England, where it became the top-selling brand.

Maurice changed the family name from Roger to Pol-Roger. He was Mayor when the Germans occupied Épernay for seven days in September 1914, during which time he withstood German threats to shoot him and burn the town to the ground. His grateful fellow townsmen voted him Mayor at every subsequent opportunity.

The most famous admirer of Pol Roger was Winston Churchill, and he proved to be the firm's greatest promoter. In November 1944, just three months after the liberation of Paris, he met Odette Pol-Roger at a luncheon party and was so captivated by her wit, charm, and intelligence that he named one of his racehorses Odette Pol-Roger (although it always ran simply as Pol-Roger). He even ordered his supply of Pol Roger to be bottled in imperial pints, so that he could drink it even when alone.

This family-owned house continues to produce the classic quality and style that Churchill adored. These Champagnes nearly always last longer and remain fresher than those of any other house.

Churchill said of Champagne that "in victory we deserve it, in defeat we need it." His favorite Pol Roger vintages were 1928, 1934, and 1947. At the launch of the firm's Cuvée Sir Winston Churchill in 1984, Lady Soames said

of her father's passion for Pol Roger, "I saw him many times the better for it, but never the worse."

Churchill once dubbed this château "the most famous address in Europe." It is still owned by the Pol-Roger family.

Louis Roederer

Jean-Claude Rouzaud knows not to exceed 2.5 million bottles a year, lest the brand's quality and exclusivity are compromised.

THIS IS THE MOST profitable house in Champagne, and as such should be an object lesson for those houses that count success in the number of bottles they sell rather than the money they make.

The Roederer house style is typified by a creamy-biscuity complexity, which is usually apparent in its nonvintage Brut Premier but can take two to three years after disgorgement to evolve in the vintage *cuvées*. The house is famous for its Cristal prestige *cuvée*, which sells like hotcakes in the US, while its least-known gem is its Blanc de Blancs. Cristal was originally produced exclusively for the Russian Imperial Court, until the Revolution of 1917 left the firm in dire straits. Unlike today, Cristal was made very sweet to suit the palate of the tsars. The first commercial vintage of Cristal was in 1945.

Nowadays, the key to true success in Champagne, as owner Jean-Claude Rouzaud demonstrates, is an impeccable reputation to secure a premium price, enough vineyards to guarantee quality for a production that is sufficient to make a lot of money, yet the self-discipline not to go beyond this turnover. Rouzaud does not, however, like to see his capital lie idle, which is why he took over Deutz *(see A–Z listing)*. That Roederer is not in debt to the bank, when most Champagne houses have overdraft facilities, also helps. Rouzaud's biggest financial worry has been deciding when the exchange rate might be best to transfer $15 million from California to France: a problem others would love to have.

A Methuselah of Cristal 2000 is opened by one of Roederer's winemakers.

This diploma of the Tsar of Russia was issued to Louis Roederer in 1908.

Louis Roederer also owns the lesser-known Théophile Roederer, which has always been a good value Champagne brand; Château Haut-Beauséjour in St-Estèphe; Roederer Estate in California; and the Port house of Ramos-Pinto in Spain.

RUINART

THIS HOUSE WAS founded by Nicolas Ruinart on September 1, 1729, and is the oldest house to trade in sparkling, rather than still, Champagne. Nicolas's uncle, Dom Thierry Ruinart, was a contemporary of Dom Pérignon *(see p18)*.

Ruinart actually started trading in linen goods, rewarding loyal customers with bottles of his Champagne, but the wine was so good that he had more orders for it than the linen, and gradually it took over his business. Nicholas's grandson Jean-Irénée was active in selling Ruinart Champagne to such famous customers as Joseph Bonaparte, King of Spain, Joachim Murat, King of Naples, and Talleyrand. He also sold wine to the Empress Josephine, but she refused to pay her bills after the divorce. Jean-Irénée was ennobled as Vicomte de Brimont by the decree of Louis XVIII, and, as Deputy of the Marne and Mayor of Épernay, he received the Empress Marie-Louise and, later, Charles X.

This high-quality Champagne has never been produced in large amounts. Even though sales quadrupled just before its purchase by Moët & Chandon in 1963, and have almost tripled since, Ruinart's turnover is still below two million bottles, which positions it between Bollinger and Louis Roederer in size. Ruinart is known for its stunning Dom Ruinart in both *blanc de blancs* and *rosé* styles, but its basic "R" de Ruinart range is all too often overlooked, and an amazing value.

Rheims, the old-fashioned English spelling of Reims, is sometimes still used by Ruinart on its labels.

The firm's cellars *(left)*, a series of Gallo-Roman chalk pits, are officially classified as a historical monument. You must write for an appointment to visit Ruinart, but it is worth the effort to see the magnificent *crayères*.

SALON

Maxim's Restaurant in Paris chose Salon's vintage *blanc de blancs* – the only style of Champagne that Salon has ever produced – as its house wine in the 1920s.

SALON SHOT TO FAME during the 1920s and 1930s, when it was the house wine at Maxim's in Paris, but after the death of its founder in 1943 it sank into obscurity.

Eugène-Aimé Salon (1867–1943) spent much of his boyhood assisting his brother-in-law Marcel Guillaume, the *chef de caves* of a small firm producing a single vineyard Champagne called Clos Tarin. Later he purchased about 12 acres of vines at Le Mesnil-sur-Oger where, in his spare time, he set about realizing a youthful ambition: to create a perfectly balanced Champagne from a single growth and from just one grape variety, Chardonnay. He used only the best fruit and exclusively the *vin de cuvée* or first pressing, selling off the rest. Furthermore, he produced only vintage Champagne. Through such strict measures, Salon mastered *blanc de blancs* and appears to have been the first to exploit this style commercially, founding the House of Salon in 1921.

Salon was taken over by Besserat de Bellefon in 1963, but its existence remained low-key until Besserat was in turn purchased by Pernod-Ricard. Paul Bergeot, the new chairman, took an active interest in Salon, relaunching it as Salon Cuvée S in 1976. Salon was acquired by Laurent-Perrier in 1989 and run for eight years by Bertrand de Fleurian, who did all he could to affirm the ascendancy of this minute, yet extraordinary, Champagne house.

Paul Bergeot was so impatient to relaunch Salon in a new, fatter bottle, he ordered what remained of the 1971 and 1973 vintages to be decanted, mixed with a light *liqueur de tirage*, and rebottled. This caused a third fermentation and was illegal, but no one realized at the time. Thus it is possible to find "old" and "new" versions of these two vintages.

Salon, relaunched in 1976, is one of the few Champagnes that does not undergo malolactic.

VEUVE CLICQUOT PONSARDIN

The Hôtel du Marc, Veuve Clicquot's house in Reims, was bequeathed by Madame Clicquot to her business partner, Édouard Werlé.

THE NAME AND IMAGE of Veuve Clicquot Ponsardin are still identified with its illustrious 19th-century owner, "the Grande Dame of Champagne", and quality is still surprisingly high for such a large operation.

What did Pushkin, Chekhov, Ian Fleming, Alfred Hitchcock, Jules Verne, the Bourbons, Romanovs, Hapsburgs, Bonapartes, and every British monarch after Edward VII have in common? They all drank Veuve Clicquot.

It is true that a satisfying quality is simpler to achieve in a full-bodied and characterful wine like Clicquot's than it is in a lighter one (because the lighter the style, the easier it is to discern the slightest flaw). It is much harder, however, to achieve finesse in a full-bodied style. Nonetheless, what comes across about Clicquot is that it is not just big but also beautiful.

The house was founded in 1772 by Philippe Clicquot-Muiron, but it was his daughter-in-law, who took over in 1805, who really established Clicquot as one of the truly great houses. She was aided by a man named Bohne, who at first criticized the mousse of the Champagne, notably claiming "this is a terrible thing that gets up and goes to bed with me: toad's eyes!" Heeding this, she employed winemaker Antoine Müller. It was through the pair's enterprise that *remuage*, a process that draws out sediment, became widespread.

Widowed at the age of 27 ("veuve" means widow), Nicole-Barbe Clicquot-Ponsardin had become the Grande Dame of Champagne by the time of her death, over 60 years later.

VILMART

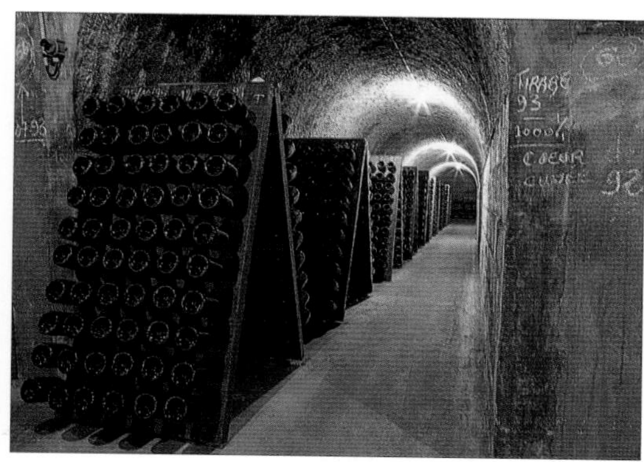

Bottles of Champagne undergo *remuage* *(see p11)* while resting at a 45° angle in V-shaped *pupitres* in Vilmart's cellars at Rilly-la-Montagne.

VILMART DATES BACK to 1890, but its breakthrough as one of the great houses of Champagne was very recent: it was only in the late 1980s that the owner, René Champs, started to make a brilliant wine.

The Champs family have always owned Vilmart, and René's son Laurent now assists his father. The location of the firm's vineyards in Rilly-la-Montagne is responsible for the fullness and complexity of its Pinot-driven style. But Vilmart's quality is less due to the vineyards' location than their low yield, which means the wine is rich and balanced by abundant ripe acidity.

Oak is another major factor. Most of the wines are fermented in large wooden ovals more reminiscent of Alsace than Champagne, but the top *cuvées* are all fermented in small oak *barriques*. Indeed, Vilmart has spearheaded a minitrend in Champagne to return to fermenting in new oak *barriques*. The policy has been implemented with too much zeal at times: the 1991 Coeur de Cuvée and the 1990 Cuvée du Nouveau Monde are too oaky.

The Champs have learned from such experiences, however, and had they not been aiming so ambitiously high in the first place, Vilmart's wines would not be as great as they are today.

René Champs is an exceptionally talented man who has designed and built his own home as well as creating a first-class Champagne. The stained-glass window showing the traditional way to crush Chardonnay grapes is just one of the building's many delightful flourishes.

This and other panes each took René Champs about 200 hours of patient and meticulous work to create.

FRANCE SPARKLING WINE REGIONS

Sparkling wines have been produced in parts of France outside of the Champagne region since at least 1820. There is a tendency to overlook French fizz alternatives, yet, of the two billion bottles of bubbly produced globally each year, the rest of France accounts for about an eighth.

APPELLATIONS

There are 50 French sparkling wine appellations. Of these, Saumur, in the Loire, is the most important and Limoux the most intriguing, but the Burgundy and Alsace appellations are more rewarding for quality and range. From the tiny region of Die comes Clairette de Die Méthode Dioise Ancestrale, one of the world's finest sweet fizzes.

ALSACE

Crémant d'Alsace, the sparkling wine appellation of the Alsace region, is dominated by the producers Wolfberger, Laugel, and Dopff Au Moulin. Dopff effectively established the sparkling wine business in Alsace in 1900. Early-picked Pinot Blanc is the most popular style. Pinot Gris makes a more superior *cuvée*, but the higher price of this grape has prevented its widespread use. Riesling is also sometimes used. *Crémant rosé* is the region's most underrated fizz: an elegant, pure Pinot Noir wine with soft strawberry or cherry fruit. Note that these wines seldom improve beyond 18 months.

Crémant d'Alsace was the first French sparkling wine appellation to adopt the term *crémant* in 1976.

Best Producers

1 Aigle (Domaine) *Roquetaillade*
2 Baumard *Rochefort-sur-Loire*
3 Bouvet *St-Florent*
4 Deliance *Dracy-le-Fort*
5 Die (Cave Cooperative) *Die*
6 Dopff Au Moulin *Riquewihr*
7 Gratien & Meyer *Saumur*
8 Picamelot *Rully*
9 Sieur d'Arques *Limoux*
10 Wolfberger *Eguisheim*

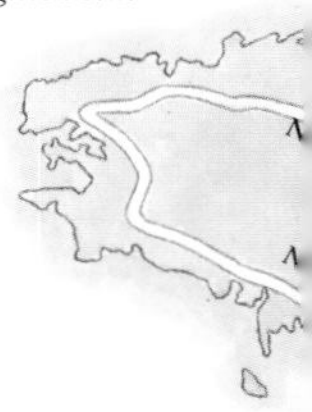

Some producers in the wir villages of Alsace make us of the extra richness and higher acidity of Pinot Gris but the grape costs 40 pe cent more than Pinot Blan

ᴾARKLING WINE ᴾPELLATIONS

ɜt of France's sparkling wines come from north and central part of the country – :hern regions such as Provence are not wn for fizz, although Limoux is interest- There are appellations for sparkling wine egions such as Bordeaux, but the best s are in Alsace, Burgundy, and the Loire.

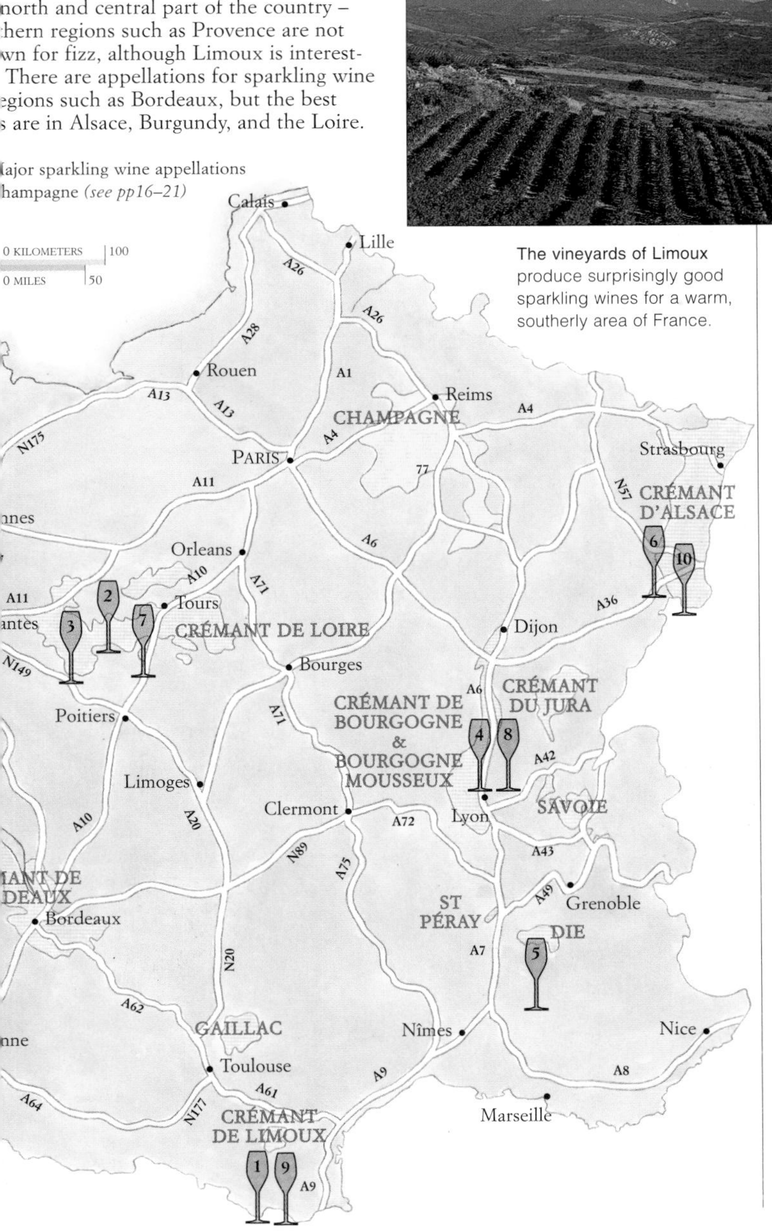

The vineyards of Limoux produce surprisingly good sparkling wines for a warm, southerly area of France.

Burgundy (Bourgogne)

There are three major production centers of sparkling wine in Burgundy: the Yonne or Chablis district, the Region de Mercurey or Chalonnaise district, and the Mâconnais. The appellation for sparkling Burgundy is Crémant de Bourgogne, which has now superseded the term Bourgogne Mousseux for all but fizzy red Burgundy.

There are some very good Crémant de Bourgogne wines, but the average quality is not as good as it should be because too many producers rely on buying grapes that are sold off cheaply after being rejected for still Burgundy. Such wines suffer from excessive sulfur levels. The sparkling wine industry in Burgundy has yet to understand that grapes must be cultivated specifically for sparkling wines if serious progress is to be made across the board.

However, when Crémant de Bourgogne is good it is usually very good and almost always a bargain. The best are invariably made purely from Chardonnay grapes. Styles range from full and toasty (often from Yonne), through rich and smooth (usually from the Chalonnaise) to fresh, light, and vivacious (mainly Mâconnais). *Crémant rosé* from Burgundy is not usually interesting, unless made from 100 percent Pinot Noir grapes. Most good-quality Crémant de Bourgogne is best consumed within three years of purchase.

The best producers include Caves de Bailly, André Bonhomme, Deliance, Picamelot, Roux Père, Simonnet-Febvre, and Caves de Viré.

The thrill of effervescing sweet wine became such a vogue in France in the 1870s that the production of another wine – sweet, still Sauternes – was under threat from the bubbly bandwagon. In *A History of Champagne* (1882), Henry Vizetelly records vast quantities of Sauternes being transported by rail to Messers Normandin Sparkling Sauternes Manufactory near Angoulême, where it was turned into award-winning sparkling wine.

Burgundy, one of France's oldest wine regions, vied with the Champagne region for royal favor in the 17th century, when both wines were still. Later, as sparkling Champagne took off, most Burgundy resolutely remained still.

Limoux

Winemaking is shown in this detail of a medieval painting from the Loire.

This small region near Carcassonne claims to have made sparkling wine more than 160 years before Dom Pérignon *(see p18)*, but this has not yet been proved. What is true, however, is that Limoux makes exceptionally fine sparkling wines for such a sunny southern location, and winemaking techniques have improved by leaps and bounds over the last decade. The style of Crémant de Limoux and Blanquette de Limoux has moved away from the distinctive character of fresh-cut grass to a much finer aroma. The best producers include Domaine de l'Aigle, Antech, Robert, Sieur d'Arques, and Héritiers Valent.

The appellation Blanquette Méthode Ancestrale, from Limoux, is made by *méthode rurale*. There is no second fermentation, which most other sparkling wines undergo. Instead, the wine is bottled before the first alcoholic fermentation is over. In the 19th century, all Blanquette de Limoux was produced in this fashion.

The Loire

If you are used to good-quality Champagne, you might find Loire sparklers difficult to appreciate. This is because the main grape used, Chenin Blanc, is too aromatic for a classic *brut* style.

Saumur is the largest French sparkling wine appellation outside of Champagne, and were it restricted to Chardonnay and Pinot Noir it would be the best. Saumur Mousseux *Rosé* can be made from several varieties, but many are pure Cabernet Franc, and the best are some of the most thrilling raspberry-flavored fizzes in the world. Some pure Cabernet Sauvignon *rosés* can also be very good, in a smoother, less overt way.

Sparkling Vouvray and, particularly, Montlouis are hard to find but can be delightfully fresh, smooth, and elegant, especially when *pétillant*. Touraine and Crémant de Loire can be good value, but too many poorly made, cheap fizzes have debased those appellations. However, there are numerous good producers throughout the Loire – too many to name here.

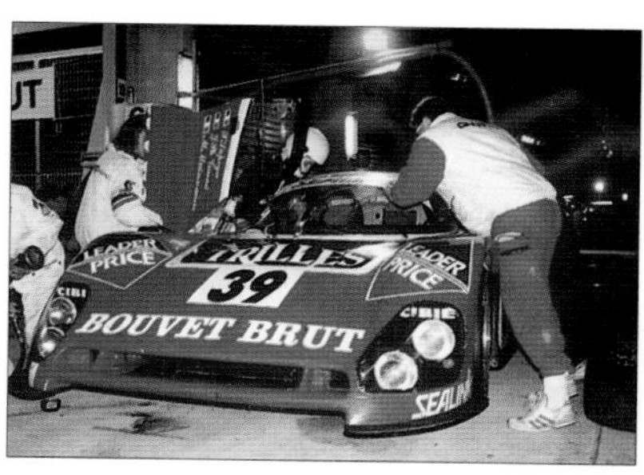

Bouvet, one of the best Saumur producers, associates itself with the sport of car racing.

SPAIN

Freixenet (pronounced roughly "freh-zhe-net") delights in a fun-loving image for its Cava.

Cava has been widely exported since the mid-1970s and is now the world's second largest bottle-fermented sparkling wine appellation. The industry is dominated by two houses: Codorníu, the oldest, largest, and most innovative firm, and Freixenet, which is probably the best known.

WHAT IS CAVA?

Cava is the generic name for bottle-fermented Spanish sparkling wine; it simply means "cellar." It was devised in 1970 for all Spanish sparkling wines made by the *méthode champenoise*, regardless of where in Spain they are made. However, when Spain joined the Common Market in 1986, Cava became subject to the EC wine regime, which is based on the integrity of origin. The EC made the Spanish choose between confining the Cava name to a geographical appellation or dropping it altogether.

This demand was cruelly ironic because at the same time the EC was failing to protect the integrity of the name "sherry" – the world's oldest geographical appellation. But Spain managed to extract its revenge simply by pinpointing every known Cava producer and drawing boundaries around individual municipalities. Cava was thus transformed overnight into a "geographical" appellation scattered across half of Spain. In practice, though, most Cava comes from the Penedès region and always has, with the area around Sant Sadurní d'Anoia producing much of the best.

VA COUNTRY

edès is Cava Country, there are pockets of a production in Rioja, 'arra, Aragón, and where. Thus the Cava ellation is geographical ' in a loose sense.

lain Cava districts

The Art Nouveau winery of Codorníu was designed in the late 19th century by José Maria Puig i Cadafalch and declared a National Historical Monument in 1976.

Codorníu began to win gold medals for its Cava in 1888.

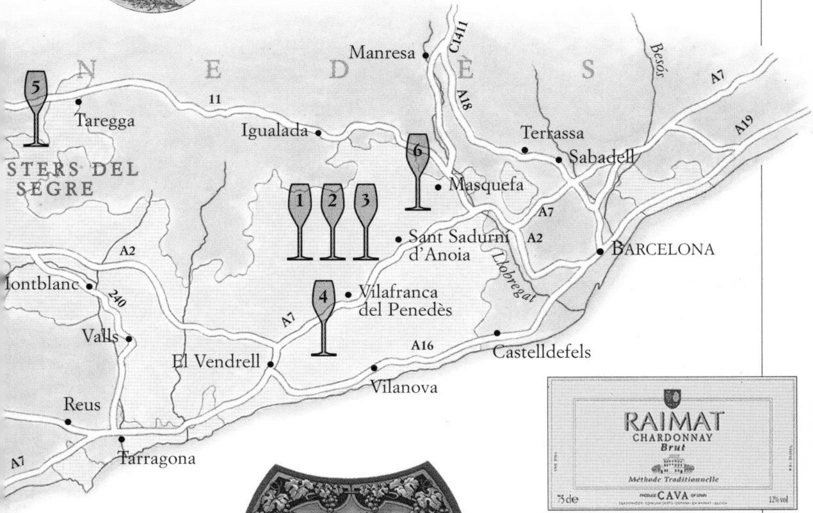

Most famous for its Cava, the Freixenet group also includes Gloria Ferrer in California, Castellblanch, and the Champagne house of Henri Abelé.

Best Producers

1 Codorníu
Sant Sadurní d'Anoia

2 Freixenet
Sant Sadurní d'Anoia

3 Gramona
Sant Sadurní d'Anoia

4 Mascaró
Vilafranca del Penedès

5 Raimat
Costers del Segre

6 Raventós Rosell
Masquefa

The Cava Industry

It was long widely believed that the first Spanish sparkling wine was made in 1872 by José Raventós, the head of Codorníu (a winery dating back to the 16th century), but recent research has revealed that it was "invented" much earlier by Luis Justo Vilanueva and first produced in 1862 by Antoni Gili. This date coincides with the migration of French Champagne producers to the region. However, there was no Cava industry as such until after World War II, and until 1974 production was so small that export statistics were not even recorded.

Gramona was founded in 1881 and started to produce Cava in 1921. The wines, shown here being corked, spend five years in darkness in Gramona's cellars before being sold.

A Soft Acidity

Cava is an obvious choice for buyers who find the acidity of even the best Champagnes too aggressive. For many drinkers, however, Cava suffers from being too soft. Not that softness is itself a shortcoming, but in a sparkling wine if the acidity is softer than the mousse, the dosage *(see p177)* will be minimal, making the wine short and hollow, with no potential for long-term maturation. Cavas that best manage to overcome these drawbacks include Codorníu, Freixenet, Gramona, Mascaró, Raimat, and Raventós Rosell.

Some of the Spanish *méthode champenoise* wines started production after the Cava boundaries were drawn up and therefore do not come under the Cava appellation. They include Xamprada (León), Oriella (Madrid), Juan de Arges (Valencia), Montsec and Ibón (Zaragoza), El Grifo (Lanzarote), and Cantares and Mantolán (Ciudad Real).

The Grapes of Cava

The three grapes used most in Cava are Parellada, Macabéo, and Xarello, which were all growing locally when Cava was first made. According to the Cava gospel, Macabéo, which is usually the base of a Cava *cuvée*, provides the fruit, Xarello the strength and body, and Parellada the softness and aroma. However, each of these grapes is problematic in sparkling wine.

The best Parellada grapes come from the highest vineyards, where they take longer to ripen.

Freixenet's headquarters are at Sant Sadurní d'Anoia, the most important Cava town in Spain, in the heart of the Penedès region.

Macabéo is not bad as a base wine, having good fruit and decent acidity, and Xarello is useful in small amounts, but Parellada has very little acidity and is prone to an internal rot that is hard to detect.

In Search of Better Grapes

Given that it took the Champenois 250 years to settle on the best three grapes for Champagne, the Cava industry has been surprisingly reluctant to try other varieties until recently. Codorníu realized the problem in the 1970s and started cultivating Chardonnay as a quality booster. Freixenet opposed this, fearing that foreign grapes would erode Cava's Spanish character (a fair point), and this stance sparked a rift between the houses.

However, this author believes that Cava can be improved through using different native grapes, especially black grapes in a white wine blend. Codorníu was the first house to try this style, and even went to the extreme of making a *blanc de noirs*, albeit with the foreign Pinot Noir, producing the most sumptuous of Spanish sparkling wines. Freixenet is now experimenting with the native black Monastrell in a white *cuvée*, which is starting to show promise.

Trepat and Garnacha have been used in experiments with *rosé* Cava. The producer Mont Marcal has used Tempranillo, the greatest of all Catalan grapes, and Can Ràfols dels Caus has even tried Merlot, both of them for pink Cava.

The Spanish terms *Fermentación en Botella*, *Vino Espumoso Natural,* and *Método Transfer* indicate the transfer method *(see p178)*. Sparkling wines stating *Vino Gasificado* or *Granvás* are carbonated in the same way as lemonade or cola.

Manuel Raventós, who took over Codorníu in 1885, commissioned posters from Catalan artists such as Ramón Casas (1866–1932).

GERMANY

Sekt, the German fizz, is now the largest sparkling wine industry in the world. In some years, production tops half a billion bottles, which is almost twice that of Champagne. However, very little Sekt has so far been exported, making this wine practically unknown outside Germany.

A German Taste

For most of the 20th century, the Germans have essentially made Sekt for themselves. The wine is off-dry with an unusual youthful tartness, which most sparkling wine drinkers elsewhere do not comprehend, let alone enjoy. Exports average barely eight percent of total Sekt sales and have dropped to as low as four percent. Yet the Germans are drinking more and more Sekt, with per capita consumption currently running at five liters, compared with less than one liter in 1960.

Early Attempts

German salesmen were widely employed by the earliest Champagne houses *(see p18)*. The first attempts to make sparkling wine in Germany date back to 1783, but because the process took a while to master, the oldest commercial producer, Kessler, was not founded until 1826. Ten years later, when it became possible to measure the amount of sugar left in a wine after the first fermentation, the number of producers significantly increased.

Sign for the town of Durbach in the southern wine region of Baden.

Best Producers

1. Deis *Mosel-Saar-Ruwer*
2. Durbach *Baden*
3. Kassner-Simon *Pfalz*
4. Kirsten *Mosel-Saar-Ruwer*
5. Knyphausen *Rheingau*
6. Ratzenberger *Mittelrhein*
7. Ress *Rheingau*
8. Winzersekt Sprendlingen *Rheinhessen*
9. Wilhelmshof *Pfalz*
10. Zahringer *Baden*

Bremm is beau fully located by the Mosel in the Mosel-Saar-Ru wine region.

SOUTHERN WINE DISTRICTS

Most of Germany's QbA delimited wine districts (Qualitätswein bestimmter Anbaugebiete) are based around the Mosel and Rhein (Rhine) River valleys in the south of the country. Sparkling wine is produced in most of these regions.

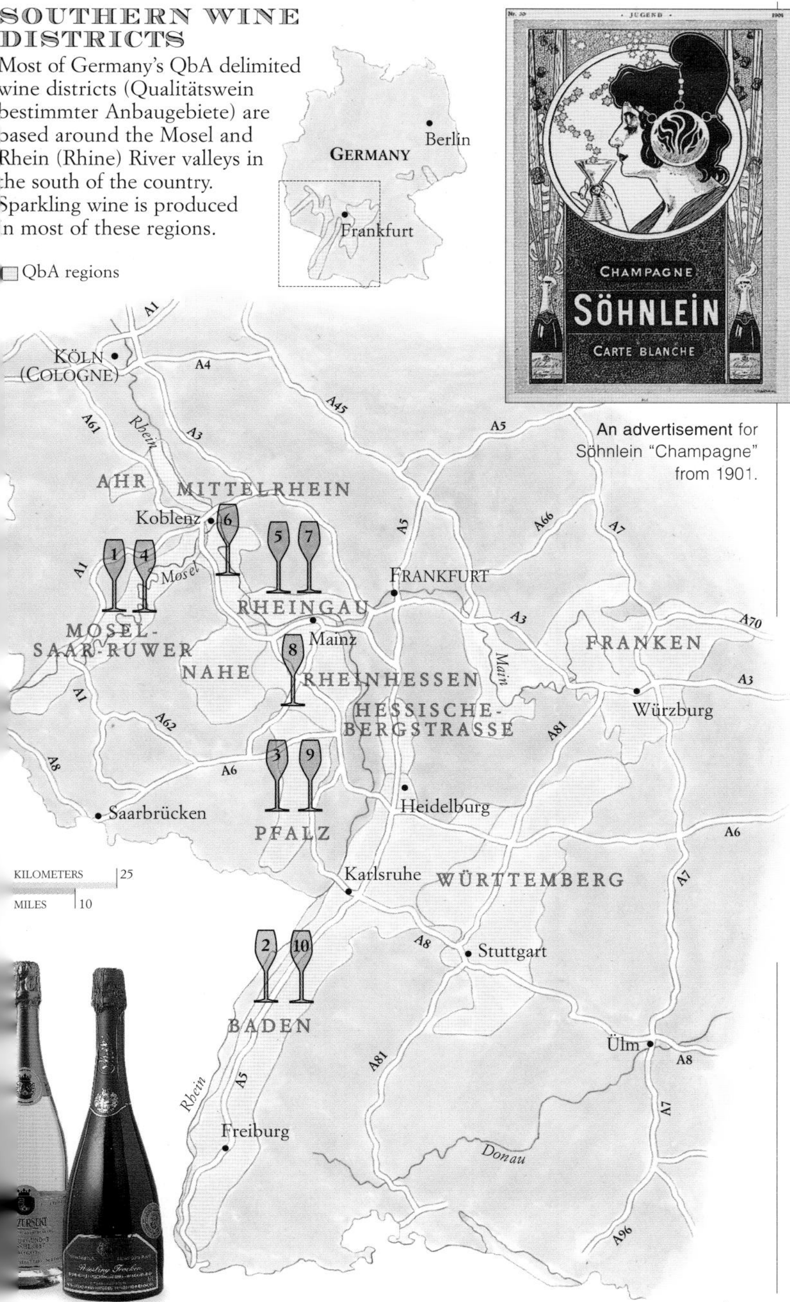

An advertisement for Söhnlein "Champagne" from 1901.

"SEKT" IS BORN

Wine presses in a museum owned by State Domaine Kloster Eberbach, in the Rheingau region.

A boom in sales came in the 1850s, coinciding with when the peculiar term *Sekt* is thought to have first been used. The classical German actor Ludwig Devrient was in the Berlin restaurant Lutter & Wegener one November night in 1852 and ordered a glass of sherry. In jocular mood, he quoted a line from Falstaff in Shakespeare's *Henry IV* to the waiter: "Give me a cup of sack, rogue. Is there no virtue extant?" Not understanding that Shakespeare's sack meant "sherry" (in turn deriving from the Spanish *sacar*: to take away or, less favorably, to loot – i.e., exported sherry!), the waiter brought him a glass of his usual German sparkling wine. After going the rounds of Berlin restaurants, it is thought that "sack" became *Sekt* and by 1900 was widely used to refer to German sparkling wine (also known as "Champagne" at the time).

The sack (sherry) of Falstaff is thought to have given its name to Sekt, in a convoluted manner.

Many of the Sekt houses that sprang up from the 1850s soon disappeared, but by 1872 production had risen to four million bottles, and no fewer than 12 Sekt houses were of sufficient size and repute to exhibit at the World Exhibition in Vienna.

Deutscher Sekt means the wine is made only with German grapes.

Rheinhessen is one of the delimited QbA wine regions.

DEUTSCHER SEKT
b.A. RHEINHESSEN
WINZERSEKT
KLASSISCHE FLASCHENGÄRUNG
SPÄTBURGUNDER
WEISSHERBST
EXTRA TROCKEN
ERZEUGERGEMEINSCHAFT WINZERSEKT GMBH · D-55576 SPRENDLINGEN

Klassische Flaschengärung is the equivalent of the French *méthode champenoise.*

The language on German wine labels is notoriously complex, and Sekt is no exception. To start, Sekt is synonymous with Schaumwein. If either term is used without qualification, the wine is probably a blend of grapes from various countries. Deutscher Sekt tells you that only German grapes have been used, and Deutscher Sekt bA and Deutscher Qualitätsschaumwein both mean that the grapes come from a specified QbA region *(see p45)*.

Moving up the quality scale, Flaschengärung means "bottle-fermented", while Flaschengärung nach dem Traditionellen Verfahren, Klassische Flaschengärung and Traditionelle Flaschengärung are all equivalents of *méthode champenoise*. Handgerüttelt means "hand-riddled", and Jahrgangsekt is vintage Sekt. At the opposite end of the scale, Perlwein is cheap, semisparkling wine made by carbonation.

Germans make merry with Sekt in this engraving from the journal *Jugend* in 1897.

)RDINARY SEKT

\lthough it started as a bottle-fermented product, irtually all Sekt is now produced by *cuve close* or ank method, and over 85 percent is made from mported foreign base wines. Most Deutscher Sekt sparkling wines made exclusively from German ;rapes) are also *cuve close* and thus little better han the ordinary Sekt of no fixed abode.

›EKT AT THE MILLENNIUM

Germany's Sekt industry underwent its largest ex›ansion in very recent times, increasing from 200 ›roducers in the late 1980s to more than 1,300 oday. Although this represents a 650 percent ncrease, total production has increased y just 25 percent, and therein lies the lue to the radical change that has ocurred at the very top of Sekt's quality cale. A small but growing band of uality-conscious estates has been craftng some truly excellent sparkling wines ince the early 1990s. Most of these are mall, go-ahead wine estates, rather than arge, old-established Sekt factories.

The most obvious development is ›ure Riesling Sekt, whereas the most unkely style evolving is pure Pinot Noir *osé*, the quality of which should bowl ›ver the most ardent Sekt-hater. It will ›ot be long before specialty importers n major export markets pick up on this emerging ew breed of Sekt. But although their numbers are ncreasing, the wines are by nature produced in such mall quantities that they will remain in short supply.

The best Sekt this author has ever tasted is the rare Wegeler-Deinhard Bernkasteler Doktor. Just two vintages were produced, 1978 and 1984, and, like Champagne, they were aged for three years but in a special vat fitted with a paddle to stir the lees.

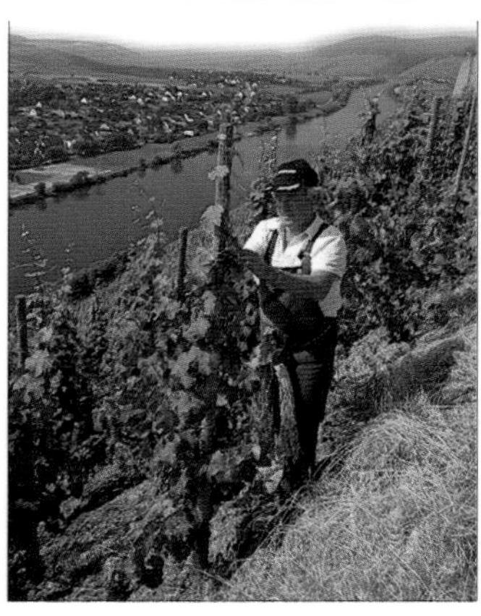

Riesling, the greatest German grape, is increasingly being used on its own to make Sekt.

ITALY

No other country has as many sparkling wine appellations as Italy, with its optional "may be *spumante*" (sparkling) clauses cluttering up more than 100 of the country's Denominazione di Origine Controllata (DOC) appellations. Yet Italy had no appellation specifically for classic *brut* sparkling wine until Franciacorta was elevated to the higher rung of Garantita (DOCG) in 1995.

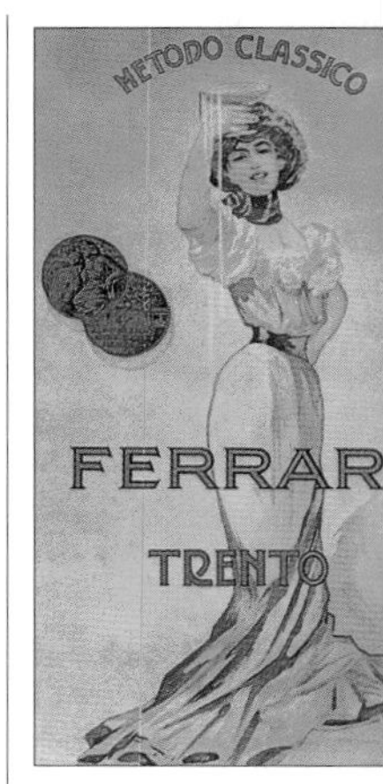

Ferrari, one of the few firm to use *metodo classico*, says that it delights in "conserving the original excellence of the *spumante*."

MYRIAD HALF-FORGOTTEN WINES

Italy's little-known sparkling wine appellations are nearly all *cuve close* (undergoing a second fermentation in a vat or tank rather than in a bottle). This is the best method for sweet sparkling wines like Asti, which has DOCG status and is Italy's best contribution to the sparkling wine world. However, *cuve close* is the worst possible method for classic *brut*. This is not because it is an intrinsically inferior method; in theory it should be able to produce *brut* sparkling wines that are every bit as good as those made in bottle, but in practice it does not. It is a bulk-production process and consequently attracts the cheapest base wines. To remedy the situation, the Italian Wine Law should require all *brut*-style DOC sparkling wines to be produced by the *metodo classico*, the Italian equivalent of *méthode champenoise*.

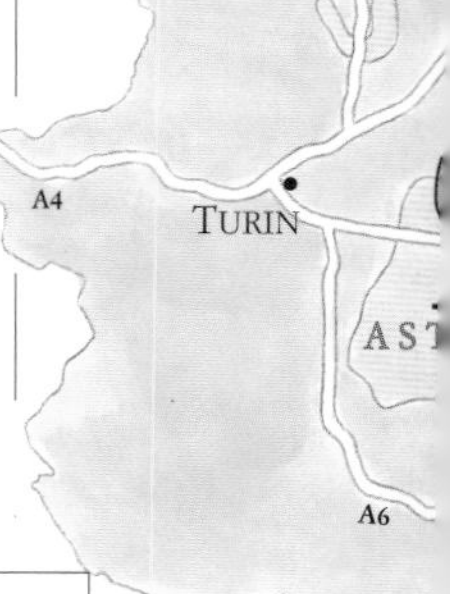

The view over Bella vista's aptly named vineyards in Lomb

ORTHERN ITALY

kling wines are made ughout Italy, but the : interesting ones are e in the north. The appellations are for sweet fizz, and ciacorta, for *brut*-style kling wine.

ain wine regions

Sophia Loren drinking classic Italian *brut* at the Venice Biennale.

Best Producers
Banfi *Tuscany*
Bellavista *Franciacorta*
Berlucchi *Franciacorta*
Ca'del Bosco *Franciacorta*
Equipe Trentino *Trentino*
Ferrari *Trentino*
Gancia *Asti*

FRANCIACORTA

The Franciacorta appellation covers various producers with vineyards on the hills around Lake Iseo northeast of Milan. The wines are made from Chardonnay, Pinot Bianco (Pinot Blanc), and up to 15 percent Pinot Nero (Pinot Noir). Franciacorta is still the only Italian classic *brut* appellation – the only wine that must be made by *metodo classico*.

The *Festa dell'uva* (Grape Harvest Festival) celebrates the wines of Northeast Italy.

Until September 1995, Franciacorta, like most Italian DOCs, was allowed to be still or sparkling. The still reds were, in fact, quite impressive. However, in a rare decision by the Italian Wine Law to put quality first, the most successful sparkling style was elevated to a super-appellation, its production restricted to the finest areas, its yield lowered, and its production method tightened up.

The still wines retain their DOC status, renamed Terre di Franciacorta. Only the sparkling wines may claim the Franciacorta DOCG. Were this uncompromising attitude applied to every appellation in the country, Italy would not only be the largest wine-producing nation in the world, as it is now, but also the greatest. With 25 months aging on its lees (if the label says *riserva* then it is 37 months), Franciacorta has the potential for producing fine, biscuity *brut*, and lightly rich *rosé* sparkling wines. The best brands include Bellavista, Berlucchi, Ca'del Bosco, and Faccoli.

The most ubiquitous cheap Italian sparkling wine is probably sparkling Lambrusco, which comes in pretty shades of red, white, and *rosé*, but much the same effect for the tastebuds can be had by putting a shot of Vodka into a soft fizzy drink.

ASTI – THE SWEET FIZZ

The town of Asti in Piedmont gives its name to the local sweet fizz made by *cuve close*. The finest Asti are the greatest sweet sparkling wines in the world – a fraction of the price of *demi-sec* Champagne, but ten times the quality. It was formerly sold as Asti Spumante, but *spumante*, which like *mousseux* in France merely means "sparkling," had become tarnished by the cheap products that also use the term, thus was dropped when Asti was promoted to the status of DOCG in 1993.

Bernhard Langer is given a silver cup filled with Berlucchi after winning the Vincitore Open d'Italia golf competition in 1997.

AC Milan shower themselves with the locally produced Ca'del Bosco after another historic win.

sti is made entirely from Mos-ato (Muscat) grapes, which come om 52 communes throughout ıe provinces of Asti, Cuneo, and lessandria. The *cuve close* meth-d of production is well suited ɔ an aromatic, sweet sparkling ine like Asti because its most ital quality – the freshness of its uit – gains nothing from the xtended yeast contact of *metodo classico.*

The best Asti has a fine mousse of tiny bubbles, fresh, grapey aroma, a luscious sweetness, and a ght yet rich flowery-fruitiness that should be ivacious and mouthwatering. The greatest examples are reminiscent of peaches, and may even have a hint of orange. One of the most important compounds in the Moscato aroma is geraniol, which is wonderful when fresh, but with bottle-age assumes an unpleasantly pungent geranium odor. Asti is not, therefore, a wine that should be kept.

Good Asti producers include Araldica, Fontanafredda, Gancia, Giuseppe Contratto, and Tosti. Gancia's special selection *cuvée*, Camilo Gancia, is a class apart.

While Asti is a pure Moscato sparkling wine, Moscato d'Asti is an entirely different product, which is not supposed to be fully sparkling, just *frizzantino* (very lightly sparkling), or even still. A Moscato d'Asti is easily recognized by its normal cork, which is fully inserted into the neck, with no mushroom top. If a wine simply states Moscato, it will be an inexpensive, fizzy blend of Moscato grapes from anywhere in Italy. Such wines rarely have the scintillating freshness of Asti, but even an average Moscato is preferable to an Asti that is too old.

Other Fizz

After Franciacorta, Tuscany and Northeast Italy are the leading areas for *brut* sparkling wines, although the grapes may be sourced from far and wide. Equipe Trentino (Trentino), Ferrari (Trentino), and Villa Banfi (Tuscany) are among the best. Of the rest, Prosecco is one of Italy's most widely available bubblies but often boringly amylic. Soldati la Scola is based in Gavi and makes various sparkling wines.

Ferrari has recently diversified its image with a range of label designs inspired by Pop Art *(left)*.

The United States

Americans were among the first to appreciate Champagne and have been producing their own fizz since the mid-19th century. The sparkling wines of California have come of age, but the states of Washington and Oregon possibly possess as much potential as their southern counterpart. A number of producers are the US arms of French Champagne and Spanish Cava houses.

Catawba, a native American grape used for both still and sparkling wines, was so famous by the 1850s that the *Illustrated London News* reported that "sparkling Catawb… … transcends the Champagne of France."

Catawba and Other Early Successes

The first American sparkling wine was made in 1842 by Nicholas Longworth, using Catawba grapes planted along the Ohio River near Cincinnati. Catawba is a native American variety with an exotic, cloying taste often described as "foxy."

The first of New York's fabled "champagnes" was made in 1865 by Joseph Masson. Five years later the Great Western Champagne brand was launched, which became the first American sparkling wine to win a gold medal in Europe. Great Western Champagnes claimed to be made in "Rheims, New York" – the winery's mailroom was cunningly named Rheims for this purpose. This "champagne" became the most important brand of sparkling wine in the country for a staggering 50 years, until Prohibition intervened.

Hollywood, eager to associate itself with rom… and the high life, strateg… places a bottle of Mumm… Bogart and Bergman.

PA, SONOMA, D MENDOCINO

ɹrnia, Washington, and ɔn are the main sparkling states, with the Napa ; Sonoma, and Mendocino cts north of San Francisco ; the lion's share.

or wine districts

Best Producers

1 Argyle *Willamette Valley*
2 Carneros (Domaine) *Napa Valley*
3 Chandon (Domaine) *Napa Valley*
4 Handley *Mendocino*
5 Iron Horse *Sonoma Green Valley*
6 J Wine *Sonoma*
7 Mumm *Napa Valley*
8 Roederer *Mendocino*
9 Scharffenberger *Mendocino*
10 Schramsberg *Napa Valley*

Carneros in Sonoma County is one of California's premier districts for sparkling wine.

CALIFORNIA

The end of Prohibition (1933) was celebrated in the most appropriate way.

The first California sparkling wine was made in about 1855 at the San Gabriel Winery, and various producers were making it by the turn of the century. The industry was going reasonably well until virtually all alcohol production came to a grinding halt in 1920. After Prohibition was repealed, in 1933, California's wine industry was painfully slow to reestablish itself. The only sparkling wine was cheap, bulk-produced, and had little to commend it.

Schramsberg was eventually the first quality California fizz. A boost came in 1973, when Moët & Chandon chose the Napa Valley to locate its first premium quality winery outside Champagne. These companies converted a sporadic production into California's fully fledged industry today. A flood of French-owned and Franco-American fizz ventures appeared on the scene in the 1980s, and the two giant Spanish Cava houses, Freixenet and Codorníu, also began to invest in California at this time. Technologically, California fizz came of age in the early 1990s, when the acidity became less "ribby" and more in tune with the fruit, giving the wines greater elegance than before. This was a surprising development because, as with many other New World sparkling wine areas, the climate is less than ideal. California producers are faced with two basic choices: pick ripe grapes that have too much sugar and insufficient acidity, or harvest much earlier, when acidity levels are higher and the grapes have an almost ideal sugar level. Unsurprisingly, most winemakers have chosen to harvest early, but they have to expend much effort overcoming numerous problems posed by grapes that have too much hard malic acid.

The clergy, of all people, demanded wine during Prohibition (for sacramental use, of course!), so a few wineries had permits for still, but not sparkling, wine for this purpose. Not satisfied with this, the Pleasant Valley Wine Company filed a suit for the right to sell bubbly to the clergy. Amazingly, it was granted. The company enjoyed a monopoly on fizz for two years until several other wineries won the same right. The end of Prohibition closed this most peculiar chapter of American law.

The best California sparkling wine areas already proven are Mendocino, Carneros, and Sonoma, but perhaps the most exciting potential for the future is the Santa Maria Valley, which was first planted for sparkling wines in the 1960s and 1970s, long before its potential for silky Pinot Noir red wines was known.

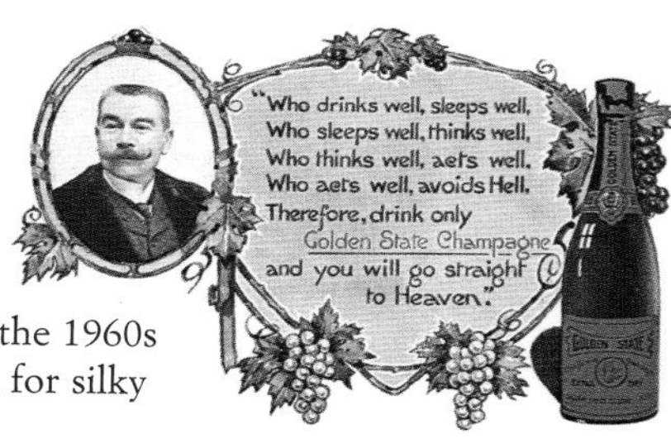

An ad for Golden State Champagne claims that those who drink it will go "straight to heaven."

"Mad Harry"

A few producers, like "Mad Harry" Osborne of Kristone, have decided to go the opposite route to other California sparkling winemakers and pick ripe grapes. Osborne challenges critics with such logic as "why harvest unripe grapes when they have no flavor and the wrong acidity, when you can harvest a larger crop of ripe grapes and simply add the acidity?" It is not as simple as that, of course, because they invariably contain too much sugar, but "Mad Harry" has managed to create a first-class product from truly ripe grapes (*see* Kristone in A–Z listing), and has helped New Zealanders to improve their bubbly, too *(see p59)*.

It is legal in the US to sell domestically produced sparkling wine as "Champagne," because the term has been used to describe American sparkling wine from very early days, and is thus defined as a generic name under Federal law. However, most serious sparkling wine producers have stopped using the term.

Washington and Oregon

These two states are slow developers in the field of sparkling wine production, yet they may have as much potential as California. In Washington, Château Ste. Michelle's sparkling wines showed great promise in the late 1970s, but they have been disappointing ever since. Dr. Michael Manz is currently making this state's most serious fizz at the Mountain Dome winery in Spokane.

Given Oregon's reputation for Pinot Noir, it is perhaps surprising that the Champenois have not shown more interest. Laurent-Perrier purchased land there in the early 1990s but made nothing of it. Another French Champagne house, Bollinger, has a financial-only interest in Argyle, in the Red Hills of Dundee, which is owned by Croser in Australia and is Oregon's best fizz by far.

Pinot Noir is picked by a vineyard worker for sparkling wine in the Willamette Valley in Oregon.

AUSTRALIA AND NEW ZEALAND

The climate and geography of New Zealand are very suited to sparkling wine production – maybe more so than anywhere else outside the Champagne region. By contrast, a vast expanse of Outback makes Australia one of the least obvious countries associated with the industry. Yet Australia's winemaking history is almost as old as its colonial history, and there are many areas where excellent sparkling wine grapes can be grown.

FLYING WINEMAKERS AND OTHER FIRSTS

The concept of the flying winemaker was born in Australia: because of the size of this continent and the staggered picking dates, consultant winemakers hop by plane from harvest to harvest. Domaine Chandon Australia (aka Green Point) has zoomed ahead of its sister company in California mainly because flying winemakers like Tony Jordan and his former partner Brian Croser have quickly identified numerous suitable vineyard areas.

Australia's first so-called Sparkling Burgundy was produced by Auldana in 1881. This was the precursor to the country's famed sparkling Shiraz, a generic style that includes wines made from Cabernet Sauvignon, Merlot, and other grapes.

Australian cricketers ce brate victory over Englar

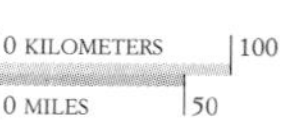

Victoria's stunning mountain scenery is the setting for Great Western's vineyards.

)UTHEASTERN
JSTRALIA

ɽkling wine production
urgeoning in the
:lborough region
Jew Zealand and
ıost winemaking
ɪs of Australia.
: best Australian
ducers are located
ɽ Melbourne and Adelaide.

Best Producers

1 Brun (Daniel Le) *Marlborough*
2 Chandon (Domaine) *Yarra Yarra Valley*
3 Croser *Barossa Eden*
4 Hunter's *Marlborough*
5 Jackson Estate *Marlborough*
6 Pelorus *Marlborough*
7 Seaview/Seppelt *Southern Vales*
8 Yalumba *Barossa Eden*
9 Yellowglen *Ballarat*

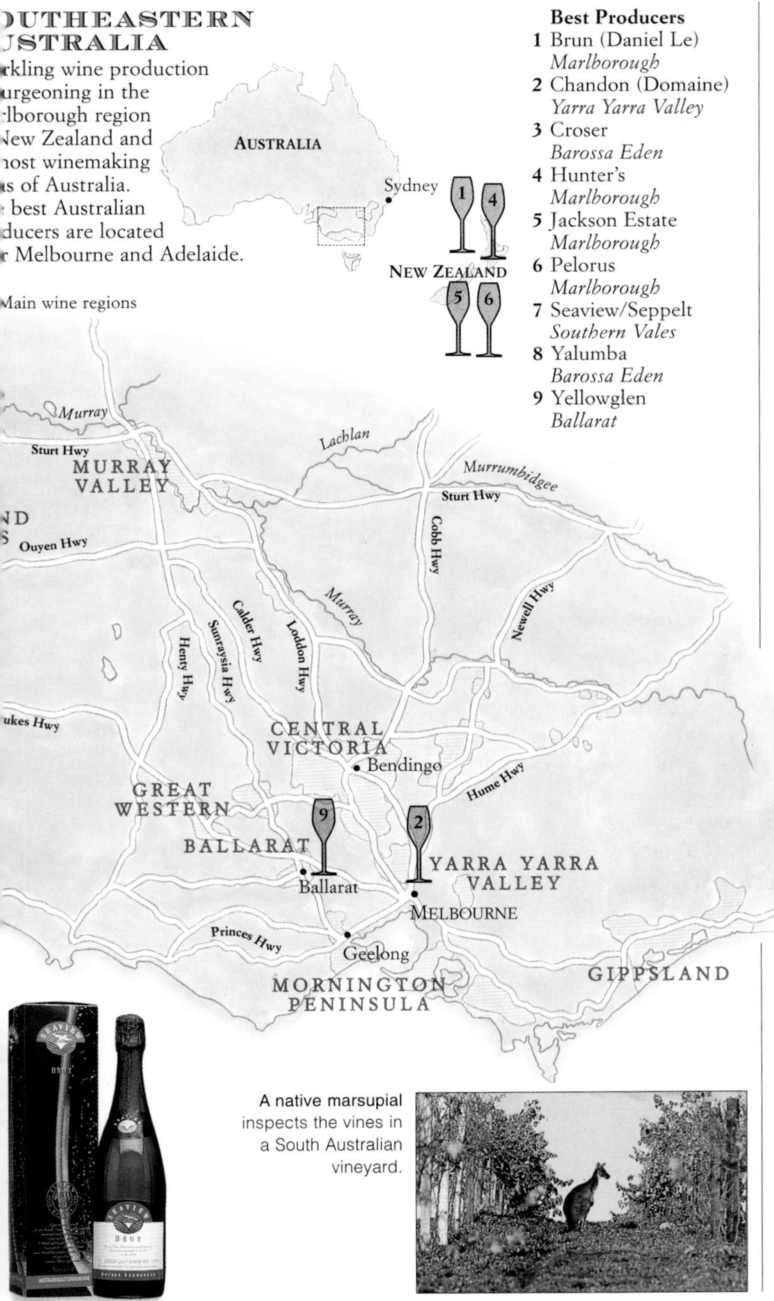

A native marsupial inspects the vines in a South Australian vineyard.

AUSTRALIAN PIONEERS

In 1843, about 50 years after the first vines were planted in Australia, the first Australian sparkling wine was made at Irrawing in the Hunter Valley, New South Wales, by James King, a free settler originally from Hertfordshire.

The Yalumba winery, founded 1849, lies in the verdant Barossa Valley.

From the late 1840s onward, South Australian winemakers, including Patrick Auld (Auldana), Thomas Hardy, Samuel Smith (Yalumba), and Joseph Ernest Seppelt (B. Seppelt & Sons; Seppeltsfield; and Chateau Tanunda), experimented with fizz. Some of these firms are still going strong.

The main development in Australia's emerging sparkling wine industry came in the 1890s when Hans Irvine purchased Great Western. He installed special equipment for sparkling wine and employed Charles Pierlot, who had trained at Pommery. Irvine's friend Benno Seppelt bought the company in 1918, thus creating Seppelt Great Western, which soon dominated the Australian fizz industry.

A year later, a French cook, Edmund Mazure, left Auldana to make his own fizz under the La Perouse label. This was taken over by Wynns, and in 1975 became the famous Seaview label.

Minchinbury was the first Australian winery to utilize the transfer method, whereby wines are filtered from one bottle to another after fermenting. Many famous Australian sparkling wines are now produced in this manner rather than strictly by *méthode champenoise*, according to which the wine must be fermented in the same bottle in which it is sold.

Eager to be acknowledged by Europe as a cultured people rather than a nation of outcasts, James King and other Australian winemakers sent their wines sailing halfway round the world to the 1855 Paris Exposition. This was at a time before settlers had crossed Australia overland from south to north.

In their official report on the wines of New South Wales, the French judges magnanimously described the "bouquet, body and flavor" of King's sparkling wine as "equal to the finest champagnes." It was chosen as one of only two wines to be served to Napoleon III at the final banquet.

Benno Seppelt owned a wine merchant's in Broken Hill, New South Wales, before buying Great Western in 1918.

SPARKLING SHIRAZ

Sparkling Shiraz has an appealing deep purple-red color and is made in two basic styles, oaky or fruity. When tasting a sparkling Shiraz for the first time, drinkers often complain that it tastes like a full-bodied red wine that just happens to be fizzy. However, for most people, the more sparkling Shiraz encountered, the more seriously the style will be taken. Sparkling Shiraz certainly has its place at the dinner table, particularly when partnering strong flavors such as Stilton sauce.

Pinot Noir grapes are harvested in the Brancott Valley of Marlborough for the New Zealand producer Cloudy Bay.

NEW ZEALAND'S LATE START

Sparkling wine did not became serious business in New Zealand until 1981, when industry giant Montana put its muscle behind the launch of Lindauer. One factor for such a late development was that few classic grape varieties had been planted. The collaboration between Montana and Champagne Deutz in 1988 then put this country on the bottle-fermented sparkling wine map. Also in that year, Cloudy Bay produced its first vintage of Pelorus under the wandering eye of "Mad Harry" Osborne *(see p55)*. It took one year longer for an expatriate Champenois, Daniel Le Brun, to demonstrate the Marlborough region's true potential for sparkling wine.

In the 1990s Domaine Chandon has produced a New Zealand *cuvée* using the facilities at Hunter's, which makes its own fizz too. This came of age in 1997 when Jane Hunter launched her compelling Mirru Mirru wine. Hopefully we will see more individually crafted sparkling wines from New Zealand, particularly Marlborough, which is capable of competing with Champagne in terms of quality as well as value.

Mate Selak made New Zealand's first fizz in 1956, although he was unable to market it at the time. The Chasselas grape he used did not work well, and, most alarmingly, many of the bottles exploded. It took 15 years of experimentation before Mate could launch his bubbly. He died in 1991, and there is now a top-of-the-range Blanc de Blancs named after him.

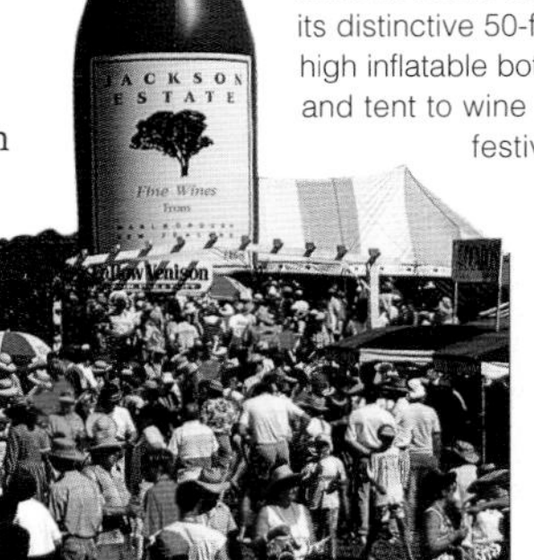

Jackson Estate takes its distinctive 50-ft-high inflatable bottle and tent to wine festivals.

SOUTH AFRICA

The ostracism of South Africa during the final phase of its apartheid period stifled developments in the wine industry. However, in the 1990s, after the country finally embraced a multiracial democracy, world markets suddenly opened up, and a fledgling sparkling wine industry gained strength.

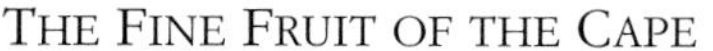

THE FINE FRUIT OF THE CAPE

Wineries are concentrated in the delimited Wine of Origin (WO) districts around Cape Town. Many produce sparkling wine, though at the moment much of it is merely fruity fizz. However, there is a fine structure and a certain delicacy of fruit about Cape grapes that promise an interesting future. The best sparkling wine brands include Graham Beck, Krone Borealis (made by Twee Jongegezellen), Jacques Bruère (made by Bon Courage), Pierre Jourdan (made by Clos Cabrière), Oak Village (made by Vinfruco), and Villiera.

FIRST PRODUCERS

The first South African sparkling wine was made by the Stellenbosch Farmers' Winery in 1929. Called Grand Mousseux Vin Doux, it was simply a still wine that had been carbonated like a fizzy soft drink. Made from the grape varieties Chenin Blanc and Clairette Blanche, Grand Mousseux Vin Doux was the market leader for 60 years, and is still a big success today, particularly in neighboring Namibia. Nederburg Première Cuvée, a *cuve close* fizz, was launched in 1945.

Nelson Mandela drinks to the postapartheid era.

Vredendal
Olifantsri
OLIFANT
RIVIER
PIKETBER
Velddrif
Bergsrivier
SWARTLAND
Moorreesburg
TULBA
Malmesbury
6
PAA
CAPE TOWN
STELLEN
BOSCH

Main map
☐ Wine of Origin
(Wyn van Oorsprong) distr

ᴘE WINE DISTRICTS

ugh wine is also made in areas between
Town and Pretoria, sparkling wine
ction is confined to the
swath of wine regions
ı 100 miles of Cape
. Terminology on
is increasingly in
sh, or both English
frikaans. A few have
e Afrikaans terms.

Best Houses

1 Beck *Robertson*
2 Bon Courage *Robertson*
3 Clos Cabrière *Paarl*
4 Oak Village *Stellenbosch*
5 Twee Jongegezellen *Tulbagh*
6 Villiera *Paarl*

0 KILOMETERS 50
0 MILES 25

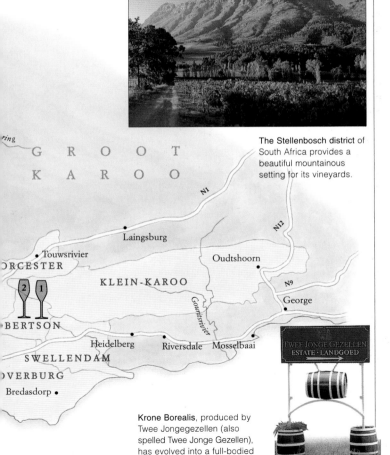

The Stellenbosch district of South Africa provides a beautiful mountainous setting for its vineyards.

ring
GROOT KAROO
N1
N12
Laingsburg
Touwsrivier
ORCESTER
Oudtshoorn
KLEIN-KAROO
N9
George
Gouritsrivier
BERTSON
Heidelberg
Riversdale
Mosselbaai
SWELLENDAM
OVERBURG
Bredasdorp

TWEE JONGE GEZELLEN
ESTATE · LANDGOED

Krone Borealis, produced by Twee Jongegezellen (also spelled Twee Jonge Gezellen), has evolved into a full-bodied quality sparkling wine.

Labels of South African wines sometimes mention a night harvest – a wise way to overcome the problems of a hot climate on newly picked grapes. Grapes harvested at night produce fresher, more aromatic, and livelier wines compared with those picked in the day.

First Hints of Quality

The first South African *méthode champenoise* sparkling wine was made by Frans Malan at Simonsig in 1971. This was called Kaapse Vonkel and was originally made primarily from Chenin Blanc, although it is now made from Pinot Noir and Chardonnay. Such was the grip of low-priced wines on the domestic market that this remained the only bottle-fermented South African wine until Boschendal produced its first *cuvée* in 1979.

The international sanctions imposed on South Africa during the 1980s affected wine exports. However, in 1984 Jeff Grier of Villiera entered into a fruitful ten-year partnership with the French winemaker Jean-Louis Denois, originally from Cumières (where his family still makes Champagne), but now one of the most innovative producers in Limoux. Since the end of apartheid, Champagne Mumm has collaborated with Nicky Krone of Twee Jongegezellen, producer of Krone Borealis, one of South Africa's best sparkling wines.

Most South African fizz is made by the *cuve close* (tank) method, and some is even made by carbonation, including virtually all those described as *perlé* or *perlant*. For higher quality fizz, watch for the words Cap Classique on the label: this has been the South African term for *méthode champenoise* since 1992.

The Cabrière Estate in the Paarl region is run by Achim von Arnim, and it owns the phenomenally successful Pierre Jourdan brand of sparkling wine.

The Cape Comes Out of Isolation

In the early 1990s, as a new South Africa began quickly to reestablish and forge new export links with other countries, it became clear that the Cape's vineyards were in a rather poor state after lengthy international isolation, and the country's viticultural knowledge was lagging ten years behind the rest of the winemaking world. The Cape wine industry, however, was eager to learn and started this process in the winery, where

fairly instantaneous results could be achieved simply through a stricter selection of grapes and also a massive investment in new wood and better winemaking equipment. More important, a visionary plan called the Vineyard Improvement Program (or VIP for short) was set up soon after sanctions were lifted, and this is being funded by a substantial proportion of South Africa's growing export income from wine.

The Cape winelands generally have a Mediterranean climate, which lends itself more to still wines than sparkling wines, but the idea that South Africa is simply too hot for sparkling wine is an exaggeration. Coastal regions have a much higher rainfall and are chilled by the icy Benguela current from Antarctica. In some places it is impossible for grapes to ripen properly, which is ideal for sparkling wine production, and the South African fizz industry will eventually gravitate toward such areas rather than rely on the inappropriate balance of early-harvested grapes.

THE FUTURE

Phase One of VIP, involving clonal selection and rootstock improvement, is under way. Nevertheless, a vine needs three years before it yields a crop, and five years before its true potential is known; thus the earliest effects of Phase One are only just now being seen.

Phase Two of the program, which is to test the suitability of Phase One clones and rootstock in the different *terroirs* of the Cape, is a very long-term project.

Although a number of South African still wines have already noticeably improved through the better winery practices, the real expected leap in quality will not start to show for a decade or so. Moreover, the learning curve for sparkling wine vinification is taking longer than for still wine. A winemaker can see the result of his or her work on a still wine within a year of its harvest, but it takes at least two years, often three, and sometimes even longer, before a serious-quality sparkling wine can be taken off its yeast lees.

Villiera has gone from strength to strength in the 1990s and now exports around the world as well as selling from the cellar door.

Other Countries

Fizz is made in several other countries. None has the sophistication of the industries already covered but some have great potential.

Countries such as Switzerland and Austria produce surprisingly little fizz given the potential of their *terroirs*, but Nyetimber has recently emerged as the UK's first world-class sparkling wine. All East European countries produce some bubbly, usually the disappointingly bland product of the Russian Continuous system. Hopefully, the same miracle that transformed Portuguese table wines will soon occur with Portuguese sparkling wines.

Harvesting Chardonnay in Argentina, a country that is likely to produce much better fizz in the next millennium.

In Canada, the Brights-Cartier group has produced top-scoring wines and now has the pioneering Inniskillin winery. British Columbia's bottle-fermented Blue Mountain is world-class, and Colio's *cuve close* Chardonnay Lily is worth trying.

South American potential is barely tapped. In Chile, Mumm's new fizz shows promise, and Miguel Torres has recently returned to form. Moët & Chandon makes a reasonable quality fizz in Brazil, but less so in Argentina, although huge new plantations of Chardonnay and a change of emphasis from *cuve close* to *méthode champenoise* will transform this firm's South American sparkling wines over the next decade. On the other side of the world, the best Asian fizz, Omar Khayyam, has been made in the Sahyadri Mountains, east of Bombay, for more than ten years.

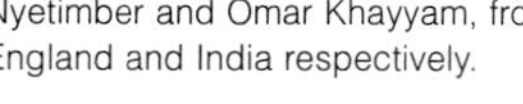

Good bottle-fermented fizz includes Nyetimber and Omar Khayyam, from England and India respectively.

Cricova in Moldova is the most intriguing sparkling wine facility in Eastern Europe. An underground "city" with 40 miles of roads and enough cellars to store a billion bottles, it was clearly built for more than just the two million bottles of fizz that it now produces. Who might have installed such opulent reception halls and marble-clad men's rooms, and a series of steel doors that could withstand a nuclear blast? Who but the now defunct Politburo!

A–Z Listing

An alphabetical listing of recommended producers and over 900 individual Champagnes and sparkling wines.

Introduction to the A–Z Listing

Recommended Wines

Almost all the wines in the listing are recommended by the author; those without a score are in an unusual developmental phase and cannot be fully judged yet but are likely to be good when ready. Most wines were tasted blind (with labels covered) at a professionally equipped facility, where producers submit samples. Real Champagnes had to score 80 or above (on a scale of 100) to qualify for this guide; other sparkling wines had to score 70 or above. Producers without any qualifying wines are not included, no matter how good their range has been in the past. The inclusion of a particular *cuvée* in the listing is not a guarantee of its availability in North America. For a listing of major US and Canadian wineries, see pages 180–86.

How the Sparkling Wines are Judged

Three elements are essential in sparkling wine: bubbles, acidity, and fruit.

Bubbles are the most obvious factor affecting quality. The strength of mousse can range from very soft at the lowest level of effervescence to firm at the highest. Most people prefer a softer mousse, but the longer you intend to cellar a wine, the firmer the mousse should be. The smaller the bubbles, the smoother the mousse feels, whether it is soft or firm, and this smoothness enhances the perception of creaminess on the finish. The only way to assess the quality of a mousse is in the mouth, not by looking at it in the glass.

Acidity maximizes finesse, gives persistence to the flavor, and is vital for graceful aging. Without sufficient acidity, a sparkling wine will either be heavy if full-bodied, or hollow and short if light-bodied. The right balance of acidity can give even the most light-bodied sparkling wine a long and persistent flavor. Without acidity the toasty and biscuity bottle-aromas that develop will lack finesse, while other finer, more complex aromas will be restricted.

Fruit is essential, although in lighter, more elegant styles this can start out as a floweriness and may develop fruitiness only after "ripening" in bottle. Simple fruity fizz is fine if it is inexpensive.

The tell-tale amylic aroma of peardrops or banana has a banal effect. Dominant buttery or butterscotch aromas indicate an overuse of malolactic *(see p11)*. A tiny whiff of free sulfur may eventually evolve into a pleasant toastiness, but leave an overtly sulfurous wine alone.

How the Wines are Described

The glossary *(see pp176–8)* includes tasting terms such as amylic, toasty, and oxidative. Besides these, I may also give two or three fruits or flowers to describe a sparkling wine. Besides aroma and taste, I tend to focus on the balance and finesse, the acidity, and the basic style of the wine; for example, light-bodied or full, fruit-driven or complex. When it is obvious to me, I say how a wine will develop over the next few years.

Findings for the Millennium Edition

With wines recommended for more than 140 producers, Champagne trounced all opposition, and so it should, having a *terroir* uniquely suited to classic *brut*-style sparkling wine. I was saddened that only a third of the wines from Alsace, Burgundy, Bordeaux, and the Loire qualified. The success rate for Cava – 23 percent – was about as expected, but I was startled by Germany's 20 percent success rate as I had expected it to be much lower! Some small estates have started producing quality Sekt not just from Riesling, as might be expected, but also from Pinot Noir in an elegant *rosé* style. I was also amazed by the number of Italian sparkling wines to qualify for this first edition – the Franciacorta appellation turns out to be of exceptional high quality.

As for the New World, quality is high and the rate of improvement is staggering. South Africa has come up so quickly that its sparkling wines now vie with those from California. There is still a lot of fruity fizz about, particularly in Australia, but at least these wines are clean and affordable.

How the Listing Works

Key

- ▩ Real Champagne
- ☐ Sparkling wine
- (99) Tom Stevenson's overall score
- ⊖ Overall score impossible to judge yet
- 🍷 Ready to drink now until year indicated
- Bottle: Preferably store until years indicated

Price Bands

The publishers have provided price bands in the A–Z listing because it is impossible to indicate exact prices for different outlets in numerous markets for an international publication.

- $ Up to $15
- $$ $16–30
- $$$ $31–54
- $$$$ $55 and above

Price in French Francs

🍇 The price in French Francs is for vineyard/cellar door sales, and given only for real Champagne, where available from the producer.

How to Find a Wine

Producer names are simplified and indexed according to wine cataloging conventions. This is usually by family name: for instance, you will find Graham Beck under "B" for Beck, not "G." Cross-references are provided where brand names differ significantly from producer names, or where confusion may arise. Contact details are given for real Champagne producers (dark-tinted boxes). Below each producer box are the full names of recommended *cuvées*. Note that some producers named elsewhere in this book do not appear in the A–Z listing, as none of their wines has qualified this year.

The 100-Point Scoring System

The 100-point scale, by which a critic makes an overall judgment on a wine, is now globally recognized.

- (70) The point at which any sparkling wine other than Champagne becomes interesting.
- (75) A reasonably good score for a sparkling wine.
- (80) Because Champagne has such advantages over sparkling wines produced in less favorable *terroirs*, this is the level at which it qualifies for inclusion in this guide.
- (85) If a non-Champagne sparkling wine scores this high, it is of exceptional quality.
- (90) A top-quality vintage or prestige *cuvée* Champagne, which will probably need three to five years' extra cellarage to achieve its full potential.
- (95) Only the greatest Champagnes score this high or above. Most could be left forgotten in a cellar for ten years.

ABBATIALE

See Locret-Lachaud

ADAM

Alsace, France

An underrated producer of varietal wines and a passable *crémant.*

JEAN-BAPTISTE ADAM NV CRÉMANT D'ALSACE, EXTRA BRUT 

Light and elegant, yet really quite rich on the nose and finely structured.

On purchase $

JEAN-BAPTISTE ADAM NV CRÉMANT D'ALSACE BRUT 

Although this has the strawlike character that detracts from so many sparkling wines, not just Crémant d'Alsace, there is a good mouthful of fruit on the palate, making it more satisfying than most.

On purchase $

ADAM-GARNOTEL

15 rue de Chigny, 51500 Rilly-la-Montagne
(326) 03.40.22 FAX (326) 03.44.47

A small house with some important vineyards, but only the nonvintage *cuvée* survived the test.

ADAM-GARNOTEL NV BRUT EXTRA QUALITY, 1ER CRU 

Deeper and richer than most nonvintage *cuvées*, with some sprightly fruitiness on the finish.

On purchase $$ 79F

AGRAPART

57 avenue Jean-Jaurès 51190 Avize
(326) 57.51.38 FAX (326) 57.05.06

The Demoiselles Rosé and vintage Blanc de Blancs are reliable, but several other *cuvées* failed the test.

AGRAPART & FILS NV CUVÉE DES DEMOISELLES BRUT ROSÉ 84

Pale peach color. Extremely fruity, but developing complexity and richness.

Now–2000 $$ 93F

AGRAPART & FILS 1989 L'AVIZOISE, BLANC DE BLANCS BRUT, GRAND CRU 86

The malolactic is too creamy-buttery for a classic *brut* style. This robs it of finesse, but it is full of smoky-creamy-rich flavor.

Now–1999 $$$ 135F

AGRAPART & FILS 1988 MILLÉSIME BLANC DE BLANCS BRUT, GRAND CRU 

Mellow creamy-biscuity aroma now, but promises to go toasty as well.

Now–2000 $$$ 93F

ALBERT

See Baron Albert

ALDRIDGE

See Cranswick

ALIGUER

See Torelló

ALLIAS

Loire, France

VOUVRAY BRUT, ALLIAS PÈRE ET FILS 

This soft and easy-drinking fizz scrapes in as one of the Loire's top ten percent.

On purchase $

ANDERSON VINEYARD

Napa, California, US

S. ANDERSON 1993 BRUT 

Zesty, crisp-sherbety aromas, with a long, fine, and delicate fruit and a very fresh finish that is developing some complexity.
Now–2000 $$

S. ANDERSON 1993 ROSÉ 

Salmon-colored, with big aromas and real flavors. Serious, complex, long, deep and beautifully balanced.
Now–1999 $$

ANGAS

See Yalumba

ANTEO

Oltrepò Pavese, Italy

Specializes in Pinot Noir fizz, using "almost organic" methods.

ANTEO BRUT, METODO CLASSICO NV PINOT NERO, OLTREPÒ PAVESE 

Streets ahead of Anteo's nonvintage Anteo Brut, which is rather mean and made by the *metodo martinotti (cuve close)*. This is a more mature and more serious *cuvée* with some malo-complexity on the nose and creamy fruit on the palate.
On purchase $

ANTEO ROSÉ BRUT NV PINOT NERO, OLTREPÒ PAVESE 

Pale in color, with very little on the nose, but quite an intense, firm-style flavor.
On purchase $

ANTEO SELEZIONE DEL GOURMET NV PINOT NERO, OLTREPÒ PAVESE BRUT 

Hinting of almonds on the nose, with rich, almost unctuous fruit. Good structure and intensity of flavor.
On purchase $

ANTICA CANTINA FRATTA

Franciacorta, Italy

ANTICA CANTINA FRATTA NV BRUT, FRANCIACORTA 

Very creamy nose, with succulent fruit on the palate and a pungent strawberry aftertaste. Too sweet for a true *brut,* otherwise it would have scored higher, but those who drink *sec* in preference to *brut* should add on a few points.
On purchase $

ANTINORI

Tuscany, Italy

Large, aristocratic Chianti producer.

MARCHESE ANTINORI NV NATURE BRUT 

Fresh, light, and elegant.
On purchase $

MARCHESE ANTINORI 1993 BRUT MILLESIMATO 

Lemony aroma following onto the palate, with good balancing acidity on the finish.
On purchase $$

ANTOINE

See Marne et Champagne

(D')ARCO

Trentino, Italy

CONTI D'ARCO 1993 RISERVA NICOLÒ D'ARCO BRUT, TRENTO 

Lively fruit acidity gives this a heightened freshness and a tingly, crisp finish.
Now–1999 $$

(D')ARENBERG

South Australia, Australia

D'Arenberg has made sparkling Shiraz on and off since the 1960s but now mostly concentrates on the Chambourcin grape, a hybrid of uncertain parentage.

D'ARENBERG 1996 THE PEPPERMINT PADDOCK CHAMBOURCIN 

Fresh, light and creamy, with a simple but enjoyable raspberry flavor. Not one of the greatest wines in this book, but one of the most interesting, this red fizz is D'Arenberg's first vintage of Chambourcin. It is not allowed into EU countries because it is made from hybrid grapes.

On purchase Ⓢ

ARNOULD

28 rue de Mailly 51360 Verzenay
(326) 49.40.06 FAX (326) 49.44.61

Michel Arnould specializes in pure Grand Cru Champagne from Verzenay.

MICHEL ARNOULD & FILS NV BRUT, GRAND CRU 

Has a rich, biscuity complexity, yet still with the potential to develop.

Now–1999 ⓈⓈ 72F

MICHEL ARNOULD & FILS NV RÉSERVE BRUT, GRAND CRU 

Richer and softer than the above, with vanilla-finesse and a lovely cushiony mousse.

Now–2002 ⓈⓈ 76F

MICHEL ARNOULD & FILS NV CUVÉE AN 2000 BRUT GRAND CRU 

Slow-building complexity of high finesse.

Now–2005 ⓈⓈⓈ 121F

ARQUES

See Sieur d'Arques

ARUNDA

Alto Adige, Italy

ARUNDA RISERVA NV EXTRA BRUT, SÜDTIROLER SEKT – ALTO ADIGE 

Tangy fruit, solid and fat, but good acidity.

On purchase Ⓢ

ASCOT

See Thames Valley Vineyard

AURIGNY

See Devaux

BACKSBERG

Paarl, South Africa

Made famous by the late Sydney Back, who was three times Champion Estate Winemaker, Backsberg continues to produce some of South Africa's most consistent and classy wines.

BACKSBERG BRUT 1991 CAP CLASSIQUE 

The nose is still developing, but the quality of the light yet rich, creamy-biscuity fruit was evident on the palate.

On purchase Ⓢ

BALARD

Bordeaux, France

This brand is used by the Union Vignerons d'Aquitaine cooperative.

BALARD NV CRÉMANT DE BORDEAUX 

Crisp, refreshing fizz.

On purchase Ⓢ

BANFI

Tuscany, Italy

Immaculate vineyards and a high-tech winery help to make Villa Banfi one of Italy's more consistent producers of sparkling wine.

BANFI BRUT PINOT NV VINO SPUMANTE 

A fresh, light, and fruity everyday fizz.

On purchase Ⓢ

Banfi 1992 Brut, Talento 72

Fat but very fresh aroma, with soft vanilla fruit lifted by the fizz on the finish.
On purchase $

Acqui Brachetto d'Acqui 1997 Banfi, Vino Spumante Dolce 71

Big, blowsy Pinot aromas followed by soft, sweet strawberry fruit on the palate.
On purchase $

Banfi Asti NV Vino Spumante Dolce 76

Sweeter than most Asti, with very fresh, light, and fluffy fruit.
On purchase $

Tener Sauvignon-Chardonnay, Banfi NV Vino Spumante Brut 

A fresh, crisp wine with a light balance, this is dominated by Sauvignon and has little Chardonnay input.
On purchase $

Barancourt

Place Tritant, 51150 Bouzy
(326) 53.33.40 FAX (326) 53.33.41

Once an interesting range, especially of mono-*cru* Champagnes, but now mostly disappointing, with a dull marzipan flavor. Devotees of the mono-*cru* should now try Delbeck or Brice.

Barancourt 1989 Brut 

Very elegant for such a full-bodied style.
Now–2000 $$$

Barnaut

13 rue Pasteur, 51150 Bouzy
(326) 57.01.54 FAX (326) 57.09.97

The grapes here are harvested later than the norm for Bouzy and always by a succession of sweeps to pick out only the ripest and healthiest grapes.

E. Barnaut NV Selection, Extra Brut, Grand Cru 

A serious old classic of some complexity.
On purchase $$ 91F

E. Barnaut NV Cuvée Douceur, Sec, Grand Cru 

Biscuity with sweetish fruit.
Now–1999 $$ 85F

Baron Albert

Grand Porteron, 02310 Charly-sur-Marne
(23) 82.02.65 FAX (23) 82.02.44

Claude Baron is an enthusiastic producer who is restricted by the limitation of his vineyards on the western outskirts of Champagne.

Baron Albert NV Brut Rosé 

Pale peach color and a fresh amylic aroma. Acidity is very good.
On purchase $$ 71F

Baron Albert NV Carte d'Or Brut 

Still lacks finesse, but has improved and picks up with food.
On purchase $$ 74F

Baron Albert 1991 Brut 

Firm, young, and lean but will it develop any finesse?
Wait and see $$$ 79F

Baron B.

See Chandon

Baron de Hoen

Alsace, France

Baron de Hoen NV Crémant d'Alsace Brut 

Lovely ripe fruit and a succulent finish that is not too *brut*. I much preferred this to Baron de Hoen's Blanc de Noirs.
On purchase $

Baron zu Knyphausen

See Knyphausen

Barramundi

See Cranswick

Bauchet

Rue de la Crayère 51150 Bisseuil
(326) 58.92.12 FAX (326) 58.94.74

One *cuvée* qualifies, but there is a general lack of finesse on the nose.

Saint Nicaise NV Brut Rosé 1er Cru, Bauchet

This apricot-gold colored Champagne just scrapes in out of curiosity: like an old Burgundy with fizz. Definitely dry, but not at all dried out, this *cuvée* has a long flavor, some aged complexity, and is definitely a food wine.

On purchase $$ 84F

Baumard

Loire, France

Before his retirement Jean Baumard was the Loire's greatest exponent of Chenin Blanc. He was a rare, gifted winemaker who could make this grape sing, even in the driest still wines, and his son Florent shares some of his father's magical abilities.

Baumard 1993 Crémant de Loire

Mature, fresh, and clean, although there is no real substance for a top score.

On purchase $

Baumard, Carte Corail NV Crémant de Loire Brut

Nice dry, easy-going, and accessible, with a perfumed aftertaste. The deliciously tangy fruit is as clean as a whistle, making this *rosé* a delight to drink.

On purchase $

Baumard, Carte Turquoise NV Crémant de Loire Brut

Drier than the Carte Corail, with less perfume and a more food-wine structure.

On purchase $

Baur

Alsace, France

This Eguisheim grower consistently produces elegant Riesling Gewurztraminer from Grand Cru Eichberg and is becoming adept at crémant.

Charles Baur 1994 Crémant d'Alsace Brut

With such lovely intensity of fruit in th Crémant d'Alsace, you can taste the quality of the grapes used. They have obviously been selected, rather than utilizing underripe leftovers.

Now–1999 $$

Beaumet

3 rue Malakoff, 51207 Épernay
(326) 59.50.10 FAX (326) 54.78.52

Flagship brand from the same stabl as Jeanmaire and Oudinot.

Beaumet 1990 Cuvée Malakoff, Blanc de Blancs Brut

Cuvée Malakoff has a soft and easy st that does surprisingly well with food. Fine cushiony mousse.

On purchase $$$

Beaumont des Crayères

64 rue de la Liberté,
Mardeuil 51318 Épernay
(326) 55.29.40 FAX (326) 54.26.30

This Champagne cooperative often outperforms the classification of its *crus* (villages) because all its memb have tiny vineyards that they atten to like gardens on weekends.

Beaumont des Crayères NV Cuvée de Prestige Brut

The nonvintage Cuvée de Prestige is fatter and has more ripeness and fine than the basic Cuvée de Réserve mad Beaumont des Crayères.

On purchase $$ 99F

Beaumont des Crayères NV Cuvée de Réserve Brut
85

:lassic, lean, and biscuity.
On purchase ⓈⓈ 85F

Nostalgie 1990 Brut, Beaumont des Crayères
87

Rich and complex, yet packed with fruit.
Now–2000 ⓈⓈⓈ 160F

Nostalgie 1988 Beaumont des Crayères, Brut

Acidity is the defining factor of this beautifully mellow, toasty rich *cuvée*. It will just get better and better and will never go blowsy.
Now–2002 ⓈⓈⓈ

Charles Leprince NV Grande Reserve Brut

Has some maturity already, but is only just beginning to build biscuity richness and has the structure for further development. A Pinot-dominated food-wine style.
Now–2000 Ⓢ

Jacques Lorent NV Cuvée Tradition Brut

This will develop a nice biscuity richness after a year or two in bottle.
1999–2000 Ⓢ

Beauregard

See Château de Beauregard

Beck

Robertson, South Africa

Graham Beck produces budget fizz under the Madeba label and reserves his eponymous brand for more serious Cap Classique with a very stylish presentation.

Graham Beck Brut NV Cap Classique

Slightly amylic, but the fruit on the palate is very elegant, fresh, and fluffy. With a year in bottle this *cuvée* usually goes zesty-toasty.
Now–1999 Ⓢ

Graham Beck Chardonnay Sur Lie NV Cap Classique

Again slightly amylic, but again the fruit on the palate is very elegant, only this time it has a more sherbety feel.
Now–1999 Ⓢ

Graham Beck Blanc de Blancs Brut 1993 Cap Classique

Nothing amylic here, so unless Beck puts his nonvintage *cuvées* through a colder first fermentation, the peardrop character will work its way out of these wines given sufficient time. This has lovely lemony-toasty fruit, like a good mature Chardonnay, but with bubbles.
Now–2000 ⓈⓈ

Graham Beck Blanc de Blancs Brut 1992 Cap Classique

There's no getting away from the New World origins of this citrusy-creamy-oaky humdinger of a wine.
Now–1999 ⓈⓈ

Bellafon

See Besserat de Bellafon

Bellavista

Tuscany, Italy

For many years this has been one of my favorite Italian sparkling wine producers, and Bellavista's 1993 Gran Cuvée Brut Rosé is the greatest dry Italian fizz I have ever tasted.

Bellavista NV Cuvée Brut, Franciacorta

A restrained nose with delicately ripe fruit on the palate and a fine, cushiony mousse. An elegant wine of some finesse.
On purchase Ⓢ

Bellavista 1993 Gran Cuvée Brut Rosé, Franciacorta

A lovely golden-sunset color here, with delicious cushiony fruit supported by lively acidity. A mini classic!
Now–2001 ⓈⓈ

Bellavista 1992 Gran Cuvée Brut, Franciacorta

Biscuity aroma, with a rich fruit flavor and good acidity for more development.
Now–2000 $$

Bell Duc

See CIGRAVI

Bellei

Emilia Romagna, Italy

Francesco Bellei 1994 Bomporto, Extra Cuvée Brut

72

The mousse has a noticeably low pressure but very fine bubbles. There is something missing from the midpalate, but the wine has a nice vanilla finesse and some complexity on the finish.
On purchase $$

Francesco Bellei NV Lambrusco di Sorbara

If only all Lambrusco were of this quality, it would not have the bad name that it does. Deep, dry, intense, seriously flavored sour-cherry fruit.
On purchase $

Bennwihr

Alsace, France

Bennwihr Riesling NV Crémant d'Alsace

I much preferred this to Bennwihr's other two *brut cuvées* even though the structure is not quite right, and this particular *cuvée* needs a slightly higher dosage.
On purchase $

Bergkelder

Stellenbosch, South Africa

Large winery that has the Fleur du Cap, Stellenryck, and Pongrácz labels.

Pongrácz Brut NV Cap Classique

72

A youthfully oxidative aroma coarsens the rich, complex flavors in this wine.
On purchase $

(Fratelli) Berlucchi

Franciacorta, Italy

Pia Berlucchi produces Franciacorta and traditionally packages his wine. Note that Fratelli Berlucchi is distinct from the best-selling, plain Berlucchi brand blended from various sources and run by Pia's cousin Guido. The latter has been good in the past, but none passed the test this year.

Fratelli Berlucchi 1993 Brut, Franciacorta

Fresh, easy-drinking fizz with a sweet twist of almondy fruit on the finish.
On purchase $$

Fratelli Berlucchi 1993 Brut, Franciacorta Rosé

The deepish color could be brighter, but the fruit-acidity balance makes this a nice, easy drinking fizz.
On purchase $$

Fratelli Berlucchi 1993 Brut, Franciacorta

This wine has oxidative complexity on the nose but no such development, as yet, on the palate, which has lovely, soft vanilla fruit on the finish.
Now–2000 $$

Besserat de Bellefon

19 avenue de Champagne, 51205 Épernay
(326) 59.51.00 FAX (326) 59.51.19

Owned by Marne et Champagne and made at Marne's mega-winery.

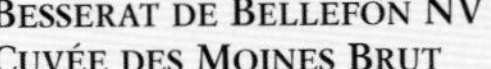

Besserat de Bellefon NV Cuvée des Moines Brut

84

Fresh aromas of some finesse and plenty of flavor on the palate, but a touch green on the finish.
On purchase $$

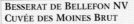

BILLECART-SALMON

40 rue Carnot, 51160 Mareuil-sur-Aÿ
(326) 52.60.22 FAX (326) 52.64.88

\ small family-owned house of ınimpeachable quality, Billecart-Salmon is currently offering one of he strongest ranges of high-quality Champagnes available.

ILLECART-SALMON RUT RÉSERVE 88

beautifully elegant nonvintage ampagne with gentle, ripe-apple fruit d soft, cushiony mousse.

Now–2000 $$

ILLECART-SALMON RUT ROSÉ 88

elicate, pale-peach color, with very sh, elegantly perfumed aromas and soft d fruit flavors.

Now–1999 $$$

ILLECART-SALMON LANC DE BLANCS 1989 BRUT 

ne acacia aroma of fresh disgorgement, th a gentle richness of creamy fruit on late. It is exceptionally fresh for the ıtage and promises to develop a creamy azil nut and walnut complexity.

Now–2010 $$$

ILLECART-SALMON CUVÉE NICOLAS-FRANÇOIS 990 BRUT 96

ery fresh, acacia-like aromas, with lots Chardonnay richness currently domi-ting the palate, and such a ripeness of ıit on the finish that it is really quite achy. The acidity and extract is so tense on the finish that you know this ne has a million places to go before it aches its peak. I cannot guess what it ll be like when it gets there, except that know it will be sensational.

2000–2015 $$$

BILLECART-SALMON CUVÉE NICOLAS-FRANÇOIS 989 BRUT 

edictably broader in style than the 990, and developing much more quickly, ıt a deliciously rich and complex *cuvée*.

Now–2002 $$$

BILLECART-SALMON CUVÉE NICOLAS-FRANÇOIS 1988 BRUT 

The 1988 has a sumptuous quality that is rare for the year. The palate is heaped high with creamy-walnutty fruit, and the creaminess pervades everything, from the nose through the finish to the aftertaste, yet it has excellent 1988 acidity to guarantee a lovely long life.

Now–2010 $$$

BILLECART-SALMON GRANDE CUVÉE 1988 BRUT 

No surprise here; this really does have 1988 typicity, with tightly sprung concentrated fruit and high acidity waiting to unleash into creamy-nutty richness.

2000–2010 $$$$

BILLECART-SALMON GRANDE CUVÉE 1985 BRUT 

At least as rich and as tightly sprung as the 1988, with promises of even greater complexity to come.

2000–2012 $$$$

BILLECART-SALMON, CUVÉE ELIZABETH SALMON ROSÉ 1988 

The first vintage of this *cuvée* was launched to build on Billecart-Salmon's great reputation for its nonvintage Rosé Brut wines, which account for an amazing one-fifth of all this producer's output. Elizabeth Salmon was immediately impressive for its creamy summer fruit notes, which made it a touch riper and richer than its nonvintage sister wine, but still every bit as delicate due to its exquisite balance.

1999–2005 $$$

BILLECART-SALMON, CUVÉE ELIZABETH SALMON ROSÉ 1989 

An elegant, slow-developing *rosé* for 1989. Billecart-Salmon deliberately prevented malolactic on some of the wines from this vintage, hence the finer balance.

1999–2005 $$$

BILLECART-SALMON, CUVÉE ELIZABETH SALMON ROSÉ 1990 

Billecart-Salmon continues the trend with its 1990 Elizabeth Salmon to create a *rosé* worth dying for. True *vin de garde*.

1999–2005 $$$

BISCHÖFLICHE

Mosel-Saar-Ruwer, Germany

BISCHÖFLICHE WEINGÜTER 1993 SCHARZHOFBERGER RIESLING SEKT BRUT 78

Perfumed Riesling aroma with soft, peachy fruit and fine acidity for freshness.
On purchase $$

BLANCK

Alsace, France

BLANCK 1995 CRÉMANT D'ALSACE, EXTRA BRUT 

Restrained malo aroma followed by malo-dominated fruit on the palate.
On purchase $$

BLIN

5 rue de Verdun, 51700 Vincelles
(326) 58.20.04 FAX (326) 58.29.67

A cooperative with vineyards in the *petit crus* of the Marne valley.

H. BLIN 1990 BRUT 

Tony Rasselet's most stunning vintage yet.
Now–2002 $$$

BLUE MOUNTAIN

British Columbia, Canada

BLUE MOUNTAIN 1993 OKANAGAN VALLEY, VINTAGE BRUT 

Creamy-malo nose, high acidity, and an oxidative hint to finish. With some fatness in the fruit it would have been world class.
Now–1999 $$

BODEGAS CHANDON

See Chandon (Argentina)

BOECKEL

Alsace, France

EMILE BOECKEL BLANC DE BLANCS 1995 CRÉMANT D'ALSACE BRUT 7

The freshest of all the Boeckel *cuvées*, and it promises to develop some biscui complexity with a little bottle-age.
Now–1999 $$

BOHEMIA

Czech Republic

With more than 28 million bottles of sparkling wine, Bohemia's productior dwarfs even that of the mighty Champagne house Moët & Chandon

BOHEMIA REGAL RED SPARKLING WINE NV LA BOHEME, DEMI SEC 7

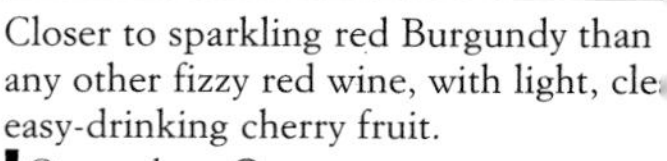

Closer to sparkling red Burgundy than any other fizzy red wine, with light, cle easy-drinking cherry fruit.
On purchase $

BOIZEL

14 rue de Bernon, 51200 Épernay
(326) 55.21.51 FAX (326) 54.31.83

BOIZEL NV BRUT RÉSERVE 8

Has fresh, fruit-driven aromas but need to crank up the finesse to compete with the top *marques*.
On purchase $$ 99F

BOIZEL NV CHARDONNAY BRUT BLANC DE BLANCS 8

Creamy and fattish, yet crisp, with plen of ripe acidity.
Now–2000 $$ 135F

BOIZEL 1990 GRAND VINTAGE BRUT MILLÉSIME 8

So fruity and succulent, the wine is almost exotic on the finish, yet it has classic structure and length.
Now–2002 $$$ 140F

EUVE BORODIN NV WHITE ABEL, BRUT, BOIZEL 83

›solutely up-front fruit-driven style :hout any of the amylic aromas that ‹ittled Boizel in the late 1980s.

›n purchase $

EUVE DELAROY NV BRUT 83

.is seriously fruity Champagne has the ucture to develop.

Jow–2000 $

BOLLINGER

16 rue Jules Lobet, 51160 Aÿ-Champagne
(326) 53.33.66 FAX (326) 54.85.59

Some tips: if you prefer fruit, buy the ıonvintage by magnum, and if you ike the toasty complexity and mellow ·ichness of a mature vintage, buy Grande Année and age it yourself, ·ather than paying for R.D. (Bolly's *·écemment dégorge* trademark – 'recently disgorged"). Also, look out ·or a special premillennium release of three R.D., including one that has nev- er been released as a Grande Année.

OLLINGER SPECIAL UVÉE (BOTTLES) 

ne of the most complex nonvintage *vées* on the market, with a lean, austere, idic, even unforgiving, character and ky echoes on the finish. Reserve wines back 15 years or so, but most of the end is young, thus when given two or ree years further aging, the wine ecomes silky-smooth, toasty, and mellow.

2000–2001 $$$ 169F

OLLINGER SPECIAL UVÉE (MAGNUMS) 

uch softer, fruit-driven and more ccessible than the same in bottles, yet omises to mature to great complexity id finesse over a much longer period.

Now–2004 $$$

OLLINGER 1990 GRANDE ANNÉE 

ig, rich, and powerfully flavored, with me vanilla on the finish. My score could e underrating this vintage; it stands for the me being, but watch this space.

2000–2010 $$$$ 236F

BOLLINGER 1989 GRANDE ANNÉE 

Beautiful, creamy-vanilla fruit, with gorgeously lush finish and the tiniest of bubbles.

Now–2009 $$$$ 236F

BOLLINGER 1988 GRANDE ANNÉE 

The 1988 is still available and now has a lovely toasty-oaky richness with a great intensity of Pinot Noir fruit.

Now–2013 $$$$

BOLLINGER 1985 GRANDE ANNÉE 96

Still available and if you still have the first release of 1985 nestling in your cellar, you have a wine of magnificent fruit, exuberance, complexity and finesse.

Now–2010 $$$$

BOLLINGER 1985 R.D. 

Dominated by the flowery, acacia-like finesse of autolysis, which all R.D. fans love, the powerful, rich-flavored fruit in this wine is awesome, but I still prefer the way the first disgorgement has developed.

Now–2010 $$$$

BOLLINGER 1982 R.D. 

Fine, flowery, acacia-like aromas are followed by really quite spicy flavors, with dried-fruit complexity.

Now–2007 $$$$

BOLLINGER 1989 VIEILLES VIGNES FRANÇAISES 

This is the wine that bred the lie that all *blanc de noirs* are big. Vieilles Vignes Françaises is big, but not simply because it is pure Pinot Noir. These particular vines are located in three minuscule parcels of ungrafted vines in the *grands crus* of Aÿ-Champagne (Clos St-Jacques, Chaudes Terres)and Bouzy (Croix Rouge). The 1989 is full, rich, and complex, with broad, creamy-ripe lushness of fruit on both nose and palate, yet a structure that is firm for such a big wine, with vanilla and oak coming through on the finish.

Now–2009 $$$$

BOLLINGER 1988 ROSÉ 

Fat, sassy, and satisfying fruit on a classic lean structure. Ideal with pheasant.

Now–2002 $$$

Bon Courage

Robertson, South Africa

Owner Andre Bruwer was Champion Estate Winemaker in 1985–6, yet if anything, the quality has gone up since son Jacques took over in 1995.

Jacques Bruère Blanc de Blancs NV Cap Classique 

Classic creamy-rich biscuity complexity.

Now–2000 $

(Alexandre) Bonnet

138 rue du Général-de-Gaulle
10340 Les-Riceys
(325) 29.30.93 FAX (325) 29.38.65

Serge and Alain Bonnet are ambitious Aubois producers who sell under the Alexandre Bonnet label.

Alexandre Bonnet NV Cuvée Prestige 

Satisfying mouthful of tingling-fresh fruit.

On purchase $$

Alexandre Bonnet 1990 Madrigal 

Behind its somewhat incongruous label this is a nicely rich, but extremely tight, Champagne that needs more post-disgorgement bottle-age.

2000–2002 $$

(Ferdinand) Bonnet

12 allée du Vignoble, 51055 Oger
(326) 84.44.15 FAX (326) 84.44.19

Part of the Remy-Cointreau group since 1992, the Ferdinand Bonnet brand still represents good value and the wines improve with further bottle-age, but they will never be the same quality as the old stocks.

Ferdinand Bonnet NV Brut Heritage 

Although it has wet-straw aromas now, this should go nice and toasty.

1999–2000 $$ 99F

Princesse de France NV Brut, Grande Réserve de Ferdinand Bonnet 8

Made by women for women, this *cuvée* was created by Cécile Rivault and Myriam Jacqueminet, two oenologists i Daniel Thibault's highly talented winemaking team. It is elegant, but more lea than soft or delicate, which are the sort adjectives the French use for the so-call feminine characteristics of a wine. Whatever your sex, I think you'll find that this is an excellent Champagne.

1999–2000 $$ 96F

Bredon NV Brut 80

Easy drinking style, with peppery fruit.

Now–1999 $

Jean de Praisac NV Brut, F. Bonnet 

Fresh, easy-going style with some pepperiness to the fruit.

On purchase $

Louis Raymond NV Brut, F. Bonnet 80

Some green hints to the fruit, but the wine scrapes in because there is a good depth of flavor in addition to this greenness, and the balance promises a mellowing development.

Now–1999 $$

Borodin

See Boizel

Boschendal

Paarl, South Africa

One of the Cape's pioneering *méthode champenoise* producers.

Boschendal Le Grand Pavillon Brut NV Cap Classique 

I have come across several samples of th current shipment that were corked, but when on form this *cuvée* has a tangy richness of fruit and a hint of complexit

On purchase $

Bosco

See Ca'del Bosco

Bothy Vineyard

Frilford Heath, England, UK

The irrepressible Roger Fisher and his indefatigable wife tend this vineyard on the outskirts of Oxford.

Bothy Vineyard 1991 Dry (78)

The more I think about this wine, the more convinced I am that it is one of the most distinctive English sparkling wines ever made, although the 1992 was a great disappointment.

On purchase $

Boucher

10 rue Pasteur, 51160 Champillon
(326) 59.48.17 FAX (326) 52.97.67

Boucher Fils NV Cuvée Fin de Siècle, Prestige (85)

The concentration of flavor blows away any lack of finesse.

1999–2001 $$ 82F

Boulard

1 et 4 rue du Tambour
51480 La Neuville aux Larris
(326) 58.12.08 FAX (326) 58.13.02

There is an amylic tendency in too many wines here. A slightly warmer first fermentation is probably needed.

Raymond Boulard NV Réserve Brut 

A touch amylic, but overshadowed by sprightly fruit on the palate.

On purchase $$ 90F

Raymond Boulard NV Brut, Grand Cru 

Richer, more sprightly fruit than the above.

On purchase $$ 99F

Raymond Boulard NV Tradition Brut 

None of the amylic aromas found in the Réserve Brut and more serious than the Grand Cru, without its sprightly fruitiness. Some true complexity and finesse.

Now–1999 $$ 118F

Raymond Boulard 1993 Brut 

Very fruity.

On purchase $$$ 102F

Bourgogne

See Haute Bourgogne

Boursault

See Château de Boursault

Boutillez-Vignon

26 rue Pasteur, 51380 Villers-Marmery
(326) 97.95.87 FAX (326) 97.97.23

G. Boutillez-Vignon NV Cuvée Prestige Brut 

Oxidative nose, but extremely rich fruit on the palate. An extra gram of finesse could add a ton of quality to this wine.

On purchase $$ 77F

G. Boutillez-Vignon 1990 Brut, 1er Cru 

There is a strange strength to the flavor of this high-acid, biscuity-rich *cuvée* that compels me to withhold judgment for at least another year.

Wait and see $$$ 99F

Bouvet

Loire, France

Bouvet NV Saumur, Demi-Sec 

Fresher and more elegant than most *demi-sec*, with plenty of sweet fruit.

Now–2000 $

BOUVET 1995 SAPHIR BRUT VINTAGE 73

Richer and softer than most Saumur, with a licorice quality to the fruit.
Now–1999 $

BOUVET EXCELLENCE NV CRÉMANT BRUT 72

This has a longer finish and is more perfumed than Bouvet's basic Brut – it can be regarded as the entry level for Bouvet.
On purchase $

BOUVET LADUBAY NV TRESOR BRUT, SAUMUR 

When first released, the fruit seemed much riper and more exotic, and it tasted more like an Australian Chardonnay with bubbles than anything from the Loire. People either loved it or loathed it, especially as it was expensive for a Loire fizz. Now it is half the price and dare I say half the wine, which will probably give it wider appeal, but there is nothing exotic or oaky, just peppery and firm.
On purchase $$

BOUVET LADUBAY NV TRESOR ROSÉ BRUT, SAUMUR 

The Tresor Rosé Brut shows little sign of its *barrique* first fermentation, but has delicate fruit underpinned by good, ripe acidity, which gives the wine excellent length in the mouth. Very fine mousse.
On purchase $$

BOUXHOF

See Domaine du Bouxhof

BREAKY BOTTOM

Lewes, England, UK

Peter Hall's fizz is enjoyable enough but has the potential for more finesse.

BREAKY BOTTOM CUVÉE RÉSERVÉE 1994 BRUT 

This was very amylic at first, although this tamed down after a few months to become a good, easy-drinking fizz.
Now–1999

BRÈQUE

Bordeaux, France

One of the oldest producers of sparkling Bordeaux wines.

RÉMY BRÈQUE NV CRÉMANT DE BORDEAUX BRUT 7

Just scraped in ahead of Rémy Brèque's prestige *cuvée*.
On purchase $

BRIANT

See Leclerc Briant

BRICE

3 rue Yvonnet, 51150 Bouzy
(326) 52.06.60 FAX (326) 57.05.07

Brice is one of the three founders of Barancourt, now doing his own thing.

BRICE NV AŸ GRAND CRU BRUT 

Firm fruit, intense and long, this wine is capable of aging.
1999–2002 $$ 130F

BRICE NV PREMIER CRU BRUT 

Light, elegant, and stylish.
Now–1999 $$ 108F

BRICE NV BOUZY GRAND CRU BRUT 81

Ripe and juicy fruit that promises to go quite toasty.
Now–2000 $$ 130F

BRISON

14 Grande Rue, 10360 Noé-les-Mallets
(325) 29.66.62 FAX (325) 29.14.59

Ambitious Aube growers. Francis Brulez ferments in well-used oak casks and prevents the malolactic.

LOUISE BRISON 1994 BRUT 

Dry, spicy, and perfumed.
2000–2002 $$$ 88F

Louise Brison 1993 Cuvée Germain Brulez Brut

Under blind conditions, I thought I detected some perfumed Meunier aromas, but after the covers came off I discovered that this *cuvée* consists of 40 percent Chardonnay and 60 percent Pinot Noir, with no Meunier whatsoever!

On purchase $$$ 200F (magnum)

Louise Brison 1993 Cuvée Tendresse Brut

I found this hard, but not in a non-malolactic way, more of a hard with a metallic taste.

Wait and see $$$ 110F

Brizé

See Domaine de Brizé

Brochet-Hervieux

10 rue Saint Vincent, 51500 Ecueil
(326) 49.24.06 FAX (326) 49.77.94

Current production is just 1,250 cases per year.

Brochet-Hervieux NV Brut Extra, Premier Cru

Quite fat and sweet for *extra brut.*

On purchase $$ 75F

Brochet-Hervieux 1990 HBH Brut, Premier Cru

Very rich malty-biscuity flavor.

Now–1999 $$$ 100F

Brogsitter

Ahr, Germany

Brogsitter Privat Sektkellerei 1995 Spätburgunder Sekt Brut

Under this awful looking label lurks a very good Pinot Noir Sekt, with an elegant cherry fruit flavor and a soft mousse. Bottle-fermented.

On purchase $$

Brouette

Bordeaux, France

Large Crémant de Bordeaux producer.

Brouette Rosé NV Crémant de Bordeaux Brut

Off-putting mature-orange color but plenty of perfumed fruit on the palate, with a delicately fruity finish.

On purchase $

Brouette Crémant de Bordeaux NV Tradition Blanc de Blancs Brut

Fresh, easy fruit with better acidity than Brouette's prestige Cuvée de L'Abbaye.

On purchase $

Brown Brothers

Victoria, Australia

Brown Brothers Pinot Noir Chardonnay NV Brut

Peachy fruit with plenty of ripe acidity.

On purchase $

Bruère

See Bon Courage

(Cellier Le) Brun

Marlborough, New Zealand

One of the New World's top sparkling wine producers, in the late 1980s Daniel Le Brun's wines began to rival the quality of good Champagne. Indeed, the 1989 Blanc de Blancs was so outstanding that it started rumors that Daniel Le Brun had imported it from his family in Champagne! The straight vintage of 1990 seemed to confirm the ascendency of this Gallic star, but Daniel flew the coop in 1996 to a new venture. Meanwhile, the priority for the new owners is surely to improve the Nonvintage Brut.

Daniel Le Brun NV Brut, Marlborough 

This fresh, fruit-driven *cuvée* is the best nonvintage from Le Brun in some time.

On purchase ⓈⓈ

Daniel Le Brun 1992 Vintage Brut, Marlborough 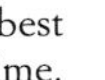

A quick whiff of sulfur, but it is free and clean and will therefore turn toasty with some more bottle-age. This is a rich and flavorsome wine that will gain complexity, but loses points for coconutty oak (although some people love that).

Now–2000 ⓈⓈ

Daniel Le Brun 1992 Blanc de Blancs Brut, Marlborough 

The current shipment is unpleasantly oxidative, but I have tasted this vintage several times and the wine is good, so I must reserve judgment for a year or two.

Wait and see ⓈⓈ

(Edouard) Brun

14 rue Marcel Mailly 51160 Aÿ-Champagne
(326) 55.20.11 FAX (326) 51.94.29

Edouard Brun & Cie NV Réserve 1er Cru Brut 

Extraordinarily fruity.

On purchase ⓈⓈ 84F

Edouard Brun & Cie NV Cuvée Spéciale Brut 

Almost as fruity as the 1er Cru Réserve but not quite as rich, although it has more room for development.

Now–1999 ⓈⓈ 76F

Edouard Brun & Cie NV Rosé Brut 

Pale salmon color, sprightly fruitiness, deep flavor, true *brut* dryness.

On purchase ⓈⓈ 90F

Edouard Brun & Cie 1990 Cuvée du Centenaire Brut 

This *cuvée* does not celebrate the end of the century, but 100 years since Edouard Brun was established in 1898. I have my doubts about how this will develop.

Wait and see ⓈⓈⓈ 119F

Bründlmayer

Austria

Vinegrowers and winemakers in Kamptal since the 17th century, the Bründlmayers currently vie with Weingut Platzer as Austria's best sparkling wine producer.

Bründlmayer 1993 Brut 

Crisp, with fine acidity, and an elegant, if slightly oxidative, complexity.

Now–1999 ⓈⓈ

Buecher

Alsace, France

The *cuvée* below is the best *crémant* from Buecher that I have tasted.

Paul Buecher, Prestige NV Crémant d'Alsace Brut 

Rich, fruity, and well-structured.

Now–1999 Ⓢ

Buisse

Loire, France

Paul Buisse NV Crémant de Loire 

This comes in a heavier, more expensive bottle than the so-called Prestige, and it is a richer, more succulent *cuvée*.

On purchase Ⓢ

Paul Buisse Prestige NV Touraine Brut 

The fresh, sweet, and peppery fruit in this wine is attractive, but not in the same class as the basic *brut* above.

On purchase Ⓢ

Buitenverwachting

Constantia, South Africa

Buitenverwachting is part of the historical Constantia estate and produces many outstanding wines.

Buitenverwachting Brut NV Cap Classique 

This perfumed yet rich and full sparkling wine makes an interesting, nonclassic, almost contradicting style.

On purchase $

Burge

See Grant Burge

Burg Hornberg

Baden, Germany

Weingut Burg Hornberg 1991 Blanc de Noirs Sekt Brut 

Made exclusively from Meunier in a true-white *blanc de noirs* style, rather than the New World synonym for *rosé*, this is one of the few Sekts that could take some aging. Bottle-fermented.

Now–2000 $$

Cabrière

See Jourdan

Cà dei Frati

Lombardy, Italy

Cà dei Frati, Cuvée dei Frati NV Brut, Lugana 

Rich, fruity aromas with fresh, easy-going fruit on the palate.

On purchase $

Ca'del Bosco

Franciacorta, Italy

Motorcycle-mad, multimillionaire Maurizo Zanella is one of Italy's most consistent sparkling wine producers, and the style is now more elegant.

Ca'del Bosco NV Brut, Franciacorta 

Fresh Mâcon-like aroma, with good, fresh fruit and acidity on the palate, but the bubbles could be smaller.

On purchase $

Ca'del Bosco 1994 Brut, Franciacorta 

Some lemony finesse on the nose, with rich fruit on mid-palate and a creamy finish, but the aftertaste lacks elegance.

On purchase $$

Ca'del Bosco 1993 Rosé Brut, Franciacorta 

A very fruity front palate, drying to a nicely focused finish.

On purchase $$

Ca'del Bosco 1992 Satèn Brut, Franciacorta 

Strong but fruity volatile acidity aromas on the nose, following onto the palate where they add a piquancy to the fruit.

On purchase $$

Ca'del Bosco 1991 Cuvée Annamaria Clementi Brut, Franciacorta 

A bit too rich for its balance to be special, but this is a nice, ripe-fruity fizz for easy drinking without food.

On purchase $$

Calixte

See Hunawihr

Callot

100 avenue Jean Jaurès, 51190 Avize

Tel (326) 57.51.57 FAX (326) 57.99.15

These Champagnes are fermented in well-used, large oak barrels, with fewer than 600 cases produced.

Pierre Callot NV Blanc de Blancs Brut, Grand Cru 

A fruity style of some depth and the potential to develop well.

1999–2000 $$ 81F

Pierre Callot NV Grande Réserve, Blanc de Blancs Brut, Grand Cru 

Not quite as overtly fruity as the standard Blanc de Blancs but with more finesse.
1999–2001 \$\$ 101F

Canard-Duchêne

1 rue Edmond Canard, Ludes le Coquet
51500 Rilly-la-Montagne
(326) 61.10.96 FAX (326) 61.13.90

This brand is practically given away in French supermarkets, but quality is better on export markets, although the Grande Charles VII Cuvée is disappointing wherever you buy it.

Canard-Duchêne NV Brut 

The Canard-Duchêne fruit-driven style plus a more classic, lean structure.
On purchase \$\$ 120F

Canard-Duchêne 1990 Brut 

One sample was old and past it, but the other was high quality for the price.
Now–2000 \$\$\$ 150F

Cape Levant

See SAVISA

Cariad

Wales, UK

Cariad Gwrid Blush 1995 Brut 

Assertive jammy fruit with a firm mousse.
On purchase \$\$

(Domaine) Carneros

Napa, California, US

The first releases were very poor, but now these wines are among the best. Even the Champenois need a year or two to get it right, it seems.

Domaine Carneros 1992 Blanc de Blancs 

Pale color, with creamy-flowery-sherbety aromas, fine and light fruit on the palate, very good acidity, and a soft mousse of very tiny bubbles.
Now–2000 \$\$

Domaine Carneros 1993 Brut 

Very fresh and fine, with nice acidity and a crisp mousse of tiny bubbles.
Now–2000 \$\$

Carolina

See Masachs

Carrington

See Orlando

Cassegrain

New South Wales, Australia

It was in 1980 that John Cassegrain established this winery at Port Macquarie, which some critics believe has too much of a maritime climate for viticulture. There have been some lows, but some of the highs have been very exciting, and the early sparklers are encouraging.

Cassegrain 1994 Brut 

This rich, smooth, full-bodied wine is spoiled by too much sulfur, and although it is clean and not fixed, thus will turn toasty, this simply should not happen in any sparkling wine.
Wait and see \$

Castell

Franken, Germany

Vineyard owners for 27 generations, the Castell-Castell family has produced wine since 1258, but Sekt is a relatively recent phenomenon here, with the first *cuvée* produced in 1973.

ÜRSTLICH CASTELL'SCHES OMÄNENAMT 1993 ASTELLER HERRENBERG IESLANER SEKT BRUT 

lees-rich Riesling-terpene style, even ough this is a *Riesling x Sylvaner* cross.
On purchase $$

(DE) CASTELLANE

57 rue de Verdun, 51204 Épernay
(326) 51.19.19 FAX (326) 54.24.81

Part of the Laurent-Perrier group, this underrated house offers brilliant value for the money, with the top *cuvées* capable of very high quality indeed.

ICOMTE DE CASTELLANE NV BRUT 

resh and fruity, with a touch of pepper.
Now $$

E CASTELLANE 1990 BRUT 

it of an old bruiser last year, but the richess now hangs well on this wine's lean ructure, with more development to come.
Now–2000 $$$ 110F

E CASTELLANE 1988 CUVÉE FLORENS DE CASTELLANE BRUT 

typically buttery-malo on the nose, but ch fruit that will go biscuity, not toasty.
Now–2000 $$$ 180F

CUVÉE COMMODORE 1989 DE CASTELLANE BRUT 

ice intensity of fruit, with a long, layered, itrusy and lime blossom complexity.
Now–2002 $$$ 160F

CROIX ROUGE DE ST ANDRÉ DE CASTELLANE NV BRUT 

uite rich and full, with a fine, fluffy finish.
Now $$

MAXIM'S NV GRANDE CUVÉE BRUT 

ush, ripe, elegant fruit with a long finish.
On purchase $$

MAXIM'S NV PRESTIGE BRUT 

ight and elegantly fruity style. Some peperyness and spicy green apple on the finish.
On purchase $$

CASTELLBLANCH

Penedès, Spain

CASTELLBLANCH 1995 CAVA BRUT ZERO 

Has the terpene character of a wine that has been stored in tank prior to second fermentation, but also good enough acidity, structure, and quality to qualify.
On purchase $

CASTELLBLANCH 1996 CAVA ROSADO BRUT 

A simple, fresh, easy-drinking style.
On purchase $

CASTILLO PERELADA

See Perelada

CATTIER

6 & 11 rue Dom Pérignon
51500 Chigny-les-Roses
(326) 03.42.11 FAX (326) 03.43.13

For many years this small house has produced one of the most individual Champagnes, its single-vineyard Clos du Moulin, which is always a blend of three vintage years. The vintages are on the back label.

CATTIER NV BRUT ROSÉ, 1ER CRU 

Pale salmon color, sprightly fruitiness, soft and succulent, with Pinot coming through on the finish. Smooth mousse, tiny bubbles.
On purchase $$ 93F

CATTIER NV BLANC DE BLANCS BRUT, 1ER CRU 

Floral style with excellent acidity and creamy aftertaste.
Now–2002 $$ 89F

CATTIER 1990 BRUT 

Exotic fruit and lovely acidity, fine and refined, with tropical fruits on the finish.
Now–2006 $$$ 93F

CATTIER 1989 CUVÉE RENAISSANCE BRUT, 1ER CRU

Still in ultrafruity mode, with a depth of fruit that makes its serious potential obvious, but it could well go through a less attractive phase between these two enjoyable extremes.

Now–2001 $$$ 140F

CLOS DU MOULIN NV CATTIER BRUT, PREMIER CRU

This particular *cuvée* is a blend of 1985, 1986, and 1988. It is already complex but needs a few years post-disgorgement aging. Having tasted future *cuvées*, I cannot wait until the amazing 1988/1989/1990 blend goes on sale.

2000–2005 $$$ 196F

CATTIN

Alsace, France

There is some inconsistency in the style of Joseph Cattin's Crémant d'Alsace because he keeps changing the *encépagement* (blend of grape varieties). Otherwise it is always an interesting wine.

BRUT CATTIN NV CRÉMANT D'ALSACE

Lots of sprightly fruitiness, strawberry-like, but finishes rather fat and needs more acidity for a higher score.

On purchase $

CAVA(S) –

See under main name

CAVALLERI

Franciacorta, Italy

CAVALLERI 1993 BLANC DE BLANCS BRUT, FRANCIACORTA

Full toasty aroma, with plenty of fruit on the palate, but needs more layers of flavor and finesse for a higher score.

On purchase $$

CAVALLERI 1993 ROSÉ, FRANCIACORTA

Fresh, fruity fizz in a sort of Latin Ang Brut *(see Yalumba)* style.

On purchase $$

CAVE(S) DE –

See under main name

(DE) CAZANOVE

1 rue des Cotelles, 51204 Épernay

(326) 59.57.40 FAX (326) 54.16.38

Always a good-value Champagne house, De Cazanove is trying to pro-duce higher quality *cuvées*. Current shipments have too much malolactic but this will no doubt be improved.

CHARLES DE CAZANOVE NV BRUT AZUR

The creamy-biscuity malolactic charact is so dominant that it tastes odd in a bli tasting amid a sea of fresh, fruit-driven Champagnes, but this *cuvée* shows its tr class and complexity at the table with fo

Now–2001 $$ 102F

CHARLES DE CAZANOVE NV BRUT CLASSIQUE

Fruit-driven style and really delicious, with classic lean structure. No domina malolactic characteristics, but it might develop some biscuitiness with age.

On purchase $$

CHARLES DE CAZANOVE NV DEMI-SEC

Simplistically sweet and clean now, but also one of the few *demi-sec* Champagn that will repay aging.

Now–2000 $$

CHARLES DE CAZANOVE 1990 BRUT MILLÉSIME

Similar creamy-malo character to the nonvintage Brut Azur, but this is richer and its more fruit-influenced style is taking longer to evolve. A safer bet tha the Stradivarius prestige *cuvée*.

Now–2005 $$$

CHARLES DE CAZANOVE 1990 STRADIVARIUS BRUT 

his wine currently has a strange boiled-hablis character – but "Strad" has had a ood string of vintages since its inaugural 985 vintage, so I am prepared to give ıis a year or two to settle down.

Wait and see $$$ 250F

CHARLES DE CAZANOVE 1990 BRUT AZUR 

ich in sweet, biscuity-ripe fruit.

Now–2005 $$$ 123F

H. LANVIN & FILS NV CUVÉE SUPÉRIEURE, BRUT 

secondary brand from the De azanove stable, this *cuvée* has simpler, ısy-going fruit and a crisp finish.

On purchase $

MAGENTA BRUT NV CHARLES DE CAZANOVE, CUVÉE SUPÉRIEURE 

nother secondary brand from De azanove, it is technically the same level s Lanvin, but softer, like an easier going ersion of the Cuvée Classique.

On purchase $

CELLAR BATTLE

See Gramona

CELLIER LE BRUN

See Brun

CHAMPAGNE –

See under main name

CHAMPALOU

Loire, France

Didier Champalou is ahead of the pack, but has some fine-tuning to do to reveal the true quality of this *cuvée*.

CHAMPALOU NV VOUVRAY BRUT 

The finesse on the nose of this wine made it stand out from most Loire bubblies, but although the fruit is initially attractive and tangy in the mouth, it is let down by a hint of dry straw on the finish.

On purchase $

(BODEGAS) CHANDON

Argentina

One of Moët & Chandon's oldest outposts. Most of the fizz is fresh, clean, and amylic, with a slightly bitter finish, but Baron B. stands out, and there are rumors of more plantings of Chardonnay for improving future *cuvées*.

BARON B. NV EXTRA BRUT CHAMPAÑA 

Just as fresh as below, but not amylic, with finer acidity and no bitter finish.

On purchase $

BARON B. ROSÉ NV EXTRA BRUT CHAMPAÑA 

Touch fatter than above and less elegant.

On purchase $

(CAVA) CHANDON

Penedès, Spain

At one time this outpost of Moët & Chandon's sparkling wine empire seemed about as interesting as its Sekt factory, but it looks as if the quality has been improved.

CAVA CHANDON NV BRUT RESERVA 

Much better acidity than this wine used to have, and above average quality for Cava, but still needs to find a more expressive character.

On purchase $

CAVA CHANDON NV BRUT NATURE 

The best Cava Chandon so far: clean, fresh, and good acidity for Cava, but definitely an early-drinking style.

On purchase $

(DOMAINE) CHANDON AUSTRALIA

Victoria, Australia

This Domaine Chandon is under the auspices of Tony Jordan. Many New World wines are dominated by malolactic aromas, but only some of the base wines are put through this. Most are lovely when released and can improve for up to 18 months. Sold as Green Point on export markets.

DOMAINE CHANDON 1995 BRUT

The best vintage so far, this *cuvée* has a lovely understated richness, Pinot-led front and mid-palate, with a smooth Chardonnay finesse on the finish, and creamy-cushiony mousse of tiny bubbles. Stunning stuff!

Now–2000 $$

DOMAINE CHANDON 1994 BRUT

Firm and tight, with nice biscuity richness.

Now–2000 $$

DOMAINE CHANDON 1994 ROSÉ BRUT

A deliciously serious *rosé*, with lovely fruit and just beginning to develop a smooth vanilla finesse on the finish.

Now–1999 $$

DOMAINE CHANDON 1993 BLANC DE BLANCS BRUT

A lovely, elegant wine, with very fresh fruit for its age.

Now–2000 $$

DOMAINE CHANDON NV CUVÉE RICHE

A soft and sensuous, beautifully balanced dessert bubbly, Cuvée Riche is no longer the amylic horror it used to be.

Now–2002 $$

(DOMAINE) CHANDON NEW ZEALAND

Marlborough, New Zealand

As Tony Jordan is Jane Hunter's consultant winemaker, it is little surprise that Hunter's has also been the testing ground for this *cuvée*.

DOMAINE CHANDON 1994 VINTAGE, MARLBOROUGH BRUT

A very malty style *cuvée*. How it might develop is anyone's guess.

Wait and see $$

(DOMAINE) CHANDON CALIFORNIA

Napa, California, US

Moët & Chandon helped to kick-start the California sparkling wine industry in the 1970s. These wines have sometimes been inclined to rely too much on weight and character and not enough on finesse and elegance although this may be changing, if the younger wines under the export label Shadow Creek are a sign of things to come. The Mount Veeder Chardonnay appellation has also begun to look interesting, especially when the malolactic is prevented. There is no doubting that winemaker Dawnine Dyer is every bit as talented as Tony Jordan in Australia – it is just that the problems they face are very different

DOMAINE CHANDON NV RESERVE

Full, spicy, and quite deeply flavored. Different than previous *cuvées*, which a somewhat terpenelike character.

On purchase $

DOMAINE CHANDON NV ROSÉ BRUT

An elegantly perfumed aroma with deli cate red fruits on the palate and a smo vanilla-style Chardonnay on the finish.

On purchase $

DOMAINE CHANDON NV BLANC DE NOIRS

Wonderfully fresh and fluffy fruit, with sherbety finish.

On purchase $

ÉTOILE

Although Domaine Chandon's prestige *cuvée* was for years much too fat and toasty, more recent blends have been more compact and better focused.

Now–1999 $$

CHANOINE

Avenue de Champagne, 51100 Reims
(326) 36.61.60 FAX (326) 36.66.62

When relaunched in 1991, Chanoine was meant to be a superior supermarket Champagne, but the wines were so good and the bottles so beautifully dressed with reproduction labels that it became a brand in its own right.

CHANOINE NV BRUT 84

Fresh, easy, and light, with a fine mousse of tiny bubbles.
On purchase $$

CHANOINE 1990 BRUT 86

A rich, full, and satisfying *cuvée*, with a succulent finish.
On purchase $$

TSARINE NV BRUT, CHANOINE 89

New prestige *cuvée* in snazzy bottle with a twisted fluting. A classy Champagne of superb value and aging potential.
Now–2005 $$

CHAPEL DOWN

Tenterden, England, UK

CHAPEL DOWN EPOCH 1993 BRUT 77

Deliciously fresh, peachy fruit underpinned by mouthwatering ripe acidity, and with an excellent mousse.
On purchase $

CHAPEL DOWN EPOCH 1995 BRUT 

Slightly less peachiness than the 1993, but with an additional violet-vanilla finesse.
On purchase $

CHARBAUT

12 rue du Pont, 51160 Mareuil-sur-Aÿ
(326) 52.80.59 FAX (326) 51.91.49

Guy Charbaut launched this grower Champagne after selling the *négociant* house of Charbaut to Vranken.

GUY CHARBAUT 1990 BRUT 

A characterful wine full of lemony richness, rather than great finesse, but it also promises to gain a toasty finesse as it ages over the next few years.
Now–2002 $$$

CHARLEMAGNE

4 rue de la Brèche d'Oger
51190 Le-Mesnil-sur-Oger
(326) 57.52.98 FAX (326) 57.97.81

Top-class *blanc de blancs*.

GUY CHARLEMAGNE NV RÉSERVE BRUT, GRAND CRU 

Flowery Chardonnay aromas, with delicious, classy fruit on the palate, and a long finish, showing both complexity and finesse.
Now–2001 $$ 82F

CHARTOGNE-TAILLET

37-39 Grande Rue, 51220 Merfy
(326) 03.10.17 FAX (326) 03.19.15

CHAMPAGNE CHARTOGNE-TAILLET NV BRUT, CUVÉE SAINTE-ANNE 

Pure gold for lovers of toasty-rich, creamy Champagne.
Now–2000 $$

CHÂTEAU DE BEAUREGARD

Loire, France

CHÂTEAU DE BEAUREGARD 1995 SAUMUR BRUT 

Very fresh and very clean, with deliciously refreshing fruit and a lively finish.
On purchase $

CHÂTEAU DE BOURSAULT

Boursault 51480 prés Épernay
(326) 58.42.21 FAX (326) 58.66.12

CHÂTEAU DE BOURSAULT NV BRUT 85

Although the least interesting wine in Boursault's range, the Nonvintage Brut should be the excellent 1995-based *cuvée* by the time this guide is published, and that will be followed by the even better 1996-based blend.

Now–1999 $$

CHÂTEAU DE BOURSAULT NV ROSÉ BRUT 

Made by *saignée* method *(see p178)*, this is always Boursault's best *cuvée*, and actually benefits from two years of aging without losing any freshness. The current shipment has delicious, cherrylike fruit of Pinot Noir, which will deepen and take on a creamy richness.

Now–2000 $$

CHÂTEAU DE BOURSAULT NV CUVÉE PRESTIGE BRUT 

Boursault's recent addition to the range is a nice fruit-driven Champagne, but the first wine is 1992-based, and the 1994-based *cuvée* is a wine of much greater finesse. This could very well be a Champagne to watch.

Now–1999 $$

CHÂTEAU DE L'HURBE

Bordeaux, France

This small château in St Laurent d'Arce has produced its own sparkling wine since 1996.

CHÂTEAU DE L'HURBE NV CRÉMANT DE BORDEAUX BRUT 

Succulent fruit intermingles with toasty aromas on nose and palate.

On purchase $

CHÂTEAU DE PASSAVANT

Loire, France

CHÂTEAU DE PASSAVANT NV CRÉMANT DE LOIRE BRUT 

An invigorating fizz with lemony fruit.

On purchase $

CHENEAU

See CIGRAVI

CHEURLIN

12 rue de la Gare
Gyé-sur-Seine 10250 Mussy-sur-Seine
(25) 38.20.27

Of the Aube's ubiquitous Cheurlins, this one is the largest and most active in developing its export trade.

CHEURLIN & FILS NV GRANDE CUVÉE BRUT 

Tangy fruit with ripe green-apples on the finish, and technically too much sulfur, but it is free, not fixed, and will go toasty

1999–2000 $$ 78F

CHEURLIN & FILS NV PRESTIGE BRUT 

Fatter and softer than the Grande Cuvée Brut but just as much free sulfur waiting to go toasty!

1999–2000 $$ 88F

CHEURLIN & FILS 1991 BRUT ORIGINEL 

Extraordinary Burgundian-like lemony-oak aromas. Obviously *barrique*-fermentec but far too much oak. Hopefully, future vintages will have more finesse.

Wait and see $$$ 136F

CHILFORD HUNDRED

Cambridge, England, UK

Buy the 1994 while you can, because I have tasted the next vintage before it is disgorged and cannot see how it can become as good as the 1994.

CHILFORD HUNDRED 1994 ALURIC DE NORSEHIDE 

Lovely old-gold color, an appealing apple-blossom aroma, and long, fruit-strewn flavor of ripe green apples and juicy Victoria plums, with just a touch c Muscat on the finish. An impressive wir

Now–1999 $

CHIARLO

Asti, Italy

Michele Chiarlo is now beginning to establish himself as one of Italy's premier sparkling wine producers.

MICHELE CHIARLO 1993 EXTRA BRUT 73

Complex biscuity aromas demonstrate that this is a serious, quality wine, but like so many Italian sparkling wines it lacks the correct acidity balance, thus misses out on length and finesse.

On purchase $$

EOS, MICHELE CHIARLO 1993 EXTRA BRUT 

This makes a fine, zesty fizz compared to most of the Italian competition. From the presentation alone this should be some avant-garde restaurant's house wine.

On purchase $$

CHIQUET

912 avenue du Général-Leclerc
Dizy, 51318 Épernay
(326) 55.22.02 FAX (326) 51.83.81

Cousins to the Chiquet brothers who own Jacquesson.

GASTON CHIQUET NV BLANC DE BLANCS D'AŸ BRUT 

This rare Aÿ *blanc de blancs* does not have the class or potential complexity of Aÿ Pinot Noir, but its succulent, creamy, juicy fruit is very tempting indeed.

Now–2000 $$ 92F

GASTON CHIQUET NV TRADITION BRUT 

A good, solid Champagne, which might not be special but is recommended for its creamy-nutty-biscuity complexity.

Now–2000 $$ 82F

GASTON CHIQUET 1989 BRUT 

Noticeably deeper yellow color than all other examples of this vintage, with a mature, full, malolactic complexity on nose and palate.

Now–1999 $$$ 110F

CIGRAVI

Penedès, Spain

Paul Cheneau is a French-owned Cava brand. CIGRAVI also produces Cava under the Masia Parera, Bell Duc, and Giró Ribot labels.

BELL DUC 1995 CAVA BRUT 

Sweet, toasty, fat, and sassy.

On purchase $

PAUL CHENEAU 1995 CAVA BRUT 

Not as lush and elegant as the 1994, this vintage nevertheless has an easy-going fruity style that is as clean as a whistle, with good acidity and a soft finish.

On purchase $

MASIA PARERA 1996 CAVA BRUT 

When so many Cavas use Chardonnay, without having a Chardonnay character, it is ironic to find one that actually does taste of Chardonnay, yet contains none! Whatever is responsible does, however, give this *cuvée* a creamy feel in the mouth.

Now–1999 $

CLICQUOT PONSARDIN

See Veuve Clicquot

CLOCKTOWER

See Thames Valley Vineyard

CLOUDY BAY

See Pelorus

CLOUET

8 rue Gambetta
Bouzy 51150 Tours-sur-Marne
(326) 57.00.82

Small grower with a large range of often complex Champagnes.

André Clouet NV Silver Brut, Grand Cru — 84

Rich, Pinot-dominated, oxidative style.
On purchase $$

André Clouet NV Grande Réserve, Brut Grand Cru — 85

Very much like the Silver Brut, just a tad smoother on the finish.
On purchase $$

Clover Hill

See Taltarni

Cockatoo Ridge

South Australia, Australia

A joint venture between Geoff Merrill, the "flying-moustache" of Mount Hurtle fame, and Yalumba.

Cockatoo Ridge NV Brut — 75

Fat and fresh, with a touch of vanilla on the finish, this is quite a serious wine for its low price point.
On purchase $

Codorníu

Penedès, Spain

Despite its ancient origins, Codorníu is the most innovative firm in the Cava industry today,

Codorníu Cuvée Raventós NV Cava Brut

Clean, elegant, and fruity, with a creamy-citrusy finish.
On purchase $

Anna de Codorníu Chardonnay 1995 Cava Brut

There used to be a Codorníu Chardonnay and an Anna de Codorníu, and they have been effectively merged as from the 1995 vintage, but it has not been a smooth transition. This has the makings of a fine wine but should still be in Codorníu's cellars.
Wait and see $

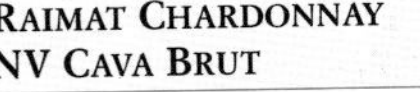

Raimat Chardonnay NV Cava Brut

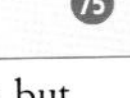

Rich and fruity, with good acidity, but usually more rustic than a properly aged Anna de Codorníu.
On purchase $

Raimat Cava NV Gran Brut — 87

Subtle barrel-fermented aromas pervade the pineapple and other tropical fruits that fill the mouth, and promise to go lightly toasty. The acidity is excellent, and the wine promises further interesting development. Great value for the money.
Now–2000 $

Codorníu Napa

Napa Valley, California, US

A high-tech facility (though all you can see is the tip of a bunker protruding from the hillside) that has come to California to do battle with Freixenet, its Catalonian adversary, which set up Gloria Ferrer in 1982.

Codorníu Napa NV Brut

Pale colored, with a firm mousse of tiny bubbles, and some malolactic complexity creeping through the lush creamy freshness on the nose. The tangy-rich fruit needs very little time to develop some biscuity complexity.
1999 $

Codorníu Napa Vintage 1992 Carneros Cuvée — 79

The aromas are young and relatively undeveloped for a California fizz of this age, yet the fruit is soft and supported by an even soft mousse of minuscule bubbles, so it should not be long before the nose catches up with the palate.
1999 $

Colio

Ontario, Canada

Founded by a group of Italian businessmen who wanted to import Italian wines, but found it easier to build a winery and make their own.

CHARDONNAY LILY 1995 COLIO ESTATE VINEYARDS, VIN MOUSSEUX

If you like a fairly sweet fizz, this *cuve close* will be preferable to more expensive Canadian *méthode champenoise*. Creamy-flowery aroma, with tempting sweet fruit, although the mousse can be a bit explosive.
On purchase $

COLLET

34 rue Jeanson, 51160 Aÿ-Champagne
(326) 55.15.88 FAX (326) 54.02.40
A low-profile cooperative in the great *grand cru* of Aÿ-Champagne.

RAOUL COLLET NV CARTE NOIRE BRUT

Lightly structured and flowery-peppery with some biscuitiness on the finish.
On purchase $$

RAOUL COLLET NV CARTE PERLE BRUT, 1ER CRU

More intensity of fruit and a more serious quality than Carte Noire, with a certain potential for development.
Now–1999 $$

RAOUL COLLET 1990 CARTE D'OR BRUT

Firm, lean, biscuity style that needs food to show at its best.
Now–2000 $$$

COMTE –

See under main name

COMTESSE DE DIE

Rhone, France
Deliciously sweet pure Muscat wines.

COMTESSE DE DIE TRADITION 1996 CLAIRETTE DE DIE, BRUT

Deliciously fresh, off-sweet richness of Muscat fruit – like Asti for grown ups.
On purchase $

CONTRATTO

Asti, Italy

CONTRATTO 1990 RISERVA GIUSEPPE CONTRATTO, SPUMANTE

Fresh, peppery fruit.
On purchase $$

CONTRATTO DE MIRANDA 1995 ASTI

Bottle-fermented Asti! Everything about this wine is a class apart even from other good Asti, from the color to the richness, sweetness, balance, and finesse.
On purchase $$

CORBANS

Auckland/Gisborne/Napier/ Blenheim, New Zealand
Many excellent upmarket wines.

CORBANS VERDE NV METHODE CHAMPENOISE

Perfectly acceptable in a firm, fizzy style, but not exactly special.
On purchase $$

CORBANS AMADEUS 1993 CLASSIC RESERVE BRUT

Not as impressive as previous vintages, but it could be in a developmental phase.
Wait and see $$

(LES) CORDELIERS

Bordeaux, France
The oldest, most famous sparkling Bordeaux producer, with showcase cellars beneath the ruined cloisters of Cordeliers in St Emilion, but a surprising number of *cuvées* failed this year.

LES CORDELIERS 1892-1992 NV CRÉMANT DE BORDEAUX BRUT

This special celebration *cuvée* has plenty of rich, clean fruit, but needs more acidity and finesse for a higher score.
On purchase $

COURBET

See Marne et Champagne

COVIDES

Penedès, Spain

A large Spanish wine cooperative formed in 1964, COVIDES has three wineries and 800 members.

DUC DE FOIX NV CAVA BRUT 75

Fatter than most Cavas, with more fruit and a better mouth-fill and acidity.

On purchase $

XENIUS NV CAVA BRUT 

This light-bodied *cuvée* shows some elegance and ripeness, but is essentially for those who prefer a sweeter-styled *brut.*

On purchase $

CRAIGMOOR

New South Wales, Australia

This Mudgee-based winery is part of the Orlando group.

CRAIGMOOR VINTAGE CHARDONNAY 1994 BRUT 

Big, malty-rich *cuvée.*

On purchase $

CRANSWICK

New South Wales, Australia

Mostly inexpensive fruity fizz, such as Barramundi and Aldridge, but also a serious Sparkling Shiraz.

ALDRIDGE ESTATE NV BRUT 

Light-bodied, gentle fruit pepped-up by a firm mousse to provide some elegance.

On purchase $

BARRAMUNDI NV BRUT 

This inexpensive fizz has developed a sweet, creamy, toffeelike complexity.

On purchase $

THE CRANSWICK ESTATE NV SPARKLING SHIRAZ 

Out of its class for Cranswick, which makes no pretensions over its inexpensive, commercial style of wine, this is a quality sparkling Shiraz with a lovely, ripeness of blackcurrant-raspberry fruit. Drier than most, with no oak at all.

On purchase $

THE CRANSWICK ESTATE NV PINOT CHARDONNAY BRUT 

The very creamy, almost oaky, smoothness underlying the zesty-lemony flavor of this fizz is quite impressive for the price.

On purchase $

CRISTALINO

See Jaume Serra

CROS

Burgundy, France

BERNARD ET ODILE CROS 1993 CRÉMANT DE BOURGOGNE BRUT 70

Fresh lemon fruit with a firm mousse.

On purchase $$

CROSER

See Petaluma

DAMPIERRE

5 Grande rue, 51140 Chenay

Tel (326) 03.11.13 FAX (326) 03.18.05

The wonderfully eccentric Comte Audoin de Dampierre is offering 2,000 magnums of an excellent 1990.

COMTE AUDOIN DE DAMPIERRE NV BLANC DE BLANCS, BRUT 82

Creamy, rich and flavorsome, with some elegance. Good value, but lacking finess

Now–1999 $$ 133F

Comte Audoin de Dampierre NV Cuvée des Ambassadeurs, Brut 87

Rich, smooth and full of biscuity fruit.
Now–1999 $$ 128F

Comte Audoin de Dampierre 1990 Brut Rosé Oeil de Pedrix 87

Delicious strawberry-cherry fruit. To be consumed as fresh as possible.
On purchase $$$ 140F

Comte A. de Dampierre 1990 Blanc de Blancs, Grand Cru, Brut 88

A delicately rich, finely tuned *cuvée* of slow-building complexity, bottled in magnum, and sealed by waxed-cord agraffe, an 18th-century method.
2000–2002 $$$

Darwin's Path

See Manquehue

D'–, De –

See under main part of name

Deidesheim

Pfalz, Germany

Riesling Sekt 1990 Deidesheimer Paradiesgarten Sekt Extra Brut 

Fresh, peachy, pure Riesling fruit, with a nice juicy finish. Bottle-fermented.
On purchase $$

Deis

Mosel-Saar-Ruwer, Germany

Matthias Deis has been producing hand-riddled Sekt by the *méthode champenois* since 1985.

Weingut Matthias Deis 1993 Riesling Sekt Trocken 

Fine, fresh Riesling with vanilla on the finish. Bottle-fermented.
On purchase $$

Delaleu

Loire, France

This has been a consistently successful sparkling wine producer over the last five years or so.

Vouvray, Cuvée Clément NV Brut, Pascal Delaleu 

Very fresh with delicate fruit lifted by a fine mousse of tiny bubbles.
On purchase $

Delamotte

7 rue de la Brèche d'Oger,.51190
Le Mesnil-sur-Oger
(326) 57.51.65 FAX (326) 57.79.29

The sister company to Salon, which is next door, Delamotte's wines are always rich, ripe, and a good value.

Delamotte NV Brut 

Fine aromas, with elegant fruit on the palate, and a touch of pepperiness, which will disappear with more bottle-age.
Now–2000 $$ 105F

Delamotte 1990 Blanc de Blancs 

A number of the 1990s had a creamy, exotic-fruit character, but this was one of the creamiest and most exotic.
Now–2002 $$$ 150F

Delaroy

See Boizel

Delatite

Victoria, Australia

DELATITE DEMELZA NV BRUT 

Ignore the awful label and you will discover that this *cuvée* has a nice creamy-richness of fruit. Apparently, it is a blend of Pinot Noir and Chardonnay from 1994 and 1995, and the label will be revamped if exported!

On purchase Ⓢ

DELBECK

39 rue du Général Sarrail, 51100 Reims
(326) 77.58.00 FAX (326) 77.58.01

An old Champagne brand that has been bought and sold so often that it has yet to establish a style.

DELBECK NV BRUT HÉRITAGE 

Firm, well-structured, high-acid fruit made without malolactic fermentation. This nonvintage *brut* could do with longer postdisgorgement aging prior to shipment or a higher dosage, however it is still early days.

1999–2001 ⓈⓈ 113F

DELBECK NV ROSÉ HÉRITAGE BRUT 

A far more mature wine than the above, with the mellow, strawberry richness of Bouzy Pinot Noir dominating.

Now–2000 ⓈⓈ 138F

DELBECK NV CRAMANT 

Pure creamy-walnutty richness.

Now–2005 ⓈⓈⓈ 145F

DELBECK NV BOUZY 

Apricot aroma with ripe Pinot Noir red fruits on the palate, and a typically Bouzy touch of fatness on the finish.

Now–2000 ⓈⓈⓈ 145F

DELBECK NV ORIGINE (90)

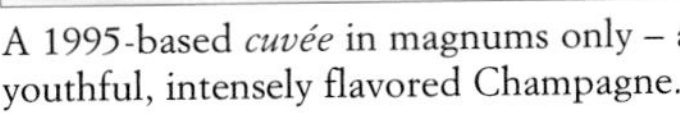

A 1995-based *cuvée* in magnums only – a youthful, intensely flavored Champagne.

2000–2010 ⓈⓈⓈ

DELBECK VINTAGE 1990 BRUT 

The 1990 vintage is a wine with young, developmental, ethereal-minerally fruit, and very fine acidity.

2000–2002 ⓈⓈⓈ 138F

DELIANCE

Burgundy, France

The two highest-scoring Crémant de Bourgogne tasted this year came from this producer, which under blind conditions speaks volumes. Made from Côte Chalonnaise grapes.

RUBAN MAUVE, CRÉMANT DE BOURGOGNE NV BRUT, DELIANCE PÈRE ET FILS (88)

Beautiful, fluffy fruit, with sherbety freshness and great acidity.

Now–2000 Ⓢ

RUBAN VERT, CRÉMANT DE BOURGOGNE NV BRUT, DELIANCE PÈRE ET FILS (88)

Lovely Burgundian Chardonnay fruit of some class and finesse. Well selected, skillfully made, with the potential to age

Now–2001 Ⓢ

DEMOISELLE

See Vranken

DÉTHUNE

2 rue du Moulin, 51150 Ambonnay
(326) 57.01.88 FAX (326) 57.09.31

Usually a rich, ripe, Pinot-driven style

PAUL DÉTHUNE 1990 BRUT (8

Tremendously rich and fruity in a easy-drinking style, yet does not lack finesse

Now–2000 ⓈⓈⓈ

DEUTZ

16 rue Jeanson, 51160 Aÿ-Champagne
(326) 55.15.11 FAX (326) 58.76.13

Deutz went through an uneven patc in the late 1980s, but everything came right in 1990. The profitability of this house suffered from under-funding until Louis Roederer acquired the firm in 1993.

DEUTZ NV BRUT CLASSIC 

Fresh, expressive fruit, with a touch of pepper, which should go minerally biscuity. Should be aged.
1999–2001 $$ 142F

DEUTZ 1990 BRUT 

As with many Deutz Champagnes, there is some pepperiness to the fruit, but the acidity is excellent. Will become complex.
1999–2002 $$$ 177F

DEUTZ 1989 BLANC DE BLANCS BRUT 88

Still tight and firm, especially for a 1989, with plenty of extract for development.
1999–2003 $$$ 240F

CUVÉE WILLIAM DEUTZ 1990 MILLÉSIMÉ BRUT 90

A flavor-packed wine with such bitterness from undeveloped extract that it promises to be complex when mature.
2000–2010 $$$ 382F

DEUTZ MARLBOROUGH

See Montana

DEVAUX

Domaine de Villeneuve, 10110 Bar-sur-Seine
(25) 38.30.65 FAX (25) 29.73.21

The Aube region's fastest-improving, most go-ahead and innovative cooperative, run by Claude Thibault.

VEUVE A. DEVAUX NV GRANDE RÉSERVE, BRUT 

This *cuvée* was strangely almondy in 1997, but the current shipment is more classic, with some biscuity character.
Now–1999 $$ 99F

VEUVE A. DEVAUX NV CUVÉE ROSÉE, BRUT 

Mature rooty-Pinot aromas, with hints of toastiness on the nose, and rich, toasty Chardonnay fruit on the palate. Rosée is not a misspelling; Devaux says that the extra "e" is intentional.
Now–1999 $$

VEUVE A. DEVAUX NV BLANC DE NOIRS, BRUT 84

This is one pure Pinot *cuvée* that will definitely go toasty, rather than biscuity.
Now–1999 $$

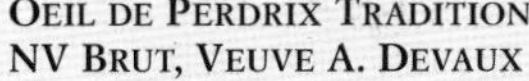

OEIL DE PERDRIX TRADITION NV BRUT, VEUVE A. DEVAUX 85

Very pale peach color, with light and delightful fruit. Elegant and tangy.
Now–1999 $$

VVE. A. DEVAUX 1990 MILLÉSIME BRUT 

With heaps of super creamy-biscuity fruit, this pure Chardonnay *cuvée* knocks the spots off the 1990 Distinction.
Now–2002 $$$

VVE. A. DEVAUX 1990 CUVÉE DISTINCTION, BRUT 

Fresh, fruity style with a hint of biscuitiness building in the middle, and an aftertaste reminiscent of apple purée.
Now–2000 $$$ 150F

VEUVE A. DEVAUX 1988 CUVÉE DISTINCTION BRUT 

Lovely salmon color with classy, creamy, slow-developing red-fruit aromas.
Now–2001 $$$

NICOLE D'AURIGNY 1992 BRUT 

The depth and structure promise good development.
Now–1999 $$$

DIE

See Comtesse de Die

DIETRICH

Alsace, France

CLAUDE DIETRICH 1994 CRÉMANT D'ALSACE BRUT 

Classy aromas are not reflected on the palate, which is okay but workmanlike. It will be interesting to see how this particular *cuvée* develops.
Now–1999 $$

Domaine Carneros

See Carneros

Domaine Chandon

See Chandon

Domaine de Brizé

Loire, France

Domaine de Brizé NV Crémant de Loire Brut 

The deep, full nose on this wine hints at botrytis (noble rot), which, real or imagined, adds to the interest. Also, the wine has plenty of fruit and gives the impression more of New World ripeness than the Old World, let alone the Loire. A serious effort.

On purchase $

Domaine de la Gloriette

Loire, France

Domaine de la Gloriette NV Cuvée Prestige, Crémant de Loire Brut 

This wine had similar botrytis-like hints on the bouquet to those of Domaine de Brizé, but without any of the "New World" fruit on the palate, although it is still very fruity.

On purchase $

Domaine de la Paleine

Loire, France

Domaine de la Paleine NV Saumur Brut 

A very fresh, easy-going, and clean wine for the Saumur appellation.

On purchase $

Domaine de Nerleux

Loire, France

Better-known for Saumur-Champigny.

Domaine de Nerleux NV Crémant de Loire Brut 

I much preferred the tangy, peppery fruit in this wine to Domaine de Nerleux's equally peppery, but dull, Saumur.

On purchase $

Domaine des Varinelles

Loire, France

This producer used to produce good Saumur-Champigny and Rosé de Loire, and now sparkling wines.

Daheuiller, Domaine des Varinelles NV Crémant de Loire Brut 

This decent, zesty fizz might only just qualify, but that makes it superior to the vast majority of Loire bubblies I tasted.

On purchase $

Domaine du Bouxhof

Alsace, France

Domaine du Bouxhof NV Crémant d'Alsace Brut 

Lots of pineapple sprightly fruitiness gives this wine a real richness, but it has the acidity to support it.

On purchase $

Domaine Ste. Michelle

See Ste. Michelle

Domaine Sylvain Gaudron

Loire, France

Vouvray Blanc de Blancs NV Brut, Domaine Sylvain Gaudron

Soft, easy, and elegant sparkler with gentle fruit and a smooth mousse of small bubbles.

On purchase $

Vouvray Pétillant NV Demi-Sec, Domaine Sylvain Gaudron

Fresh, creamy fruit.

On purchase $

Dom Pérignon

See Moët & Chandon

Dom Ruinart

See Ruinart

Don Perejón

Spain

The white *cuvée* would have been hard pushed to score 10 points out of 100, but the *rosé* scraped in.

Don Perejón NV Mencía Rosé Brut

Although not a Cava, this is made by the *método tradicional* and its accessible fruit made it more enjoyable than many Cavas.

On purchase $

Dopff au Moulin

Alsace, France

Pierre-Etienne Dopff puts a personal face on the Moët & Chandon of Alsace.

Dopff au Moulin, Cuvée Bartholdi 1993 Crémant d'Alsace Brut

A richly flavored wine that has consistently aged well since its inception. This vintage will peak in five or six years.

Now–1999 $$

Dopff au Moulin, Cuvée Julien NV Crémant d'Alsace Brut

72

There is a good weight of fruit for a correctly lean structure here.

Now–1999 $

Doquet-Jeanmaire

44 Chemin Moulin Cense Bizet
(326) 52.16.50 FAX (326) 59.36.71

Doquet-Jeanmaire NV Blanc de Blancs, Carte Or Brut

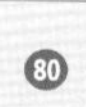

Sprightly fruitiness on nose, with extremely rich fruit on the palate.

On purchase $$ 71F

Doquet-Jeanmaire NV Blanc de Blancs, Réserve, Demi-Sec

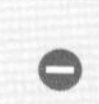

The first bottle had very little fizz, the second only a bit more, and both were deep yellow, with a mature sweet flavor and coconutty complexity that had nothing to do with oak, and everything to do with age. Curious, but not disliked.

On purchase $$ 85F

Doquet-Jeanmaire 1989 Blanc de Blancs Brut

Very soft and creamy, and needs to lengthen on the palate, but does not have the balance to age. Scrapes in on current enjoyment only.

On purchase $$$ 90F

Down St. Mary

Crediton, England, UK

Simon Pratt is determined to produce the best English sparkling wine of which his vineyard is capable.

Down St. Mary Bubbly 1994 Dry

The 1992 was too oxidative, but this is far more skillfully made, with a fruit-driven style that promises to go toasty rather than oxidative after a year or so.

Now–1999 $

DRAPPIER

Grande rue, 10200 Urville
(25) 27.40.15 FAX (25) 27.41.19

Ultra-fruity Champagnes that quickly attain a lovely biscuity complexity.

DRAPPIER NV CARTE D'OR BRUT (88)

Succulently fruity when first released, this goes deliciously biscuity within a year.
Now–1999 $$ 80F

DRAPPIER NV ROSÉ BRUT (88)

Rich, creamy-fruity that is already developing biscuity bottle-aromas.
Now–1999 $$

DRAPPIER NV SIGNATURE BRUT (89)

Extremely rich and fruity, this will go very toasty after another year in bottle.
Now–2000 $$ 90F

DRAPPIER 1990 CARTE D'OR BRUT (88)

Incredibly fruity when first launched, this now has a great depth of intense fruit infused with biscuity complexity.
Now–1999 $$$

DRAPPIER 1989 GRANDE SENDRÉE (90)

Rich, sweet and pure, with complex after-aromas and great finesse, this is a single-vineyard Champagne from 70-year-old vines grown on soil with ash in it.
Now–2000 $$$ 120F

DRAPPIER 1995 CUVÉE DE L'AN 2000 (88)

The quality was evident although it is not commercially disgorged until May 1999. Capable of great finesse.
2000–2002 $$$

DUC DE FOIX

See COVIDES

DUMANGIN

3 rue de Rilly, 51500 Chigny-les-Roses
(326) 03.46.34 FAX (326) 03.45.61

J. DUMANGIN FILS NV CARTE D'OR, DEMI-SEC, 1ER CRU (84)

Fresh fruity aromas followed by soft, mellow sweetness.
On purchase $$ 78F

J. DUMANGIN FILS 1992 BRUT, 1ER CRU (84)

Firm, but more fruit-driven than biscuity
Now–1999 $$$ 110F

J. DUMANGIN FILS 1993 CUVÉE 2000 (–)

Under blind conditions I noted the biscuitiness building and gave this wine 83 points. However, this is not yet a fully commercial product, so I will reserve judgment.
Wait and see $$$ 125F

J. DUMANGIN FILS 1991 BRUT MILLÉSIMÉ, 1ER CRU (84)

Full-flavored style with mellow-ripeness.
Now–1999 $$$ 110F

DUMONT

11 rue Gambetta, 51500 Rilly-la-Montagne
(326) 03.40.67 FAX (326) 03.44.82

A respected grower from the same village as Vilmart.

DANIEL DUMONT NV PREMIER CRU GRANDE RÉSERVE BRUT (85)

This has grown richer, and fuller in bottl
On purchase $$ 73F

DANIEL DUMONT NV GRANDE RÉSERVE ROSÉ BRUT (82)

Deepish salmon-peach color, with sprightly fruit on the nose. Little finesse, but bags of fruit in a big, rich, soupy way.
On purchase $$ 73F

DANIEL DUMONT 1988 CUVÉE D'EXCELLENCE, BRUT (86)

Creamy-biscuity richness.
Now–1999 $$$ 97F

DURBACH

Baden, Germany

WINZERGENOSSENSCHAFT DURBACH 1994 DURBACHER KOCHBERG ROSÉ SEKT BRUT 

An old gold color with hues of a setting sun. Gorgeously rich Pinot fruit on the palate, gently cushioned by an impeccable mousse of tiny pinhead bubbles.
On purchase $$

DUVAL-LEROY

69 avenue de Bammental, F-51130 Vertus
(326) 52.10.75 FAX (326) 57.54.01
This house has always produced elegant Champagne of good value, and the quality improved in the 1990s.

FLEUR DE CHAMPAGNE NV DUVAL-LEROY 

Very fresh, fragrant style of Chardonnay-dominated Champagne.
On purchase $$

FLEUR DE CHAMPAGNE BLANC DE NOIRS NV DUVAL-LEROY 

Made from Pinot Noir and Meunier, yet relatively more full-bodied than the *rosé*, which is just Pinot Noir. Fuller and more intense than other Duval-Leroy.
On purchase $$

FLEUR DE CHAMPAGNE SAIGNÉE ROSÉ NV DUVAL-LEROY 

A pure Pinot Noir *cuvée,* this delicious, easy-drinking *rosé* is teeming with beautiful, elegant, juicy ripe fruit.
On purchase $$

FLEUR DE CHAMPAGNE BLANC DE BLANCS NV DUVAL-LEROY 

Very fresh, floral aromas with light, fluffy fruit and a juicy-sweet finish.
On purchase $$$

FLEUR DE CHAMPAGNE BLANC DE BLANCS 1995 DUVAL-LEROY 

Its fresh, lime-blossom aromas and fluffy-citrusy fruit are so inviting that for this wine to be released any time after the legal minimum January 1999 would not be too soon. And the 1996 has such beautifully ripe acidity that I cannot wait for 2000.
Now–2005 $$$

FLEUR DE CHAMPAGNE 1995 DUVAL-LEROY 

Similar comments to the Blanc de Blancs 1995, but with sweeter, creamier fruit.
Now–2005 $$$

FLEUR DE CHAMPAGNE 1990 DUVAL-LEROY 

Wonderful richness of cream for such light body and elegant structure, with a lovely sweet-vanilla finish.
Now–2005 $$$

EDWARDS & CHAFFEY

See Seaview

EHRHART

Alsace, France

ANDRÉ EHRHART NV CRÉMANT D'ALSACE BRUT, ROTENBERG 

Some biscuity complexity with sweet, malty fruit.
Now–2000 $

ELSTREE

See Highfield

EMRICH

Nahe, Germany

CHRISTIAN UND RICHARD EMRICH 1995 KREUZNACHER BLAUER SPÄTBURGUNDER SEKT EXTRA SEKT TROCKEN 

An off-dry *rosé* with soft, elegant cherry fruit and fine acidity. Bottle-fermented.
On purchase $$

ENDRIZZI

Trentino, Italy

ENDRIZZI NV COLLEZIONE MASETTO BRUT 

Satisfying clean richness of fruit, a firm mousse and very small bubbles.
On purchase $

ENGEL

Alsace, France

A family enterprise with vineyards at the foot of Haut-Koenigsbourg.

ENGEL TRADITION NV CRÉMANT D'ALSACE BRUT 

Touch of Chablis-like character, with firm fruit, structure and acidity. Could develop.
Now–1999 $

FACCOLI

Italy

My first encounter with Faccoli, and an extremely happy one it was too. One of Franciacorta's top producers.

FACCOLI NV BRUT ROSÉ, FRANCIACORTA 

Old gold color, with mature, toasty aroma, but very fresh apricot fruit on the palate.
On purchase $

FACCOLI NV EXTRA BRUT, FRANCIACORTA 

Rich toasty aromas and superior acidity balance for an Italian sparkling wine.
On purchase $

FACCOLI NV BRUT, FRANCIACORTA 

Seriously fine, mature aromas of toast and coffee follow perfectly onto the palate. A Champagne-lover's Italian fizz.
On purchase $

FAHRER

Alsace, France

This grower has a certain reputation for Rouge de St-Hippolyte, but only just passes muster on his *crémant*.

MICHEL FAHRER NV CRÉMANT D'ALSACE BRUT 

Very fresh fruit, but would benefit from a more individually expressive style.
On purchase $

FAUSTINO MÁRTINEZ

Rioja, Spain

One of a small number of Rioja wineries producing Cava. The firm's Reserva and Gran Reserva still red wines are also very good.

FAUSTINO MARTINEZ NV CAVA EXTRA SECO 

Fresh and simple tropical fruit flavor.
On purchase $

(DE) FAVERI

Veneto, Italy

Only six Prosecco survived the test, two of which were from this producer, including the highest scorer.

DE FAVERI, PROSECCO DI VALDOBBIADENE NV VINO SPUMANTE BRUT 

Similar to, but a lighter version of, the De Faveri in the prestige bottle below.
On purchase $

DE FAVERI, PROSECCO DI VALDOBBIADENE NV VINO SPUMANTE BRUT 75

Same name as above, but in a prestige-shaped bottle. Very fresh, Mâcon-style fruit on nose and palate, with the freshness and elegance following right through to the aftertaste.
On purchase $

FAZI-BATTAGLIA

Italy

This producer's makes the excellent Verdicchio di Castelli di Jesi Le Moie, a still wine, as well as this *spumante*, which just scraped in.

Fazi-Battaglia NV Vino Spumante Brut 

Ripe fruit overlaid with wet straw.
On purchase $

Ferrari

Trentino, Italy

To maintain the motoring theme, Ferrari is acknowledged by many as the "Rolls Royce" of Italian fizz,

Ferrari NV Brut, Trento 

A firm, rich flavor of some complexity, although it still has room to develop.
Now–2000 $

Ferrer

See Gloria Ferrer

Feuillatte

CD 40a Chouilly, 51206 Épernay
(326) 54.50.60 FAX (326) 55.33.04

This Champagne brand has improved over the last 10 years, but the performance is still patchy for a cooperative that has so many good vineyards at its disposal.

Nicolas Feuillatte 1992 Blanc de Blancs Brut, Premier Cru 

A rich, clean, and flavorsome *cuvée* that promises to develop some complexity. It is nice to see Nicolas Feuillatte succeed in a relatively modest vintage.
Now–1999 $$$ 109F

Nicolas Feuillatte 1988 Cuvée Spéciale Brut, 1er Cru 

This biscuity *cuvée* is very mature for a 1988, showing its age particularly on the finish. This is one of two prestige *cuvées*, the other being Palmes d'Or, and only the first vintage of the latter (1985 Palmes d'Or) has lived up to the expectation of a luxury Champagne.
On purchase $$$ 130F

Firmato

Trentino, Italy

Firmato NV Brut, Trento 

Rich, smooth fruit, firm mousse and a tasty finish.
On purchase $

Fitz

Pfalz, Germany

The oldest Sekt-producing house in the Pfalz, dating from 1837.

Fitz NV Riesling Sekt Extra Brut 

This is an elegant pure Riesling with a hint of peaches. Made by *cuve close*.
On purchase $$

Fluteau

5 Rue de la Nation, 10250 Gyé-sur-Seine
(325) 38.20.02 FAX (325) 38.24.84

This Aubois house run by Thierry and Jennifer Fluteau is the smallest in Champagne, even smaller than Salon.

G. Fluteau NV Blanche Brut 

Rich and fruity, with good weight, with a gentle mousse of medium-small bubbles.
On purchase $$

G. Fluteau 1993 Blanche Brut 84

Richer and fruitier, with tinier bubbles in the mousse than the above.
Now–2000 $$

Foix

See Covides

Forget-Brimont

11 route de Louvois, 51500 Craon de Ludes
(326) 61.10.45 FAX (326) 61.11.58

FORGET-BRIMONT NV CARTE BLANCHE, EXTRA BRUT 83

Lacks a bit of finesse on the nose, but is really quite rich and ripe on the palate.
Now–1999 $$ 82F

FOURNY

5 rue du Mesnil, 51130 Vertus
(326) 52.16.30 FAX (326) 52.2013

VVE FOURNY NV BLANC DE BLANCS, BRUT PREMIER CRU 

Lovely fresh and fluffy sherbety fruit.
On purchase $$ 80F

FRATI

See Cà dei Frati

FREIXENET

Penedès, Spain

The Freixenet group includes Castellblanch, Segura Viudas, Conde Caralt and Canals Nubiola, Gloria Ferrer in California, and an operation in Mexico, plus the Champagne house of Henri Abelé, but it is most famous for its black bottle Cava.

FREIXENET MONASTRELL-XARELLO NV CAVA BRUT 

Now on the third or fourth release of this ground-breaking *cuvée* (the first commercially available white Cava to include black grapes), this wine shows a hint of black grape color, some creamy-richness, and a flowery perfume on the finish.
On purchase $

FREIXENET 1991 CAVA BRUT NATURE 

The nondosage, vintage version of Cordon Negro was fine in 1997 when the 1991 was on the shelf – one of the best vintages of this *cuvée* since the 1975 – and it will still serve you well. (Not so the 1994 Brut Nature vintage.)
On purchase $

GAILLARD-GIROT

43 rue Victor Hugo, 51530 Mardeuil
(326) 51.64.59 FAX (326) 51.70.59

GAILLARD-GIROT NV BRUT 

Rich, fruity, and tasty, with creamy-biscuity finesse building on the finish.
Now–1999 $$ 66F

GALLIMARD

18-20 rue du Magny, 10340 Les Riceys
(325) 29.32.44 FAX (325) 38.55.20

Jean and Didier Gallimard have recently received a fair bit of well-deserved attention in the French press for their sparkling wines.

GALLIMARD NV CUVÉE DE RÉSERVE BRUT 

Has a fine, flowery finesse and an incredibly long finish.
Now–1999 $$ 70F

GALLIMARD 1992 CUVÉE PRESTIGE BRUT 

Very rich and biscuity.
Now–2000 $$$ 80F

GALLO

California, US

It is almost too much to comprehend, but E&J Gallo has a total production under numerous brands equal to one-and-a-half times the entire output of Australia. The latest sparkler only just scrapes in, but this is the sort of producer that could, with investment and the right consultant, produce a world class sparkling wine. We will have to see whether Indigo Hills is as ambitious as Gallo gets or the blueprint for something more serious.

INDIGO HILLS 

An easy-drinking fizz in a clean, fresh, ar fruity style that is a tad too sweet, but probably just right for the mass market.
On purchase $

GARDET

13 rue Georges Legros
51500 Chigny-les-Roses
(326) 03.42.03 FAX (326) 03.43.95

A small house with a good reputation among British traditionalists. The wines can sometimes be too heavy and oxidative, but when there is enough fruit, these elements come together to make *cuvées* of stunning richness and potential complexity.

GARDET 1988 BRUT — 85

Very fruity with none of the oxidative aromas that can detract from some Gardet *cuvées*. Could do with more finesse, but there is an interesting peppery character that promises to mellow, and a certain richness.

1999–2002 ⓈⓈⓈ 113F

CUVÉE CHARLES GARDET 1995 BRUT — 85

An advance sample shows fine balance and potential, providing it is not left on its lees longer than three years.

2000–2005 ⓈⓈⓈ

GATINOIS

7 rue Marcel Mailly, 51160 Aÿ
(326) 55.14.26 FAX (326) 52.75.99

Pierre Cheval sells part of his production to Bollinger, but increasingly makes more of his own Champagne.

GATINOIS NV TRADITION — 85

This is an easy-to-drink *cuvée*. However, it does need 18–24 months to smooth down the raw elements of the floral aromas that pervade this young, soft, elegant Champagne.

2000 ⓈⓈ

GATINOIS NV RÉSERVE — 87

This is the Tradition with an extra year or two yeast-contact, and the raw-floral notes have disappeared to be replaced by fine autolytic aromas. Consequently, this is ready to drink but also offers more serious, age-worthy potential.

Now–2003 ⓈⓈ

GATINOIS 1991 BRUT

I was not convinced by this vintage, but the 1985 is full of delicious, honeyed fruit, so I will reserve my opinion for now, hence the lack of an overall score.

Wait and see ⓈⓈⓈ

GATINOIS 1992 BRUT

Similar feelings to the 1991.

Wait and see ⓈⓈⓈ

GAUCHER

10200 Arconville
(325) 27.87.31 FAX (325) 27.85.84

This Aube producer is currently on as good a form as I can remember.

BERNARD GAUCHER NV CARTE D'OR BRUT — 86

A full, strong Pinot style that builds in the mouth. This *cuvée's* high extract is supported by a fine structure, making it a good food wine, but there is already some complexity and the finish is beginning to mellow out.

Now–1999 ⓈⓈ

GAUDRON

See Domaine Sylvain Gaudron

GAUTHIER

See Marne et Champagne

GENET

22 rue des Partelaines, 51530 Chouilly
(326) 55.40.51 FAX (326) 59.16.92

An inconsistent producer in my experience.

MICHEL GENET NV BLANC DE BLANCS BRUT, GRAND CRU

Fresh and rich, but rather too almondy for a classic *blanc de blancs*.

On purchase ⓈⓈ

GEOFFROY

150 rue du Bois-des-Jots
Cumières 51480 Damery
(326) 55.32.31 FAX (326) 54.66.50

The Geoffroys are quality-conscious, in both the vineyard and winery, harvesting grapes in sweeps, using oak foudres and preventing the malolactic.

René Geoffroy NV Cuvée Prestige, Brut

Softer and smoother than the Cuvée de Réserve, with some finesse.
On purchase $$ 108F

René Geoffroy NV Cuvée de Réserve Brut, Premier Cru

Fine flavors and good acidity, with more finesse than the current Cuvée Sélectionnée.
Now–1999 $$ 75F

René Geoffroy 1993 Cuvée Sélection Brut

A fresh and zesty *cuvée* that is drinking well but will age gracefully.
Now–2001 $$

GERMAIN

38 rue de Reims, 51500 Rilly-la-Montagne
(326) 03.40.19 FAX (326) 03.43.11

The basic nonvintage is boringly amylic, although some of the top *cuvées* can be excellent value.

Henri Germain 1990 Brut

Very exotic, rich, and fulsome fruit. Huge fun when tasted, but will probably go through an awkward developmental stage before emerging in a more classic, complex style. A second sample via the importer had a creamy-toffee malolactic richness.
Now–2002 $$$

Henri Germain NV Brut Reserve

I was glad to find no amylic aroma in the latest *cuvée,* which is fresh and fruity, with some mellow-vanilla on the finish. The best nonvintage Germain in memory.
Now–1999 $$

GERMANIER

See SAVISA

GIANNI

Asti, Italy

Gianni NV Asti

Sweet, fresh, rich, and piquant, this wine had the most muscatty fruit of all the As tasted this year.
On purchase $

GIERSBERGER

Alsace, France

Giersberger NV Crémant d'Alsace Brut

Oxidative complexity with sweet fruit o the palate.
On purchase $

GIESEN

Christchurch, New Zealand

This is almost as good as Giesen's wonderful still Pinot Noir.

Voyage, Special Cuvée Brut NV Giesen Wine Estate

Beautifully bright Pinot fruit. A stunner
Now–1999 $

GIMONNET

1 rue de la République, 51530 Cuis
(326) 59.78.70 FAX (326) 59.79.84

All Gimonnet vineyards are planted exclusively with Chardonnay, hence every wine is a *blanc de blancs*, which is a rare phenomenon in Champagne, even among growers on the Côte des Blancs. Quality can be exceptionally high and prices very reasonable.

PIERRE GIMONNET & FILS NV BLANC DE BLANCS BRUT, PREMIER CRU 

Clean, rich flavor. Should develop well.
Now–2000 ⓈⓈ 87F

PIERRE GIMONNET & FILS NV OENOPHILE, BLANC DE BLANCS MAXI-BRUT 

Patience!
1999 ⓈⓈ 113F

PIERRE GIMONNET & FILS 1993 GASTRONOME, BLANC DE BLANCS BRUT 

Huge mouthful of flavor with an extremely persistent finish.
1999–2003 ⓈⓈⓈ 96F

PIERRE GIMONNET & FILS 1992 GRAND CRU - CHARDONNAY BRUT 

Rich and fruity, but too young to drink yet.
2000–2002 ⓈⓈⓈ 115F

PIERRE GIMONNET & FILS 1990 FLEURON, BLANC DE BLANCS BRUT 

A classy combination of succulent fruit, richness, and finesse.
Now–2003 ⓈⓈⓈ 108F

PIERRE GIMONNET & FILS 1989 BLANC DE BLANCS BRUT 

A big, flavor-packed wine that needs either food or time.
Now–2005 ⓈⓈⓈ 127F

GISSELBRECHT

Alsace, France

The Auxerrois *crémant* failed muster this year, while the *rosé* scraped in.

W. GISSELBRECHT BRUT ROSÉ NV CRÉMANT D'ALSACE 

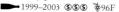

Soft, pure Pinot fruit.
On purchase Ⓢ

GLORIETTE

See Domaine de la Gloriette

GLORIA FERRER

Sonoma, California, US

The Spanish Cava house Freixenet founded this in California in 1982, and it is named after the wife of José Ferrer, the president of Freixenet.

GORIA FERRER SONOMA BRUT NV FREIXENET SONOMA CAVES 

Light and creamy with fat, sassy fruit and a sherbety finish.
On purchase Ⓢ

GLORIA FERRER BLANC DE NOIRS BRUT NV FREIXENET SONOMA CAVES 

A few years ago, this *cuvée* had raw fermentation odors, but the current shipment is deliciously fresh and juicy.
On purchase Ⓢ

GOERG

4 Place du Mont Chenil, 51130 Vertus
(326) 52.15.31 FAX (326) 52.23.96

A superior cooperative Champagne that is usually good for vintage *cuvées*, but I was not able to recommend the 1992 submitted for tasting.

PAUL GOERG NV BLANC DE BLANCS BRUT 

Rich flavors supported by a structure that will be better after a little bottle-age.
1999–2001 ⓈⓈ 75F

GOLAN HEIGHTS WINERY

Israel

This winery in the Golan Heights is famous for its still wines, but it still has a lot of fine-tuning to do to its sparkling wine *cuvées*.

YARDEN BLANC DE BLANCS NV GOLAN HEIGHTS WINERY BRUT 

Shipments of this wine seem to vary. A lightly rich malo style with elegant, mellow fruit on the finish.
On purchase Ⓢ

(Michel) Gonet

196 avenue Jean-Jaurès, 51190 Avize
(326) 57.50.56 FAX (326) 57.91.98

An inconsistent grower who hits as many lows as highs.

Michel Gonet NV Blanc de Blancs Brut Grand Cru 87

Fruity, with nice finesse on finish.
Now–1999 $$ 90F

Michel Gonet 1989 Blanc de Blancs Brut Grand Cru 87

A bit of a contradiction, this, with its fresh, delicately perfumed aromas sitting on an unexpectedly firm structure, as if there were some Pinot Noir in the blend.
1998–2001 $$$ 100F

(Philippe) Gonet

1 rue de la Brèche d'Oger
51190 Le-Mesnil-sur-Oger
(326) 57.51.07 FAX (326) 57.51.03

Philippe is Michel's cousin (above).

Philippe Gonet 1988 Blanc de Blancs Brut 

Creamy-nutty style with low dosage.
1999–2000 $$$ 140F

Gosset

69 rue Jules Blondeau
51160 Aÿ-Champagne
(326) 55.14.18 FAX (326) 51.55.88

I queried the quality of Gosset recently, but I am now sure that the quality is as good as it has ever been.

Gosset Brut Excellence 

Fresh, sweet, easy-drinking fruit.
Now–1999 $$ 129F

Gosset NV Grande Réserve Brut 

A lovely depth of flavor, plenty of finesse, and great potential complexity in a smooth, nonoxidative biscuity style.
Now–1999 $$$ 218F

Gosset Grande Millésime 1989 Brut 89

Maturing relatively quickly on the nose for Gosset, but there is a strand of freshness running through the richness on the palate, hinting that it might well go through another stage of development.
Now–2002 $$$ 284F

Gosset Grande Millésime 1985 Brut 

The depth of flavor in this wine is incredible, and it gets deeper and more sustained each time I taste it. Although it already has the rich, biscuity complexity and finesse that Gosset drinkers expect, it will be even greater in five years.
Now–2015 $$$

Gosset Celebris 1990 Brut 91

New prestige *cuvée* with a significantly higher proportion of Chardonnay. Almost too delicious to be true, but it has a classic structure and will develop well.
Now–2010 $$$$

Gosset Celebris 1988 Brut 91

Great promise, but needs lots more post disgorgement aging.
2003–2018 $$$$ 390F

Gosset Grand Rosé 1990 Brut 

This exotically creamy-floral *cuvée* seems atypical for Gosset, but it is superb nonetheless and is still very young.
Now–2002 $$ 296F

Gosset Grand Rosé 1988 Brut 

Refined and strongly perfumed in its youth, this is now taking on the smooth, biscuity finesse expected from Gosset.
Now–2002 $$

Goutorbe

9 rue Jeanson, 51160 Aÿ-Champagne
(326) 55.21.70 FAX (326) 54.85.11

Henri Goutorbe has produced some excellent Champagnes in the past, but nothing to touch the quality and complexity of the 1990 vintage now on the market.

HENRI GOUTORBE NV CUVÉE TRADITIONNELLE BRUT 84

Fine, perfumed, and elegant.
Now–2001 $$ 75F

GOUTORBE NV BRUT, CUVÉE PRESTIGE 

Rich citruslike fruit.
Now–2000 $$ 84F

HENRI GOUTORBE 1990 BRUT, GRAND CRU 91

Blockbusting combination of succulence and complexity, with a touch of vanilla on the finish.
Now–2005 $$$ 116F

GRAEGER

Rheinhessen, Germany

GRAEGER PRIVAT RESERVE 1995 SPÄTBURGUNDER SEKT BRUT 74

The intensity of Pinot Noir fruit in this wine is so satisfying and mellow it is almost gamey. Bottle-fermented.
On purchase $$

GRANDIER

See Manquehue

GRANT BURGE

South Australia, Australia

Owner-winemaker Grant Burge originally founded Krondorf (now part of Mildara Blass). He has a solid foundation of good vineyards and in just ten years has quickly built up a reputation for the richness and consistency of his eponymous brand.

GRANT BURGE NV METHODE TRADITIONELLE BRUT 

I did not like the green-malic Pinot Chardonnay *cuvée* tasted a couple of months earlier, but this is softer with a touch of vanilla finesse on the finish.
On purchase $

GRAMONA

Penedès, Spain

This small family-owned firm has its own vineyards, and regularly produces some of the best Cavas available.

III LUSTROS 1991 CAVA BRUT 

Creamy-cedary fruit and good underlying acidity enable this *cuvée* to scrape in. Last year it had lovely lemony-toasty fruit that would have warranted a score of 80 points, but, unfortunately, terpene aromas have developed over the last 12 months.
On purchase $

CELLAR BATTLE 1989 CAVA BRUT 

Terpenes have also appeared on the nose of this vintage since I tasted it one year ago (80 points then). This has leached away some of the finesse, but it is still packed with creamy-peachy-vanilla fruit on the palate, and a sweet vanilla finish.
On purchase $

GRATIEN

30 rue Maurice Cerveaux, 51201 Épernay
(326) 54.38.20 FAX (41) 51.03.55

This is one of my favorite producers, but I was surprised by the small selection submitted for the organized tastings (especially compared to the large number of Loire *cuvées* from its sister company Gratien & Meyer).

ALFRED GRATIEN NV BRUT RÉSERVE 

Alfred Gratien's Brut Réserve is a full, firm, classic-structured *cuvée* that shows rich, spicy fruit of excellent finesse. This wine is capable of considerable longevity and ultimate complexity, which is a tribute to the much-maligned Meunier grape, since it accounts for more than 45 percent of this blend.
Now–2002 $$

ALFRED GRATIEN 1989 BRUT 

Astonishing acidity underscores an intensity of fruit that promises to become very complex in a few years.
2000–2010 $$$

Gratien & Meyer

Loire, France

One of the top fizz producers in the Loire, this was founded in 1864 at the same time as Alfred Gratien.

Gratien & Meyer NV Cuvée Royale, Crémant de Loire Brut

Very rich, fresh, fruity aroma. I much preferred this to Gratien & Meyer's Saumur Brut, although the "same" wine under the own-label of The Wine Society (UK) was distinctly better.

On purchase $

Gratien & Meyer NV Harmonie Dry, Saumur

The freshest *sec* on the nose, and as rich and sweet as a *demi-sec* on the palate, with nice juicy fruit that I preferred to Gratien & Meyer's Demi-Sec.

Now–2000 $

Gratien & Meyer NV Cuvée Flamme, Saumur Brut

Apricots and custard on the nose, with elegant apricot fruit and a twist of tangerine on the palate. An expressive Loire sparkling wine that shows some potential for complexity, it is the best Loire fizz I have tasted in recent memory.

Now–2000 $

Gratien & Meyer NV Brut Rosé, Cuvée Flamme, Saumur

A well-structured *rosé* capable of some improvement in bottle.

Now–2000 $

Gratien & Meyer, Cardinal NV Noir de Noirs, Vin Rouge Mousseux, Demi-Sec

72

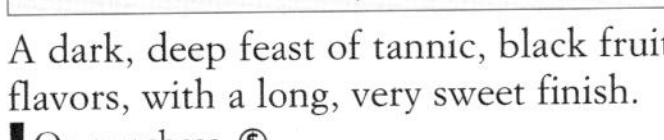

A dark, deep feast of tannic, black fruit flavors, with a long, very sweet finish.

On purchase $

Gratien & Meyer Collection 1989 Blanc de Blanc, Saumur Brut

Mature, creamy-fruit aroma and flavor. This is a serious Saumur that some Loire devotees would probably rate higher.

On purchase $$

Green Point

See Chandon Australia

Grenelle

Loire, France

Louis de Grenelle NV Saumur Rosé Sec

Fresh and sweetish, with very clean, easy-drinking fruit.

Now–1999 $

Louis de Grenelle NV Saumur Brut

Tight, lemony fruit of some specificity. Expressive.

Now–2000 $

Grésille

Loire, France

Anne de la Grésille NV Crémant de Loire Brut

A slight oxidative complexity adds a dimension of interest to the clean, lean fruit in this wine. Good length.

On purchase $

Gruss

Alsace, France

A few wines from this Eguisheim grower, including two good *crémants*.

Gruss Brut Prestige NV Crémant d'Alsace

77

Lovely, fat and sassy fruit, and a nice cushiony mousse, but it would have scored even higher with more acidity.

On purchase $

Joseph Gruss & Fils NV Crémant d'Alsace Brut

Very fruity aroma, sherbety fruit, cushiony mousse, and a fresh, breezy finish.

On purchase $

HAGNAU

Baden, Germany

WINZERVEREIN HAGNAU 1995 HAGNAUER BURGSTALL KERNER SEKT EXTRA TROCKEN 

I'm not overly fond of the Kerner grape, but this *cuvée* is a good example of how fresh, flowery, off-dry fizz should be. Bottle-fermented.

On purchase $$

HAMBACHER SCHLOSS

Pfalz, Germany

This cooperative has 150 members who produce 50,000 cases of Sekt each year by the transfer method.

HAMBACHER SCHLOSS 1993 HAMBACHER REBSTÖCKEL DORNFELDER SEKT TROCKEN 

Very winey style. A curiosity.

On purchase $$

HANDLEY

Mendocino, California, US

Méthode champenoise specialist in the top-performing Anderson Valley.

HANDLEY 1992 BLANC DE BLANCS 

Even when a vintage has lacked acidity, the soft, creamy-lemony Chardonnay fruit in the Blanc de Blancs makes it stand out.

Now–1999 $$

HANDLEY 1992 BRUT 

Good acidity and a soft mousse of tiny bubbles add a crisp dimension to the creamy-vanilla richness in this *cuvée*.

Now–1999 $$

HARDY'S

South Australia, Australia

Hardy's Nottage Hill is a real winner.

HARDY'S NV BRUT 

Malo-dominated nose and palate here, with deep, malty richness of fruit, and a good balance.

On purchase $

SIR JAMES NV SPARKLING SHIRAZ 

Soft spicy red fruits put this sparkling Shiraz in a different class to the 1993 white Sir James Hardy Brut.

On purchase $

NOTTAGE HILL SPARKLING CHARDONNAY 1996 BRUT 

A fresh, fluffy, gently rich and creamy fizz that hits the spot. Not great quality, but certainly a satisfying wine that offers great value for the money.

On purchase $

OMNI NV BRUT 

A more individual character than most at this price point, with a reasonable structure of firm, creamy fruit.

On purchase $

YARRA BURN CHARDONNAY PINOT NOIR 1993 BRUT 

This zesty-lemony *cuvée* is a very fresh sparkling wine, with its five years of age only just beginning to mellow the sherbety fruit on the finish.

On purchase $$

LEASINGHAM CLASSIC CLARE 1991 SPARKLING SHIRAZ 

Classic cedary-oaky sparkling red Shiraz.

On purchase $

HARTENBERGER

Alsace, France

Normally one of the best Crémant d'Alsace producers, particularly for Pinot Gris, but the current *cuvées* are somewhat below par.

HARTENBERGER, BLANC DE BLANCS NV CRÉMANT D'ALSACE BRUT 

Rich and ripe, with more than enough fat for mouthfill and a rather sweet finish. Needs more acidity for a higher score.

On purchase $

HASELGROVE

South Australia, Australia

Established in 1980 by Nick Haselgrove, who laid down a *solera* for his increasingly popular Sparkling Garnet as recently as 1991. The notes below were based on SG3 (1995-based) and SG4 (1996-based), both of which were uncannily similar in style and quality, I am glad it is such a young *solera* because old *soleras* have too many drawbacks for sparkling wine in terms of terpenes and coarse oxidative characteristics.

HASELGROVE NV MCCLAREN VALE SPARKLING GARNET

Full of tangy, bilberry and cranberry fruit, this lavishly flavored fizz is marked by its fresh, billowy mousse.

On purchase $

HAUTE BOURGOGNE

Burgundy, France

This cooperative started producing Crémant de Bourgogne in 1994.

LES VIGNERONS DE HAUTE BOURGOGNE NV DEMI-SEC, CRÉMANT DE BOURGOGNE

Some creamy-biscuity malolactic complexity on the nose, with rich, sweet, caramel fruit on the palate, and a touch of vanilla on the finish.

Now–2000 $

HAUTES-CÔTES

Burgundy, France

Grapes grown in the Hautes-Côtes de Nuits and Hautes-Côtes de Beaune.

CRÉMANT DE BOURGOGNE NV BRUT, LES CAVES DES HAUTES-CÔTES

Some biscuity maturity on the nose, with good acidity underpinning light, elegant fruit on the palate.

Now–1999 $

CRÉMANT DE BOURGOGNE BLANC DE BLANCS NV BRUT, LES CAVES DES HAUTES-CÔTES

74

Creamy-malo-biscuity aromas, good length of flavor, plenty of ripe acidity.

Now–1999 $

HEEMSKERK

See Jansz and Rebecca Vineyard

(CHARLES) HEIDSIECK

4 Blvd. Henry Vasnier, 51100 Reims
(326) 84.43.50 FAX (326) 84.43.99

This is the home of Daniel Thibault, the maestro of master blenders who built up a stock of reserve wines to create the top-performing Brut Réserve. This has now been relaunchec in three versions based on the date of bottling, which is confusing even for wine critics. The quality is as brilliant as ever, but I hope that fractionalizing the Brut Réserve image does not divide its loyal customers. Meanwhile, look out for a release of mature Champagne "Charlie" vintages.

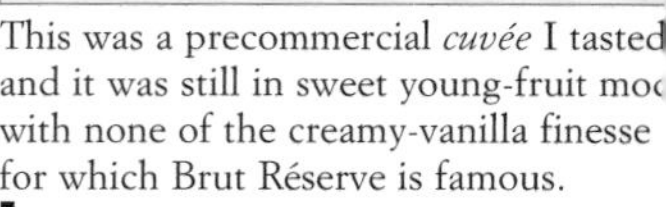

CHARLES HEIDSIECK NV BRUT RÉSERVE, MIS EN CAVE 1995

8

This was a precommercial *cuvée* I tasted and it was still in sweet young-fruit moc with none of the creamy-vanilla finesse for which Brut Réserve is famous.

Now–2003 $$

CHARLES HEIDSIECK NV BRUT RÉSERVE, MIS EN CAVE 1994

90

Extraordinary finesse for such a rich an full wine, this has the finest bead (tiny bubbles) of the Mis en Cave *cuvées*, wit the most cushiony mousse and smoothe palate. Beautifully balanced dosage.

Now–2002 $$ 130F

CHARLES HEIDSIECK NV BRUT RÉSERVE, MIS EN CAVE 1993

88

Soft and mellow, this is the easiest Mis e Cave to drink, but the 1994 offers more interest on the palate.

Now–2001 $$ 145F

CHARLES HEIDSIECK NV BRUT RÉSERVE, MIS EN CAVE 1992

You would not think that this was the oldest of the three *cuvées* originally launched. Still quite tight when tasted, it will loosen up by Christmas 1999.

1999–2003 ⓈⓈ 160F

CHARLES HEIDSIECK 1990 BRUT 93

Rich and creamy, but still building, this vintage was a change of style for Charles Heidsieck, with more emphasis on Chardonnay fruit, going for intensity and elegance, rather than Pinot weight.

Now–2010 ⓈⓈⓈ 180F

CHARLES HEIDSIECK 1989 BRUT 90

Extraordinarily successful for the vintage, this was the bridge in style between the old Charles Heidsieck vintages as last expressed by the 1985, and the new direction of 1989.

1999–2004 ⓈⓈⓈ

CHARLES HEIDSIECK 1990 CUVÉE DES MILLÉNAIRES 92

The creamy-rich fruit in this *cuvée* has the slow-building capacity for which Millénaires has quickly become noted, and promises an exceptional balance of finesse and complexity in years to come.

Now–2005 ⓈⓈⓈ

CHARLES HEIDSIECK 1985 CUVÉE DES MILLÉNAIRES

The second vintage of this *cuvée* is even more intensely flavored than the first, and has taken just as long to reveal its true mellow-biscuity richness.

Now–2005 ⓈⓈⓈ 250F

(PIPER-)HEIDSIECK

51 Boulevard Henri Vasnier, 51100 Reims
Tel (326) 84.41.94 FAX (326) 84.43.49

Marilyn Monroe used to claim that a glass of Piper each morning spread a little warmth throughout her body! The house has been part of Remy-Cointreau since 1990, prior to which it had built its reputation as a non-malolactic Champagne, but, through the advice of Daniel Thibault, all *cuvées* now undergo the malo.

PIPER-HEIDSIECK NV BRUT 85

The real jump in Piper's quality came with the 1992-based blend, two years after Thibault started making it. The non-vintage is lighter than Charles Heidsieck's Brut Réserve, with a more straightforward plumpness and bright southern ripeness in the fruit. Underneath, however, there is a minerally finesse, and if allowed to age it curiously develops a Charles-like creamy-vanilla richness. Lay down a few bottles.

Now–2000 ⓈⓈ 110F

PIPER-HEIDSIECK 1989 BRUT

There was no such thing as a straight Piper vintage until this *cuvée* was launched in 1997. It is not special, though, and you will have to wait for the excellent 1990 before you get to taste a Thibault-made Piper vintage.

Now–2000 ⓈⓈⓈ 160F

PIPER-HEIDSIECK 1989 BRUT SAUVAGE 89

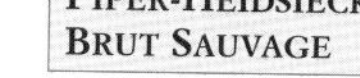

Ever since this *cuvée* went from non-vintage to vintage, the fruit has appeared to be more low-dosage than the non-dosage that its label suggests. The 1989 has been in something of a time warp since 1996 when it has had a lovely toasty-richness of fruit, with a long, mellow-flavored finish.

Now–2000 ⓈⓈⓈ

HEIDSIECK MONOPOLE

17 avenue de Champagne
51205 Épernay Cedex
Tel (326) 59.50.50 FAX (326) 51.87.07

Belgian-born entrepreneur Paul Vranken purchased Heidsieck & Co Monopole from Mumm and put the stock in Charbaut's old cellars.

HEIDSIECK & CO MONOPOLE NV BRUT

Light, fresh, and easy.

On purchase ⓈⓈ

HEIDSIECK & CO MONOPOLE 1989 BRUT

Creamy-malo fruit supported by high acidity.

Now–2004 ⓈⓈ

HEIM

Pfalz, Germany

The Heim'sche Privat-Sektkellerei has been making the unusual sparkling wine below since 1989.

MARTIN HEIM 1994 GEWÜRZTRAMINER TROCKEN SEKT

This was one of only two German fizzy Gewürztraminers I tasted, and it was far better balanced than I imagined such a product could be, with the sort of clean, truly pungent spicy fruit that most producers of still Gewürztraminer outside of Alsace can only dream about.

On purchase $$

HEIM IMPERIAL

See Westhalten

HEITZMANN

Alsace, France

A capable producer of Pinot Gris and Vendange Tardive, and this *crémant* is also surprisingly good.

LÉON HEITZMANN NV CRÉMANT D'ALSACE BRUT

Despite the strawlike aroma, there is a nice, fat, fruity flavor, a hint of spice, and good acidity.

On purchase $

HENRIET-BAZIN

9 rue Dom Pérignon, 51380 Villers-Marmery

(326) 97.96.81 FAX (326) 97.97.30

D. HENRIET-BAZIN 1990 CARTE D'OR, BRUT 1ER CRU

One for the buttery-malo brigade, this wine has so much butterscotch fruit that it has lost all hope of finesse, but some drinkers go for this style.

On purchase $$$

M.N. HENRIET 1989 CUVÉE PRESTIGE BLANC DE BLANCS, BRUT 1ER CRU

82

Sprightly fruitiness on the nose, with a very rich finish.

On purchase $$$

HENRIOT

3 Place des Droits de l'Homme

51100 Reims

(326) 89.53.0 FAX (326) 89.53.10

Look to Henriot for good bottle-age and unrelenting high quality from the former head of Veuve Clicquot.

HENRIOT NV SOUVERAIN BRUT

88

Creamy-peppery-biscuity aromas, with long, lush, creamy fruit on the palate. This Champagne is one of the best that Henriot has ever produced.

Now–2000 $$ 105F

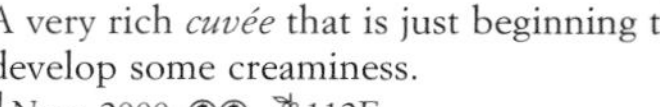

HENRIOT NV BLANC DE BLANCS BRUT

85

A very rich *cuvée* that is just beginning t develop some creaminess.

Now–2000 $$ 112F

HENRIOT 1989 BRUT MILLÉSIMÉ

Toasty aroma with peppery fruit on the palate, and very good acidity.

Now–2001 $$$ 130F

HENRIOT 1988 BRUT MILLÉSIMÉ

Exclusively for those who love to be reminded of farmyard fruit when drinking sparkling wine, which counts me out.

On purchase $$$ 130F

HENRIOT 1988 ROSÉ MILLÉSIMÉ BRUT

85

A mature fruitiness, truly dry, but gentle and soft, with peppery undertones.

Now–2000 $$$ 140F

HENRIOT 1985 CUVÉE DES ENCHANTELEURS BRUT

The slow-building toasty complexity of this Champagne, and its high acidity make it a must with food.

Now–2000 $$$ 190F

HÉRARD

31 Grande Rue, 10250 Neuville-sur-Seine
(325) 38.20.14

I have always found this Aube producer reliable and good value, especially for bright and sunny, fruit-driven *blanc de noirs*.

PAUL HÉRARD NV BLANC DE NOIRS BRUT 84

Ultrafruity aromas with strawberry-like fruit on the palate.
On purchase $$

PAUL HÉRARD NV BLANC DE NOIRS, DEMI-SEC 86

An ultrafruity aroma followed by a *demi-sec* flavor that tastes sweeter and more complete than others, perhaps because the acidity was initially very high and thus could carry substantially more dosage, although there is nothing green about the finish.
Now–2000 $$

HERTZ

Alsace, France

PRINCE ALBERT NV CRÉMANT D'ALSACE BRUT, ALBERT HERTZ 

A curiosity, this! Tastes like sparkling Muscat to me, but whatever it actually is, it needs some sweetness, and would be an absolute stunner in a rich *demi-sec* style.
On purchase $

HIDDEN SPRING

Horam, England, UK

Martyn Doubleday and Chris Cammel won the English Sparkling Wine Trophy in 1997 for their first fizz.

HIDDEN SPRING VINEYARD NV PINOT NOIR BRUT 

Pale salmon color, with some cherry-not. May develop well over the next couple of years.
Now–2000 $

HIESTAND

Rheinhessen, Germany

Erich Hiestand has made Sekt since 1990 by the *méthode champenoise*.

WEINGUT HIESTAND 1992 GUNTERSBLUMER EISERNE HAND PINOT BLANC SEKT BRUT 

Crisp, clean, and very pale with a gentle, slow-rising bead. A fine food wine in a tall Rhine bottle. Bottle-fermented.
On purchase $$

HIGHFIELD

Marlborough, New Zealand

This Anglo-Japanese-Kiwi-owned estate initially turned to Champagne Drappier, but now makes its Elstree sparkling wine independently.

ELSTREE 1993 MARLBOROUGH 

As rich as it has been in the past, but more malty in style than the creamy-vanilla character it used to have.
On purchase $$

HILL

Penedès, Spain

The origins of this old Cava firm go back to Mr. Hill, an Englishman who established a vineyard at Moja.

CAVAS HILL 1995 RESERVA ORO SECO 

Much better than the 1994, this vintage has some flowery finesse on the nose, but the lightweight fruit lacks mouthfill, despite the higher dosage.
On purchase $

HILL OF HOPE

New South Wales, Australia

From the former Saxenvale winery, this changed name in 1996 when it was bought by pharmacist Michael Hope.

HILL OF HOPE 1996 BLANC DE NOIR BRUT 

Although I liked the ripe, sweet, succulence on the finish of this wine, I am concerned by the maturity of its fruit and deep yellow color.
Wait and see $

HOCHRIEGL

See Kattus

HOEN

See Baron de Hoen

HOLLICK

Coonawarra, Australia

HOLLICK 1994 SPARKLING MERLOT, COONAWARRA 

Huge fruity-oak flavor with rich, floral aromas and cherry, plum, and blackberry fruit. Drier than other Australian fizzy reds.
Now–2001 $$

HORNBERG

See Burg Hornberg

HOUËT & TESSIER

Loire, France

HOUËT & TESSIER NV SAUMUR BRUT 

Just scrapes through on fruit and length.
On purchase $

HUGUET

Penedès, Spain

Some of the best Cava available.

HUGUET 1993 CAVA BRUT NATURE 77

Very tight and young, but promising.
1999–2000 $

HUGUET 1993 CAVA BRUT CLASSIC 80

Wonderful, sweetish fruit.
1999–2000 $

HUNAWIHR

Alsace, France

CALIXTE NV CRÉMANT D'ALSACE BRUT 70

Fresh, finely balanced, elegant style.
On purchase $

HURBE

See Château de L'Hurbe

HUNTER

Sonoma, California, US

Pinot Noir was not in demand in the early 1980s, but Robert Hunter's vineyard was full of the stuff. He had no idea what to do with it until his friend Dan Duckhorn suggested he make sparkling wine.

ROBERT HUNTER 1993 BRUT DE NOIRS 

Always a richly flavored *cuvée* with plent of complexity, yet still quite young.
Now–1999 $$

HUNTER'S

Marlborough, New Zealand

Jane Hunter owns one of New Zealand's best wineries, and her services to wine were rewarded a few years ago with an OBE. Her vintage Brut is starting to show promise, and the new export Mirru Mirru is excellent.

IUNTER'S MIRRU MIRRU NV BRUT 

was lip-smacking good when first re-ased, but quickly tightened up and ecame almost unpleasantly sharp. A few onths more, and Mirru Mirru had eveloped great depth of flavor, classic ructure, and evolved into a serious wine.
On purchase or wait six months $$

INDIGO HILLS

See Gallo

IRON HORSE

Sonoma, California, US

Iron Horse is one of those rare New World sparkling wines that can not only take plenty of post-disgorgement aging but positively needs it. The fruit structure here has always been superb for *méthode champenoise*.

RON HORSE 1993 BRUT 

eep, beautifully intense fruit. A class act.
Now–2000 $$

RON HORSE 1993 BLANC DE BLANCS 

it and weighty with creamy-complexity.
Now–2000 $$

RON HORSE 1993 ROSÉ 

wickedly deep strawberry color, with uit so brash that it slaps you in the face!
On purchase $$

J WINE COMPANY

Sonoma, California, US

It was not until the elegant 1991 hit the shelves that the "J" brand was established as a world-class fizz.

J" 1993 BRUT 

nce the 1991 vintage this *cuvée* has en lovely to drink when the fruit is ung and elegant. Great finesse.
On purchase $$

JACKSON ESTATE

Marlborough, New Zealand

This was originally intended to be a specialist sparkling wine brand, but the owners have made still wines too.

JACKSON ESTATE 1993 MARLBOROUGH 

Not as good as the inaugural 1992 vintage (82 points). It should benefit from additional bottle-age, gradually acquiring a creamy-toasty complexity.
Now–1999 $$

JACQUART

6 rue de Mars, 51066 Reims
(326) 07.20.20 FAX (326) 57.78.14

An ambitious cooperative brand that grew in quality in the 1990s. It uses the initials NM (for "house") in its matriucation number instead of CM (for "cooperative") because a new company was formed in which the members simply became shareholders.

JACQUART NV BRUT TRADITION 

A fresh, clean, youthful nose belies the creamy-biscuity richness on the palate.
Now–1999 $$ 121F

JACQUART NV BRUT MOSAÏQUE 85

Sweeter, riper, and fatter than the Brut Tradition, but not as biscuity, and more fruit-driven than creamy.
Now–2000 $$ 127F

JACQUART 1990 BRUT 

This was brilliant in 1997, with massive fruit and potential, but started developing complexity in 1998, and this has not made it shine as well as it used to or will be. Preferably leave until the Millennium.
2000–2005 $$$

JACQUART 1992 CUVÉE MOSAÏQUE, BLANC DE BLANCS 

A creamy-malo aroma adds some complexity to the richness of fruit on the palate. But will it go the same way as the 1990 vintage (an early demise)?
Now–2000 $$$ 163F

Jacquart 1990 Cuvée Mosaïque, Blanc de Blancs
80

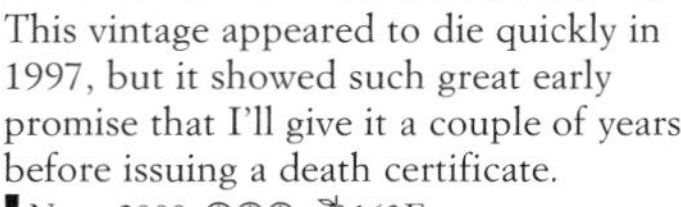

This vintage appeared to die quickly in 1997, but it showed such great early promise that I'll give it a couple of years before issuing a death certificate.
Now–2000 $$$ 163F

Jacquart Cuvée Mosaïque 1990 Brut Rosé

Soft fruit, starting to mellow, but should develop nicely over the next few years.
Now–2002 $$$ 163F

Jacquesson

68 rue du Colonel Fabien, 51200 Dizy
(326) 55.68.11 FAX (326) 51.06.25
Quality-conscious house on par with Billecart-Salmon, but with more emphasis on complexity, less on elegance.

Jacquesson & Fils NV Perfection Brut

Very fresh, fine and delicious in an easy-drinking style.
Now–1999 $$$ 119F

Jacquesson & Fils NV Perfection Rosé

Succulent, creamy-soft, red fruits served on a pincushion mousse.
Now–1999 $$$ 134F

Jacquesson & Fils 1990 Blanc de Blancs

This was extravagantly fruity when first released, then went through a strange phase before emerging as a beautiful, creamy-walnutty *cuvée* that has fine acidity to insure future evolution.
Now–2005 $$$ 160F

Jacquesson & Fils 1990 Signature Brut

Champagnes like this humble the taster because it was coarse, oxidative, and not very attractive when tasted prior to commercial disgorgement. Now, however, it has beautifully pure fruit of great concentration and such high acidity that it needs time to show its full potential. A great *vin de garde rosé* like this is a rare beast indeed.
Now–2005 $$$

Jacquesson & Fils 1989 Signature Brut
90

Superb walnutty complexity, with huge promise for future development, and excellent high acidity for a 1989 vintage
Now–2008 $$$ 233F

Jacquesson & Fils 1988 Signature Brut
91

This went through a strangely coarse period a couple of years ago, but had previously shown its great potential, and has developed beautifully over the last year. It has a huge amount of fruit with complex bottle-aromas only just beginning to emerge, but will eventually be suffused with toasty finesse.
Now–2005 $$$

Jacquesson & Fils 1990 Signature Rosé Brut
91

This went through a strangely oxidative stage a few years ago, but is back on trac as one of the most delicious, delicately succulent *rosé* Champagnes available.
Now–2005 $$$ 257F

Jacquesson & Fils 1985 Dégorgement Tardif (bottle)
–

An intensely flavored Champagne, though there was a touch too much sulf when it was first released as a late-disgorged vintage. Since this fault might not appear in a future shipment, I will reserve judgment until next year.
Wait and see $$$$ 300F

Jacquesson & Fils 1985 Dégorgement Tardif (magnum)

The magnum is a totally different wine: a *blanc de blancs* as opposed to the tradi tional blend of three Champagne grapes in the 75cl bottle. It actually indicates *blanc de blancs* on the magnum label, whereas there is no such mention on the ordinary bottle-size, although the labels in both cases are very intricate (beautifu 19th-century replicas). What is not on th magnum's label, however, is that this *blanc de blancs* is also a mono-*cru*, made exclusively from Avize grapes. It is not classic, but it is rather wonderful in a fat creamy, exotic fashion.
Now–2010 $$$$ 700F

JACQUINET-DUMEZ

26 rue de Reims, 51370 Les Mesneux
(326) 36.25.25 FAX (326) 36.58.92

ACQUINET-DUMEZ 1992 UVÉE L'EXCELLENCE BRUT

ch lean fruit of an impressive depth, th lots of finesse.

Now–2000 $$$ 100F

(SIR) JAMES

See Hardy's

JANSZ

Tasmania, Australia

Formerly majority-owned by Louis Roederer and, dare I say, significantly better after it was sold to the Heemskerk Group in 1994. However, the Jansz brand has recently been sold again, to Samuel Smith & Son of Yalumba fame.

ANSZ TASMANIA 1993 BRUT CUVÉE

ovely creamy-biscuity complexity, classic an structure, yet juicy fruit acidity.

Now–2003 $$

ANSZ TASMANIA 1992 BRUT CUVÉE

ot in the same class as Janz 1993; it has coffee aftertaste and lacks finesse.

On purchase $$

JECHTINGEN

Baden, Germany

WINZERGENOSSENSCHAFT ECHTINGEN 1994 PINOT SEKT BRUT

ood full, fruity style, with expansive feel the Pinot Blanc character, and a soft, ashiony mousse. Bottle-fermented.

On purchase $$

JONGEGEZELLEN

See Twee Jongegezellen

JORDAN

See J Wine Company

JOURDAN

Paarl, South Africa

Highly regarded fizz from the Cabriere Estate, which is owned by Achim von Arnim, who used to be the winemaker at Boschendal.

PIERRE JOURDAN NV BRUT

Just scrapes in on the fresh and fruity ticket, but needs layering with more flavors and a touch of finesse to make the grade of a top estate fizz.

On purchase $

PIERRE JOURDAN NV BLANC DE BLANCS, CLOS CABRIÈRE BRU

The extraordinary mint-caramel character of this wine is almost certainly derived in part from malolactic and/or oak, but exactly where the mint comes from is anybody's guess. Certainly it's a first in sparkling wine, giving this wine some novelty value, and the higher acidity gives it the edge over most other Pierre Jourdan *cuvées*.

On purchase $

PIERRE JOURDAN NV BRUT SAUVAGE, CLOS CABRIÈRE

Too much creamy-caramel malolactic dominates the nose and detracts from the potential finesse of the wine. It has a very rich, soft, fat, caramel and vanilla flavor but needs more acidity. A fascinating concoction.

On purchase $

PIERRE JOURDAN NV CUVÉE BELLE ROSÉ

A golden color with barely any hint of pink, but plenty of soft, succulent fruit.

On purchase $

KAAPSE VONKEL

see Simonsig

KALIFELZ

Mosel-Saar-Ruwer, Germany

KALIFELZ RIESLING 1995 RIESLING SEKT EXTRA BRUT 74

Satisfying peachy fruit with a fresh floweriness on the finish. Bottle-fermented.

On purchase $$

KARTHÈUSERHOF

Mosel-Saar-Ruwer, Germany

KARTHÈUSERHOF 1995 TYRELL RIESLING SEKT BRUT 

Fresh, fruit-driven style. Bottle-fermented.

On purchase $$

KASSNER-SIMON

Pfalz, Germany

KASSNER-SIMON 1994 RIESLING SEKT EXTRA BRUT 

Elegant flowery fruit. Bottle-fermented.

On purchase $$

KASSNER-SIMON 1994 RIESLING SEKT EXTRA SEKT TROCKEN 

Let down by a touch of sulfur on the nose, but there was so much richness of fruit that it deserved recommendation.

On purchase $$

KATNOOK

South Australia, Australia

KATNOOK NV BRUT 

Too much malolactic, but there is promise underneath.

Wait and see $$

KATTUS

Austria

HOCHRIEGL EXTRA TROCKEN 70

Fresh, applelike Sekt style.

On purchase $

KIRSTEN

Mosel-Saar-Ruwer, Germany

WEINGUT KIRSTEN 1992 WEISSER BURGUNDER SEKT BRUT 74

Very flowery aroma with soft, elegant fruit on the palate.

On purchase $$

WEINGUT KIRSTEN 1993 RIESLING SEKT BRUT 80

Some classy, ripe-peachy Riesling fruit.

On purchase $$

KLOSTERMÜHLE

Nahe, Germany

KLOSTERMÜHLE 1995 MONFORT PINOT NOIR SEKT BRUT 76

A very clean and well-focused *rosé* with red-fruit pastilles on the nose and crisp acidity on the palate. Bottle-fermented.

On purchase $$

KNYPHAUSEN

Rheingau, Germany

Just 250 cases of Sekt annually, made from Spätlese grapes. The 1990 was one of the three best Sekt wines tasted this year, and the greatest Riesling Sekt of the tasting.

BARON ZU KNYPHAUSEN 1993 RIESLING SEKT EXTRA BRUT 

A seriously glugable pure Riesling Sekt that is just beginning to develop gasoline like bottle-aromas.

On purchase $

ARON ZU KNYPHAUSEN 1990 IESLING SEKT EXTRA BRUT 

ass and elegance were the first two words come to mind as soon as I tasted this ne, terpenelike Riesling Sekt with its vely peachy-ripeness of fruit on the nish. Like most German so-called *extra uts*, it is dry, but not especially dry.

On purchase $$

KOEHLY

Alsace, France

Koehly is a brilliant producer of varietal wines, and the richness and ripeness of his style comes through especially in this *crémant*.

OEHLY, CRÉMANT ST-URBAIN OSÉ NV CRÉMANT D'ALSACE 

ttractive aroma of creamy cherries, soft d easy on the palate, with fat fruit minating the finish.

On purchase $

KÖWERICH

Mosel-Saar-Ruwer, Germany

The Köwerichs include Beethoven's mother in their family line, thus when they started making Sekt in 1989, they named the *cuvée* below after the great composer. (Perhaps this was in the hope that one day someone might describe the wine as "music to their ears," but, like Beethoven, I will remain deaf to that!).

WEINGUT GESCHWISTER KÖWERICH 1994 LUDWIG VAN BEETHOVEN RIESLING SEKT BRUT 

he first bottle I tried was unfortunately rked, but the back-up sample was very pe, round, and perfumed. Bottle-rmented.

On purchase $$

KRIPTA

See Torelló

KRISTONE

Santa Maria, California, US

Kendall-Jackson's prestige sparkling wine is the pet-project of "Mad Harry" Harold Osborne, who was Schramsberg's first winemaker and more recently a consultant for Pelorus.

KRISTONE BLANC DE BLANCS 1992 CALIFORNIA CHAMPAGNE 

Like a classy oaked California Chardonnay on the nose, with no aromas that hint it might be sparkling. This is not as blowsy as the 1991, but still very toasty and too oaky on the palate. Too rich for the balance, it needs a bucketful of acid!

On purchase $$$

KRISTONE BLANC DE BLANCS 1991 CALIFORNIA CHAMPAGNE 

Much better than I imagined, especially on the nose, which was so toasty and blowsy when first released, but has developed an amazing cappuccino aroma. I would love to taste this side-by-side with Billecart-Salmon's Blanc de Blancs 1973, which is cappuccino right down to the sprinkling of chocolate powder. Kristone gets its toast from the barrel before it's even bottled.

On purchase $$$

KRISTONE BLANC DE NOIRS 1992 CALIFORNIA CHAMPAGNE 

Like the 1991, this is an authentic *blanc de noirs*, which is to say white not pink. Also like the 1991, this is fruit-driven rather than *barrique*-dominated, thus has far more elegance, soft, creamy fruit, and better acidity.

On purchase $$$

KRISTONE BRUT ROSÉ 1992 CALIFORNIA CHAMPAGNE 

Toasty nose, very rich, ripe and sweet red-fruit flavors, particularly strawberry. Needs more acidity.

On purchase $$$

KRONE BOREALIS

See Twee Jongegezellen

KRUG

5 rue Coquebert, 51100 Reims
(326) 84.44.20 FAX (326) 84.44.49

Krug is Krug is Krug. It is purchased by a relatively small number of Krugist aficionados around the world, and the price steadily increases at auction.

KRUG NV GRANDE CUVÉE 95

The aromas on this prestige *cuvée* are the epitome of finesse, even when with age it develops huge, lemony-oak aromas; the palate becomes so succulently rich and so fruity that, but for the classic lean structure, would seem fat and exotic. Buy Grande Cuvée by the magnum and keep it perfectly cellared for five years, and you will be assured of the most fabulous supply of exquisite Champagne.

Now–2008 $$$$

KRUG NV ROSÉ

I have to reserve opinion about the current *cuvée* because it was overly mature. Normally this very pale *rosé* is fine and refined, with an exquisitely clean summer-fruit flavor of exceptional length for such a light balance. I have always considered this to be a great *rosé* that improves with an extra year or two in bottle, but some critics have damned it for being too young and austere, so it is possible that Krug could have reacted to this by issuing a more mature *cuvée*. On the other hand, it could be a duff bottle!

Now–2008 $$$$

KRUG VINTAGE 1989 94

Released prior to the 1988, this *cuvée* already has an opulent creamy-walnutty fruit, with a silkiness on the palate and softness of acidity on the finish. A gorgeous mouthful now, it still has plenty of development ahead.

Now–2009 $$$$

KRUG VINTAGE 1988 96

Not released at the time of writing, the 1989 was launched in preference because of the blistering ripe-acidity in this wine. In time this will prove to be one of Krug's greatest vintages, although rumor has it that the 1990 is even better!

Now–2008 $$$$

KRUG VINTAGE 1985 93

When first released, the complexity and class of the 1985 stood out, but it has since clammed up, and will take a few years to emerge in Krug's typically honeyed-rich, mellow, and even more complex second life.

2002–2015 $$$$

KRUG CLOS DU MESNIL 1989 96

I put my hands up: tasted blind I thoug this was the 1988, with its alpine-fresh, fluffy, lemon-pie fruit. Pure delight now it will be fascinating to see how the 1989 develops beside the 1988. This might w be the surprise winner at Krug tastings the future; most of the money will be o the 1988 Clos du Mesnil coming out on top in the long run, whereas the Krugs themselves will probably back the Vintage over Clos du Mesnil. And shou someone slip in a magnum of 1988-base Grande Cuvée, we might all end up wit egg on our faces!

Now–2009 $$$$

KRUG CLOS DU MESNIL 1988 95

Even lighter, fluffier lemon-pie fruit tha the above, but this has the distinctive vanilla and cream aromas of new oak.

Now–2009 $$$$

KWV

Paarl

A huge national cooperative that officially controlled the South African wine industry until privatized in 1995.

LABORIE BRUT 1993 CAP CLASSIQUE 82

Classic biscuity fruit supported by high acidity for length, and satisfying mid-palate mouthfill.

On purchase $

LABORIE BRUT 1992 CAP CLASSIQUE 73

Nice toasty aromas intermingling with malolactic creaminess, and although the is a soft violety-vanilla smoothness on th finish, it lacks mid-palate mouthfill, depriving the wine of a higher score.

On purchase $

Laborie

See KWV

Lacrima

See Lavernoya

Lafitte

See Vranken-Lafitte

Laisement

Loire, France

This producer is well known for his excellent Vouvray Moelleux, and I have enjoyed the sparkling Vouvray before, but it did not pass this year, whereas the Touraine *cuvée* did well.

Touraine Rosé NV Brut, Jean-Pierre Laisement

Not great in a classic sense, but so rich and succulent that it is definitely yummy.

On purchase $

Lamiable

8 rue de Condé 51150 Tours-sur-Marne

(326) 58.92.69 FAX (326) 58.94.96

Lamiable NV JLP Brut, Grand Cru

Very sweet and undemanding style.

On purchase $$

Lancelot-Pienne

1 allée de la Foràt, 51530 Cramant

(326) 57.55.74 FAX (326) 57.53.02

Albert Lancelot's family have been growers in Champagne for about 120 years. I preferred his basic Blanc de Blancs to the classic Brut Sélection.

A. Lancelot-Pienne NV Blanc de Blancs Brut

Fresh, zingy-zippy sherbety fruit with a mouthwatering crisp finish.

Now–1999 $$ 76F

Lang

Rheingau, Germany

Hans Lang wastes nothing; after bottling his best wines, including 2,500 cases of Sekt, he not only distills the leftovers for Weinbrand (brandy), but the skins and pips for Testerbrand (grappa), and even the yeast for Hefebrand (yeast-brandy).

Johann Maximilian 1993 Riesling Sekt Extra Brut, Hans Lang

Fresh sherbety pure Riesling fruit, quite fluffy, with a satisfying almondy complexity on the finish.

Chardonnay & Weissburgunder 1992 Hans Lang

Just scrapes in for those sparkling wine drinkers who like butterscotch aromas. Those with a more classic bent might prefer to see Hans Lang use a malolactic culture that produces much less diacetyl, but this is a curiosity nonetheless. Bottle-fermented.

On purchase $$

Langenbach

Rheinhessen, Germany

This large commercial bottler is best known for its Crown of Crowns Liebfraumilch, but it also produces a passable sparkling Chardonnay.

Langenbach NV Chardonnay Extra Brut

Although not Deutscher Sekt, this sparkling Chardonnay, which was made in Germany from grapes of no fixed abode, has good varietal fruit and a fresh elegant style.

On purchase $

LANGLOIS

Loire, France

Owned by Champagne Bollinger, Langlois-Château places emphasis on blending a wide selection of wines from a diversity of *terroirs*,

LANGLOIS NV CRÉMANT DE LOIRE BRUT 73

Firm, assertive flavor set against a soft mousse backdrop, and an intense finish. I much preferred it to Quadrille de Langlois-Château, which should be the Bollinger of the Loire, yet sadly is not.

Now–1999 $

LANGLOIS ROSÉ NV CRÉMANT DE LOIRE BRUT

The *rosé* is made in typical Bollinger food-wine fashion. A serious wine with firm fruit.

Now–1999 $

LANGLOIS RÉSERVE 1993 CRÉMANT DE LOIRE BRUT

Lovely biscuity aromas illustrate the sort of bottle-aged complexity expected from a mature sparkling wine, but it does not quite follow through on the palate. But it shows that some winemakers in the Loire are serious about increasing quality.

On purchase $

LANSON

12 Boulevard Lundy, 51100 Reims

(326) 78.50.50 FAX (326) 78.50.99

Shortly after the purchase of this famous and popular *grande marque* by Marne et Champagne, the Champagne market plummeted, and rumor has it that it will take the owner 390 years to repay the loan.

LANSON NV BLACK LABEL BRUT

I would not bother to taste Lanson Black Label until it had undergone at least two years in my cellar, preferably five, after which I would serve it blind to Masters of Wine, asking them to name the house and year of vintage.

2000–2003 $$

LANSON NV BRUT ROSÉ 8

Pale-salmon color suggests age, but beautifully fresh, with a long, elegant fruit flavor. Has finesse and works with or without food.

Now–1999 $$

LANSON NV DEMI-SEC 8

Very strong flavor with plenty of sweetness that currently lacks harmony, but promises to develop with bottle-age

1999–2000 $$

LANSON 1993 GOLD LABEL, BRUT 86

Promises to be a relatively quick develo ing vintage in Lanson terms. Nice alreac and will improve, but not top stuff.

1999–2002 $$$

LANSON 1990 GOLD LABEL, BRUT 88

Very soft and easy for Lanson when launched, this vintage now has a nice toastiness, but has developed slower tha I had initially imagined.

Now–2005 $$$

BLANC DE BLANCS DE LANSON 1990 BRUT

Mature, forward, and well developed, bu with expansive fruit underneath.

Now–2000 $$$

NOBLE CUVÉE DE LANSON 1988 BRUT

Still miles away from showing its full potential, this wine can be useful with food now – in fact it needs food – but true Champagne lovers will lay this dowr until well into the next millennium.

2000–2012 $$$$

BARON EDOUARD MASSÉ NV BRUT

Once itself a *grande marque*, but little more than the *sous marque* of Lanson these days, this *cuvée* is very fruity, with fine aromas that will soon go toasty.

Now–2000 $$

LANVIN

See Cazanove

LARMANDIER

30 rue du Général Koenig, 51130 Vertus
(326) 52.12.41 FAX (326) 52.19.38

Of the several Larmandiers on the Côtes des Blancs. Guy Larmandier can be relied on to produce clean, precise, elegantly fruity Champagne.

;uy Larmandier NV :ramant Grand Cru, ;lanc de Blancs, Brut

oral-fruity aromas, with clear, precise ıvors on palate, and clean, well-focused .iit on finish.

Now–1999 $$

;uy Larmandier NV ;rut Premier Cru

emon-blossom aroma, with a flowery ıesse to the fruit on the palate, and a trusy finish.

Now–2000 $$

LARMANDIER-BERNIER

43 rue du 28 août, 51130 Vertus
(326) 52.13.24 FAX (326) 52.21.00

.armandier-Bernier NV Blanc de Blancs ;rut, 1er Cru

ery rich, but not in the same class as the ieilles Vignes Cramant or the Grand ru 1990.

Now–1999 $$ 89F

.armandier-Bernier, Vieilles /ignes de Cramant NV ;lanc de Blancs, Extra Brut

uscious, crisp, creamy fruit – this is onderfully fresh and just beginning to evelop creamy-walnutty richness.

Now–2002 $$$

.armandier-Bernier 1990 Grand Cru Blanc de Blancs Brut

ot quite as rich as the Vieilles Vignes, ut certainly not lacking in richness. lore slow-building biscuity than creamy-alnutty, but equally high finesse.

Now–2002 $$$

Larmandier-Bernier 1992 Grand Cru Blanc de Blancs Brut

Plenty of grip and intensity, but it is almost stern and not ready for drinking.

2000–2002 $$$

LATEYRON

Bordeaux, France

The second-oldest producer of sparkling Bordeaux wine, having been established in 1897.

Paulian NV Crémant de Bordeaux Brut, Lateyron

Lime is commonly found in top quality Australian Semillon, but it is unusual to have such a distinctive lime aroma and flavor in a Bordeaux wine. Intriguing.

On purchase $

LAUFFEN

Württemberg, Germany

Winzergenossenschaft Lauffen-am-Neckar 1995 Lauffener Katzenbeisser Schwarzriesling Sekt Brut

Bit of a mouthful for a pure Meunier *blanc de noirs*, but this fine, fresh *cuve close* also offers quite a mouthful of tangy fruit, and scored higher than any of the bottle-fermented Sekt of the same style.

On purchase $$

LAURENT-PERRIER

Domaine de Tours-sur-Marne
51150 Tours-sur-Marne
(326) 58.91.22 FAX (326) 58.77.29

Laurent-Perrier is back on top after a period when this firm's finances were overstretched with holdings in Bordeaux, Burgundy and beyond. The group will now concentrate on Champagne, including the tiny but great house of Salon, Delamotte, De Castellane, Joseph Perrier, and Lemoine.

LAURENT-PERRIER NV BRUT L.P. 85

Much bigger and more forceful than Brut L.P., with rich citrus-toasty overtones. The only characteristic reminiscent of the L.P. style is its hint of undeveloped peppery-fruit. A good nonvintage Champagne, but regular L.P. consumers will be confused, to say the least.
Now–2001 $$ 139F

LAURENT-PERRIER NV CUVÉE ROSÉ BRUT

Unlike most nonvintage *rosés*, this salmon gold-colored wine always repays keeping in a cellar for a year or two.
Now–2000 $$$ 197F

LAURENT-PERRIER NV CUVÉE ULTRA BRUT 

The most distinctive of the nondosage *cuvées* on the nose, with a tart-toastiness on the palate. Needs food.
On purchase $$$ 173F

LAURENT-PERRIER 1990 VINTAGE BRUT 

Apart from a small number of off bottles circulating in early to mid-1997, this *cuvée* has always promised to be one of the best 1990s, and the sample tasted for this guide fulfilled that potential. A beautiful wine full of delicious fruit that still has a long way to go.
Now–2005 $$$ 173F

LAURENT-PERRIER GRAND SIÈCLE "LA CUVÉE" 

The original Grand Siècle and still my favorite, this is always a blend of three different vintage years and half-and-half Chardonnay and Pinot Noir. The *cuvée* at the time of publication is 1990/1988/1985 and as these three exceptional vintages suggest, the wine is one of the greatest *cuvées* in a long line of extraordinarily great Champagnes. It has fine, crisp fruit with a hint of violets, and biscuity aromas starting to build, and is a Champagne of great finesse and length. I have tasted every blend of "La Cuvée" (the first was a sumptuous blend of 1955/1953/1952), and they all age as gracefully, which brings me to ask again – why doesn't Laurent-Perrier indicate the component years on the back label as Cattier does?
Now–2010 $$$$

LAURENT-PERRIER GRAND SIÈCLE 1990 EXCEPTIONELLEMENT MILLÉSIMÉ 9

I have always preferred the classic "La Cuvée" to the vintaged version of Grand Siècle, which began with the 1982 sold in the US. The 1985 and 198 were both superb, but not quite in the same class as "La Cuvée" when it is of a comparable age. However, although I have my preferences, they are by no means prejudices, and the sublime dept of fruit and finesse in this wine is incontestable. The magnums will be eve more spectacular in 10 or 20 years.
Now–2020 $$$$ 368F

LAURENT-PERRIER GRAND SIÈCLE 1988 ALEXANDRA ROSÉ 92

Firmer than the 1985 or 1982 Alexandr Rosé, the 1988 is not as immediately accessible as either of those two vintage but its rich fruit is softening, and the balance makes for finesse.
Now–2020 $$$$ 440F

LAURENT-PERRIER GRAND SIÈCLE 1985 ALEXANDRA ROSÉ 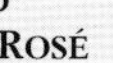

Exquisite fruit and finesse.
Now–2010 $$$$

LAVERNOYA

Penedès, Spain

An old-established firm, Cavas Lavernoya was founded in 1890,

LACRIMA BACCUS RESERVA 1995 CAVA BRUT 

This spicy concoction is better than the almonds and aldehydes in the 1993.
On purchase $

LACRIMA BACCUS RESERVA 1995 CAVA SEMI SECO 77

This *cuvée* has some real richness and depth of fruit, with excellent acidity.
On purchase $

LE, LES –

See under main name

Leclerc Briant

67 rue Chaude Ruelle, 51204 Épernay
(326) 54.45.33 FAX (326) 54.49.59

The launch of three single-vineyard Champagnes (Les Chèvres Pierreuses, Les Crayères, and Les Clos des Champions) was a bold nitiative, flawed by the nonvintage status of these *cuvées*. If this has made it difficult for critics to plot the progress of each wine, it has made it virtually impossible for customers to know how old the wines are and whether to lay them down. However, the Lot number reveals the year of bottling: the system starts with 43 for 1991, then jumps 10 digits per year – 53 for 1992, 63 for 1993, etc. In most cases, the wines are from a single vintage in the year prior to the bottling year. I urge readers to wait for the 1995s (L83) and the super 1996s (L93) before judging these *cuvées*.

ECLERC BRIANT 1988 DIVINE BRUT 87

you can bring yourself to buy such a udy bottle, you will be rewarded with a uity Champagne that promises some mplexity in the future.
Now–2000 $$$ 157F

ECLERC BRIANT, LE CLOS DES CHAMPION NV LES AUTHENTIQUES COLLECTION BRUT

ery fruity, but lacks the finesse shown y the first release of this *cuvée*.
On purchase $$ 103F

LECLERC BRIANT, LES CHÈVRES PIERREUSES NV LES AUTHENTIQUES COLLECTION BRUT

his is *cuvée* L43CH, which is like a ature Mâcon with bubbles, but it should ave been consumed a few years ago.
On purchase $$ 103F

Leasingham

See Hardy's

Lenoble

34 rue Paul-Douce, 51480 Damery
(326) 58.42.60 FAX (326) 58.65.57

A.R. LENOBLE NV RÉSERVE BRUT 85

Very ripe and fruity.
On purchase $$ 85F

A.R. LENOBLE 1990 BRUT 86

Creamy-rich, easy, gluggy fruit.
On purchase $$$

Le Phantom

See Saxenburg

Lépitre

4 rue de l'Eglise
51390 Coulommes-la-Montagne
(326) 49.78.20 FAX (326) 49.27.26

JEAN-CLAUDE LÉPITRE 1989 BRUT PRESTIGE

Oxidative, creamy-biscuity aroma with a whiff of clean, free sulfur, which will eventually go toasty. Requires more finesse for a higher score.
On purchase $$$ 70F

Leprince

See Beaumont des Crayères

Lété-Vautrain

11 rue Semars, 02400 Château-Thierry
(323) 83.05.38 FAX (323) 69.98.29

LÉTÉ-VAUTRAIN NV TRADITIONNEL BRUT

Has a flowery aroma, and there is a rather off-putting explosive foaminess to the mousse, but it is also very rich and fruity, with a creamy finish.
Now–1999 $$ 67F

LÉTÉ-VAUTRAIN NV GRANDE RÉSERVE BRUT 

Light, creamy-malo style.
On purchase $$ 76F

LEVASSEUR

Loire, France

CLAUDE LEVASSEUR NV BRUT, MONTLOUIS 

More correct than special, with more of a sugary sensation than any true ripeness of fruit. This wine just scrapes in, but I have had some truly excellent Montlouis Pétillant in the past.
On purchase $

CAPE LEVANT

See SAVISA

LILBERT

223 rue du Moutier51200 Cramant
(326) 57.50.16 FAX (326) 58.93.86

A consistent producer of firm *blanc de blancs* that show finesse and age gracefully, particularly the vintage *cuvées,* although the fruity non-vintage is definitely for drinking now.

LILBERT-FILS NV BLANC DE BLANCS BRUT, GRAND CRU 

Sprightly fruitiness, with a pure, clean, fresh, precise, fruit-driven palate.
On purchase $$ 80F

LINDAUER

See Montana

LOCRET-LACHAUD

40 rue Saint-Vincent, 51160 Hautvillers
(326) 59.40.20 FAX (326) 59.40.92

DE L'ABBATIALE NV BRUT, 1ER CRU

Made by Locret-Lachaud, the De L'Abbatiale Premier Cru *cuvée* has go acidity, and is building some creamine for the nose and palate, but it is let dc by the mousse, which could have finer more cushiony, bubbles.
1999–2000 $$ 115F

LORENT

See Beaumont des Crayères

LORENTZ

Alsace, France

Lorentz is one of Alsace's best-known producers, located in the beautiful village of Bergheim.

LORENTZ NV CRÉMANT D'ALSACE BRUT

The terpene aromas in this *cuvée* sugg there is Riesling in the blend, although there is no mention of Riesling on the label of the bottle. Good acidity.
On purchase $

LUBIANA

Tasmania, Australia

A family-owned wine company established in 1990 by Steve "Stefano" Lubiana and Monique Lubiana, whose first sparkling wine was made as recently as 1993.

STEFANO LUBIANA NV BRUT

Stefano Lubiana's basic Brut has complex, malty aromas on the nose, wi rich, tangy fruit on the palate.
On purchase $

STEFANO LUBIANA 1995 BRUT

This young, deliciously sherbety fizz is currently spoiled by amylic aromas, although these might drop out after a while in bottle.
1999–2000 $

Lugny

Burgundy, France

This well-known cooperative has been producing sparkling Burgundy since 1975.

Crémant de Bourgogne NV Brut Rosé, Cave de Lugny

The sample I tasted appeared to be very recently disgorged, so I will forgive it having a slight whiff of free sulfur, which should disappear before this guide is published and will eventually end up as part of the wine's toasty complexity. Lots of lovely red fruits on the palate, with a hint of vanilla on the finish.

On purchase $

Lustros

See Gramona

Mailly

28 rue de la Liberation
51500 Mailly-Champagne
(326) 49.41.10 FAX (326) 49.42.27

This mono-*cru* cooperative produced Champagnes of exceptional value and character throughout the 1970s and much of the 1980s, but there has been a certain lack of finesse in some of the *cuvées* on the market during the 1990s. Mailly is, however, back on form, pruducing its best Champagnes in over ten years.

Mailly NV Brut Reserve, Grand Cru

There is a fine flowery-Pinot aroma with really rich fruit underneath, but this *cuvée* is best drunk young.

On purchase $$

Mailly NV Blanc de Noirs, Grand Cru, Brut

Full, flowery-Pinot aroma of some finesse, followed by rich fruit, with some biscuitiness building.

Now–2000 $$ 131F

Mailly 1990 Brut, Grand Cru

A whiff of sulfur, but it is clean and free, and will turn toasty after a year or so. On the other hand, there is a strangely undeveloped character about this wine, and it compels me to withhold judgment for at least another year.

Wait and see $$$

Mailly Champagne NV Cuvée des Echansons, 100% Grand Cru Brut

Very full Pinot aroma, with big, intense fruit on the palate, yet it shows some elegance as well.

Now–2000 $$$

Mandois

66 rue du Gal-de-Gaulle, 51200 Pierry
(326) 54.03.18 FAX (326) 51.53.66

Henri Mandois NV Cuvée de Réserve Brut

Soft, fresh, elegant, this is definitely a fruit-driven style of Champagne made for early and easy drinking.

Now–1999 $$ 76F

Henri Mandois NV Brut Rosé, Premier Cru

Bright, cherry fruit aromas, with ripe, elegant fruit on the palate.

Now–1999 $$

Henri Mandois 1993 Chardonnay Brut, Premier Cru

Succulent fruit, with a surprisingly intense finish, suggesting this has more potential aging capacity than Mandois *cuvées* normally offer.

Now–2001 $$$ 86F

Manquehue

Chile

Viña Manquehue makes both *méthode champenoise* and *cuve close* wines. Grandier is called Darwin's Path on some export markets, and wines are also sold under the Rabat label.

GRANDIER 1996 VIÑA MANQUEHUE BRUT 

This surprised me by the lovely succulent fruit on the nose, but it needs a lighter hand on the palate to inject more freshness and elegance.
On purchase $

MANSARD

14 rue Chaude Ruelle, 51200 Épernay
(326) 54.18.55

Quite how this obscure producer has recently managed to grow into a house half as big again as Bollinger is perplexing, but there are some interesting *cuvées* here, including at least one of exceptionally fine quality.

MANSARD NV BRUT 

Light structure, ultrafruity aroma and flavor, with fresh finish.
On purchase $

MANSARD NV PREMIER CRU BRUT 

Just as fruity as the basic nonvintage, but with a more serious quality about it.
Now–1999 $$

TRADITION DE MANSARD 1993 GRANDE CUVÉE BRUT 

Fresh and firm with good fruit structure. A different style than all the rest.
Now–1999 $$$

MANSARD 1990 BLANC DE BLANCS, GRAND CRU 

An odd-looking, discordant label on the bottle, but the wine inside certainly does not lack harmony, with its lovely, mellow-toasty aromas and succulent, sweet, toasty-fruit on the palate.
Now–2000 $

MARIENBERG

New South Wales, Australia

This winery was established in 1966 by Australia's first woman winemaker, Ursula Pridham, who retired in 1990. The new winemaker is Grant Burge.

MARIENBERG PINOT NOIR CHARDONNAY NV BRUT 75

Fine, firm fruit showing some biscuity complexity, yet still age-worthy.
On purchase $

MARGAINE

3 avenue de Champagne
51380 Villers-Marmery
(326) 97.92.13 FAX (326) 97.97.45

Basic *cuvées* are often too amylic, but the Cuvée Club is a good find.

A. MARGAINE 1989 CUVÉE CLUB BLANC DE BLANCS 87

Very rich fruit, yet lean structure, with excellent acidity.
Now–2003 $$$

MARIE STUART

8 Place de la République, 51059 Reims
(326) 77.50.50 FAX (326) 77.50.59

Recently acquired by Alain Thienot, who has his own eponymous brand.

MARIE STUART NV CUVÉE DE LA REINE BRUT 

A real treat, this is light, fresh and elegant, yet complex, with clean fruit and lovely slow-building biscuitiness.
Now–2000 $$$ 133F

MARIE STUART 1991 BRUT 84

A classless depth of crisp fruit with a mellow finish.
Now–1999 $$$ 100F

MARINGER-THEES

Mosel-Saar-Ruwer, Germany

MARINGER-THEES 1988 TRITTENHEIMER ALTRÄCHEN RIESLING SEKT BRUT 

Quite sweet for a so-called *brut*, but the rich and concentrated fruit is very fresh for a ten-year-old Sekt.
On purchase $$

MARLBOROUGH

See Montana

MARNE ET CHAMPAGNE

22 rue Maurice-Cerveaux, 51205 Épernay
☎ (326) 78.50.50 FAX (326) 54.55.77

In addition to Lanson and Besserat de Bellefon, which operate as individual houses (although Besserat de Bellefon *cuvées* are all made here), Marne et Champagne markets in excess of 200 labels. A number of bargain wines have won Vincent Malberbe the Sparkling Winemaker of the Year award at *Wine* magazine's International Wine Challenge.

MARC ANTOINE NV CARTE NOIRE BRUT

Amylic, but scrapes in because of its easy-drinking fruit.

On purchase Ⓢ

CHARLES COURBET NV SPECIALE CUVÉE, BRUT

In pure quality terms this should not even scrape in, because it is too amylic, too fat, and too soft, but it has its use for those who insist on serving Champagne even though they usually find it too acidic.

On purchase ⓈⓈ

GAUTHIER NV BRUT GRANDE RESERVE

Fresh, light, and fruity. Nothing amylic.

Now–1999 ⓈⓈ

GAUTHIER 1988 BRUT

The toasty Chablis-like fruit would make a very good own-label Champagne for a merchant who likes to offer a more mature product at the bottom of the range, yet this will also improve with further age.

Now–2000 ⓈⓈ

MARNIQUET

8 rue des Crayères, 51480 Venteuil
☎ (326) 58.48.99

JEAN-PIERRE MARNIQUET NV BRUT

Not a classic by any means, this *cuvée* has a Muscat-like exotic twist to the fruit that until now I would have thought must be alien to Champagne, but it is an enjoyable sparkling wine within its own right.

On purchase ⓈⓈ

MARQUÉS DE MONISTROL

Penedès, Spain

Owned by Martini & Rossi, this Cava firm was established in 1882 and now owns 400 hectares of vineyards.

MARQUÉS DE MONISTROL GRAN COUPAGE NV CAVA SEMI SECO RESERVA

Very sweet, even for *semi-seco (demi-sec)*, which is why it beats its competitors hands down. Drinkers of this style want and expect a seriously sweet sparkler, but despite its high degree of sweetness this *cuvée* is light and elegant.

On purchase Ⓢ

MARTINEZ

See Faustino Martinez

MASACHS

Penedès, Spain

Josep Masachs is a family-owned Cava firm that owns more than 100 acres of vineyards, and started sparkling wine production in 1940.

LOUIS DE VERNIER BLANC DE BLANCS NV CAVA BRUT

Fresh and clean, in an uncomplicated fruit-driven style.

On purchase Ⓢ

CAROLINA DE MASACHS NV BRUT NATURE RESERVA

This one is light, elegant, and fruity, with good acidity.

On purchase Ⓢ

MASCARÓ

Penedès, Spain

Don Narcisi Mascaró Marcé was born into a family of well-established distillers, but set up this winery in 1945 in order to produce exclusively sparkling wines.

MASCARÓ NV CAVA BRUT NATURE 

Mascaró's Brut Nature is a richly flavored sparkling wine of good depth and nice acidity, without any of the coarseness that blights many Cavas.

On purchase $

MASIA PARERA

See Cigravi

MASOTTINA

Italy

One of only six Prosecco recommended in this guide, and I preferred it to the two non-Prosecco submitted.

MASOTTINA NV PROSECCO DI CONEGLIANO E VALDOBBIADENE, EXTRA DRY 

Fresh, light, amylic-style fruit, but with more elegance than most.

On purchase $

MASSÉ

See Lanson

MATHIEU

Les Riceys, 10340 Avirey-Lingey

(25) 29.32.58 FAX (25) 29.11.57

This small, immaculately equipped producer makes the most elegant Champagnes of any grower in the Aube region of Champagne.

SERGE MATHIEU NV CUVÉE TRADITION, BLANC DE NOIRS BRUT 84

Soft, easy fruit with a touch of elegance.

On purchase $$ 75F

SERGE MATHIEU NV SELECT, TÊTE DE CUVÉE BRUT 87

An object lesson for anyone who does not think that the Aube can produce finesse.

Now–1999 $$ 99F

SERGE MATHIEU NV CUVÉE PRESTIGE BRUT 85

Elegantly rich fruit.

On purchase $$ 81F

MATUA VALLEY

Waimauku, New Zealand

This superbly equipped winery is renowned for expressive wines of excellent focus and purity of fruit.

MATUA VALLEY NINETEEN NINETY TWO BRUT 

Rich, yet fluffy, fruit, with a fine balance that somehow reveals the serious quality of the wine.

Now–1999 $$

MAXIM'S

See Castellane

MERCIER

68/70 avenue de Champagne

51200 Épernay

(326) 51.22.00 FAX (326) 54.84.23

Although seen by many as a down-market brand compared to Moët & Chandon, it is Mercier that is the brand-leader in France, and it always has been. The style is generally fuller, riper, and less elegant than that of Moët, although some of the vintages can be dark horses, while the Cuvée du Fondateurs offers extraordinary quality for the price.

MERCIER NV BRUT 

What this *cuvée* lacks in finesse it more than makes up for in frank, unashamed Aube fruit ripeness.

On purchase $$ 89F

EUGÈNE MERCIER NV CUVÉE DU FONDATEUR BRUT 

Fat and rich, and what this wine lacks in finesse, it more than makes up for with flavor and value for the money. It works especially well at the table.

Now–1999 $$ 105F

MERCIER 1993 VENDANGE BRUT 

There is an attractive light richness here in what appears to be a quick-developing vintage *brut*.

Now–1999 $$$ 115F

MERCKLÉ

Alsace, France

I have been disappointed with M. Mercklé's *crémant* in the past, even when it has won a gold medal at Dijon, but I take off my hat to him for this impressive *cuvée*.

ANDRÉ MERCKLÉ NV CRÉMANT D'ALSACE BRU 

Good fruity acidity gives a tangy-pineapple finish, which should go toasty with a year or two bottle-age.

Now–1999 $

(DE) MERIC

17 Rue Gambetta, 51160 Aÿ-Champagne

(326) 55.20.72 FAX (326) 54.84.12

This small house is owned by Christian Besserat, whose family founded Besserat de Bellefon.

DE MERIC NV CATHÉRINE DE MEDICI 

This prestige *cuvée* is a very special Champagne that is best enjoyed with food and rewards true Champagne aficionados with sublime finesse and seductively mellow bottle-aromas.

Now–2002 $$$ 119F

(LE) MESNIL

Union des Propriétaires Récoltants

51390 Le Mesnil-sur-Oger

(326) 57.53.23

Only an occasional glitch mars the exceptional potential in quality of this cooperative.

LE MESNIL NV BLANC DE BLANCS, BRUT 

Smooth and rich, with fine acidity.

Now–1999 $$

LE MESNIL 1990 RÉSERVE SÉLECTION, BLANC DE BLANCS BRUT 

Excellent crisp, rich, fullness of fruit with mellowing toasty aromas and finesse.

Now–2002 $$$

MESTRES

Penedès, Spain

The methods are traditional and the style very much the sort of thing that lovers of well-matured Cavas adore.

MESTRES COQUET NV CAVA BRUT NATURE 

Fresh, light, and slightly amylic.

On purchase $

LOS CUPAGES DES MESTRES NV CAVA BRUT NATURE 

Firmer, tighter, and capable of some aging.

Now–1999 $$

MESTRES CLOS NOSTRE SENYOR 1990 CAVA BRUT NATURE 

Honeyed terpenes.

On purchase $$

MESTRES CLOS DAMIANA 1987 CAVA BRUT NATURE 

Honeyed, with a toffee richness.

On purchase $$

MESTRES RESERVA 1986 MAS VIA BRUT 

A ripe-mature sweetness with honeyed aromas.

On purchase $$

MEURGIS

Burgundy, France

MEURGIS, CUVÉE BLANC DE NOIRS 1995 CRÉMANT DE BOURGOGNE

A light, early-drinking wine with a perfumed Pinot aroma and some elegance.

On purchase $$

MEURGIS, CUVÉE BLANC DE NOIRS 1994 CRÉMANT DE BOURGOGNE

Not an outstanding wine by any means, but there is nothing wrong with it, and it just scrapes through because of its exceptionally fine mousse.

On purchase $$

MEYER FONNÉ

Alsace, France

My first encounter of this producer, who started making *crémant* as recently as 1992.

MEYER FONNÉ NV CRÉMANT D'ALSACE BRUT EXTRA

Fresh, fizzy Chablis style.

On purchase $

MIGNON & PIERREL

24 Rue Henri Dunant, 51200 Épernay

(326) 51.93.39 FAX (326) 51.69.40

Floral-patterned, shrunk-wrapped Champagne bottles are Mignon & Pierrel's specialty.

MIGNON & PIERREL NV BRUT, PREMIER CRU

If you can bring yourself to buy the extravagantly decorated bottle, then you will be rewarded by a *cuvée* of light but satisfying richness, with some serious, creamy biscuitiness. This applies to the wine in the bottle with a blue floral pattern: beware of the green!

Now–1999 $$ 120F

MILAN

6 route d'Avize, 51190 Oger

(326) 57.50.09 FAX (326) 57.78.47

Traditional producers who use oak barrels for some of their *cuvées*, although not for the one below.

JEAN MILAN NV BRUT SPÉCIAL, GRAND CRU

Fresh, with fine aromas and lean fruit.

Now–1999 $$ 81F

MILLS REEF

Bay of Plenty, New Zealand

A typical boutique-style winery that has quickly developed a reputation for the consistency of its oaky fizz.

MILLS REEF CHARISMA NV METHODE TRADITIONELLE, HAWKES BAY

Heaped with rich coconutty fruit, this *cuvée* is always far too oaky for my liking, but I recognize the quality of fruit and the excellent level of ripe acidity.

On purchase $$

MOËT & CHANDON

20 avenue de Champagne, 51200 Épernay

(326) 51.20.00 FAX (326) 51.20.37

Moët is the largest and most popular Champagne house, and surely the only way it can expand further is to attract those who have been put off by its high-volume operation. Even wine snobs acknowledge the quality of Cuvée Dom Pérignon, and the new *rosé* and Brut Premier Cru should also attract quality-seeking customers.

MOËT & CHANDON NV BRUT IMPÉRIAL

If judged for drinking on purchase, the world's greatest-selling nonvintage *cuvée* might just scrape in with 80 points, but if kept for 12 months, it picks up toasty aromas and a nice mellowed elegance.

1999–2000 $$ 125F

MOËT & CHANDON NV BRUT PREMIER CRU 85

This relatively new *cuvée* is restricted to the French market. Interestingly, Moët has not gone for anything bigger or richer, just an extra dimension of finesse.
On purchase $$$ 140F

MOËT & CHANDON NV BRUT ROSÉ

Wonderfully fresh, delicately floral fruit aromas, elegant and long. I love the mellowed richness of the vintage *rosé*, but the extra finesse in this new nonvintage *cuvée* makes it significantly superior.
Now–1999 $$

MOËT & CHANDON 1992 BRUT IMPÉRIAL ROSÉ

Apricot-gold color, perfumed Pinot aromas, and a mellow fruit flavor.
Now–1999 $$$ 155F

MOËT & CHANDON 1992 BRUT IMPÉRIAL

Not a top Moët vintage, but going toasty, and is at least as good as a well-matured, nonvintage Brut Impérial.
Now–1999 $$$ 55F

CUVÉE DOM PÉRIGNON 1990 BRUT

The toasty bottle-aromas have evolved quicker than the extract on the palate, which promises further development, but you might have a more recently disgorged bottle, which will be pure, creamy-fruit. Indisputably a great wine, but its disgorgement should have been left to 2000.
2000–2015 $$$$ 420F

CUVÉE DOM PÉRIGNON 1988 BRUT

Floral-toasty aromas and firm, pineapple-fruit. Very linear, with a heightened perception of acidity on the finish.
1999–2015 $$$$

CUVÉE DOM PÉRIGNON 1985 BRUT

Fruit-driven aromas with toastiness peeping through very tightly focused fruit on the palate. There is a huge concentration on the finish that promises to go biscuity, with some Christmas cake complexity.
1999–2015 $$$$

MÖLLER

Pfalz, Germany

SEKTKELLEREI MÖLLER 1995 CHARDONNAY SEKT

An apricot and custard concoction that just scrapes in for its curiosity value. Bottle-fermented.
On purchase $$

MONISTROL

See Marqués de Monistrol

MONMOUSSEAU

Loire, France

MONMOUSSEAU, CUVÉE J.M. 1992 BLANC DE BLANCS BRUT, TOURAINE

Clean, fresh, ripe, and fruity for a Touraine sparkling wine of this age.
Now–1999 $

PRINTEMPS GRAND VIN PÉTILLANT NV VOUVRAY, MONMOUSSEAU

For those wine drinkers who prefer a less sweet style of *demi-sec,* this fresh-flavored fizz has quite intense fruit.
On purchase $

MONTANA

Marlborough, New Zealand
New Zealand's largest wine producer, with an excellent new Blanc de Blancs.

LINDAUER NV BRUT

This high-volume transfer-method fizz is normally fresh and fluffy, with lemon-meringue fruit, but the current shipment is fuller, fatter, and richer, with a certain complexity and not lacking in finesse. Is this a deliberate change in style or simply an effect of age on a quick-moving *cuvée*?
On purchase $

LINDAUER NV SPECIAL RESERVE BRUT 81

Exquisite finesse for such mouthfilling fruit. Soft fruits, sweetish vanilla smoothness on finish.

On purchase $

DEUTZ MARLBOROUGH NV BRUT 78

Refreshing, fruity style with a serious edge when young, this wine usually develops a toasty, high-acid Chablis character with bottle-age.

Now–1999 $

DEUTZ MARLBOROUGH 1991 BLANC DE BLANCS 

Were you to set a standard, then 1991 would be a seriously mature Cava, and most Cavas of this age would be well past their best. In fact, this *cuvée* is so young that it needs more time. Will turn into creamy-rich nectar in the future.

1999–2004 $$

MONTAUDON

6 rue Ponsardin, 51100 Reims
(326) 47.53.30 FAX (326) 47.88.82

Established by Auguste-Louis Montaudon, the winemaker at Bouvet-Ladubay. The nonvintage and vintage have always been okay but not special, but this *cuvée* was better.

MONTAUDON NV CHARDONNAY PREMIER CRU BRUT 

Starting to go very toasty, so what it lacks in finesse is compensated for drinkers who like their Champagnes to come complete with a continental breakfast.

Now–1999 $$ 100F

MONTE ROSSA

Franciacorta, Italy

MONTE ROSSA NV FRANCIACORTA BRUT 

Very fruity, everyday drinking style.

On purchase $

MONTE ROSSA NV FRANCIACORTA BRUT SATÈN 75

Some creamy-malo finesse showing through slow-building toasty aromas, with toast, coffee, and a twist of lemon on the palate.

On purchase $

MONTE ROSSA 1992 FRANCIACORTA BRUT 72

A distinctive fresh pepperiness on the nose, and soft, sweet fruit on the palate, this wine would have received a higher score but for a hollow touch on its finish.

On purchase $$

MONT MARÇAL

Penedès, Spain

MONT MARÇAL CAVA NV GRAN RESERVA BRUT 

Creamy-malolactic aromas dominating rich, mellow fruit, but it lacks the finesse necessary for a higher score.

1999–2000 $

MONT MARÇAL CAVA 1993 BRUT NATURE 

Young and firm, with plenty of promise and a delightful cushiony mousse.

1999–2000 $

MÔRESON

Paarl, South Africa

SOLEIL DU MATIN BRUT NV CAP CLASSIQUE 

Fresh and obviously young, the flavor is quite long for such a light-bodied wine, but otherwise unexceptional. It would normally score 70 points, but I am in uncharted water here, and it could develop far more favorably.

Wait and see $

MORIANO

Trentino, Italy

Moriano Brut NV Trento 

The fruit is good, if a little oaky, but the structure could be leaner.

Now–2000 $

Morris

Victoria, Australia

Established in 1897, and now part of the French-owned Orlando group, Morris is actually famous for its fortified wines but has also been producing sparkling wine since 1989. Although this winery belongs to one of Australia's four largest groups, the original owners are still involved, with the *cuvée* below having been made by David Morris.

Morris Shiraz-Duriff NV Brut 

Very creamy-oaky style of red fizz. Confusingly, in California the Duriff (more commonly spelled Durif) is called the Petite-Sirah, which writers go to pains explaining is not related to the true Syrah or Shiraz. However, in recent years many of the so-called Petite-Sirah have been identified as authentic Syrah!

On purchase $

Morton

Bay of Plenty, New Zealand

This white-wine specialist produces one of New Zealand's finest and potentially complex sparkling wines, but there is a high incidence of bad corks.

Morton Estate NV Sparkling Brut, Methode Traditionelle 

One sample at the tasting had sweet, ripe fruit that was spoiled by green-apple on the finish, the other was more complex, less fruit-driven.

Now–1999 $$

Moulin

See Dopff au Moulin

Mountadam

South Australia, Australia

The Mountadam vineyard in the Eden Valley belongs to Adam Wynn, who was one of the founders of the legendary Wynns Coonawarra Estate, which now belongs to Southcorp. Wynn makes his sparkling wines with a pale *rosé* hue because he believes that all the best non-*rosé* Champagnes are not decolorized and are thus "usually pink" (whereas in reality the best Champagne producers actually take a pride in making the palest possible *cuvée* without resorting to artificial means).

Mountadam 1992 Brut 

With so much toffee-malo and creamy-coconut character dominating the wine, any finesse that was once present has unfortunately been lost, but I cannot help admiring the richness of this *cuvée* and the obvious high quality of the raw materials used.

On purchase $

Mountadam 1991 Brut 

Like the 1992, this is too heavily malo-dominated but should appeal to anyone who likes Devon toffees.

On purchase $

Mountain Dome

Washington, US

Dr. Michael Manz has worked hard to produce a classic sparkling wine, and this year the *rosé* was best.

Mountain Dome NV Brut Rosé 

A succulent melange of strawberry-dominated red-fruits. This lovely *rosé* is very soft, fresh, and fruity with an excellent mousse of tiny bubbles.

On purchase $$

Mountain Dome NV Brut 

Rich coconutty fizz with a label depicting "little people."

On purchase $$

MOUTARD

Buxeuil, 10110 Bar-sur-Seine
(25) 38.50.73 FAX (25) 38.57.72

The full name of the house is Moutard-Diligent – the brand is simply called Moutard, although there is a second label called François Diligent. Most Moutard *cuvées* are pure Chardonnay.

MOUTARD NV ROSÉ BRUT 85

Salmon-pink, with nice Pinot Noir aromas, this *cuvée* is rich, flavorsome, and crisp, with a firm mousse.

Now–1999 (S)(S) 70F

MOUTARD NV CUVÉE PRESTIGE BRUT

Some biscuity complexity, but let down by a touch of coarseness, which robs the wine of any finesse, and a touch of green fruit on the finish.

On purchase (S)(S) 91F

MOUTARD NV VIEILLES VIGNES, CÉPAGE ARBANE

Not recommended, but included as a curiosity because it's made from Arbane, an ancient and almost extinct variety that is still technically permissible in Champagne. Apparently, local producers can pick out its distinctive floral aroma even if it represents less than one percent of a blend – and this one is a pure example!

Wait and see (S)(S) 109F

MOUTARD NV RÉSERVE BRUT

A sprightly nose, with soft, billowy fruit on the palate.

On purchase (S)(S) 68F

MOUTARD 1983 BRUT MILLÉSIME

Licorice-fruit intensity, with a spicy-dry finish. Worth keeping an eye on.

Wait and see (S)(S)(S) 101F

MOUTARD NV CUVÉE SANS DOSAGE, EXTRA BRUT

The pungent nose suggests this wine is over the hill, but upon tasting there is a lot of undeveloped extract, which goes well with food, particularly game dishes. It might have been better if disgorged two years ago and given a full *brut* dosage!

On purchase (S)(S) 91F

MOUTARDIER

51210 Le Breuil
(326) 59.21.09 FAX (326) 59.21.25

Run by Englishman Jonathan Saxby. Le Breuil is one of the best sites for Meunier, and the Carte d'Or, Rosé Brut, and Millésime are made exclusively from this grape. These are not Moutardier's best, but I still hope that one day Saxby will make the world's greatest pure Meunier *cuvée*.

JEAN MOUTARDIER NV CARTE D'OR BRUT

An initial whiff of sulfur, but it was clean free sulfur, and disappeared after a good swirl of the glass. Fresh, light, and fruity palate, with a hint of vanilla.

Now–1999 (S)(S) 75F

JEAN MOUTARDIER NV SÉLECTION BRUT

Still the most complete Champagne in th Moutardier range, this is on par with the Centenaire *cuvée*.

Now–1999 (S)(S) 87F

JEAN MOUTARDIER NV LA CENTENAIRE BRUT

A richly flavored *cuvée* with some malo-dominated complexity, and plenty of clean fruit.

Now–1999 (S)(S) 95F

JEAN MOUTARDIER NV ROSÉ BRUT

Apricot-peach color, with a fresh, easy-drinking fruity style.

Now (S)(S) 85F

JEAN MOUTARDIER 1990 MILLÉSIME BRUT

This vintage was very good when I tasted it for *Decanter* magazine in 1997, but the sample submitted more recently was not at all special. Judgment reserved.

Wait and see (S)(S)(S) 82F

MOUZON-LEROUX

16 rue Basse des Carrières, 51380 Verzy
(326) 97.96.68 FAX (326) 97.97.67

PH. MOUZON-LEROUX NV BRUT ROSÉ, 1ER CRU 82

lthough this distinctly pink-looking *rosé* as an amylic aroma, it is richly flavored, as a long, crisp finish, and will age well.
Now–2000 $$ 82F

PH. MOUZON-LEROUX NV GRANDE RÉSERVE BRUT, 1ER CRU 

iscuity, but rustic in character, with a ather disjointed balance.
On purchase $$ 72F

PH. MOUZON-LEROUX NV CUVÉE PRESTIGE BRUT, 1ER CRU 

icher than the Grande Réserve, with etter balance, and it could even develop touch of finesse.
Now–1999 $$ 92F

MULLER

Alsace, France

CHARLES MULLER ROSÉ NV CRÉMANT D'ALSACE BRUT 

'ery soft fruit, hinting of cherries and trawberries, with a smooth mousse of ny bubbles.
On purchase $

MUMM

29 rue du Champ-de-Mars, 51053 Reims
(326) 49.59.69 FAX (326) 40.46.13

While Pierre-Yves Harang produced some of the cleanest Mumm wines for a long time from the 1995 harvest, it is the 1996s that indicate a return to the light, pure, fluffy style for which Mumm used to be renowned. The 1995-based nonvintage *cuvées* should be on the shelf for the millennium.

MUMM CORDON ROUGE NV BRUT 

'his shipment has a light, biscuity-malo roma with a really quite dry flavor. This s Mumm Cordon Rouge on the up, and here should be better *cuvées* to come.
On purchase $$ 110F

MUMM CORDON ROUGE 1989 BRUT MILLÉSIMÉ 

The hint of malolactic on the nose does not show through on the palate, which is dominated by sprightly fruit.
On purchase $$$ 128F

MUMM DE CRAMANT NV BLANC DE BLANCS BRUT 

This *cuvée* (originally called Crémant de Cramant) would benefit from less, rather than more, time on yeast, about 15–18 months. This would result in an even lighter, fresher, and fluffier style.
On purchase $$ 213F

MUMM CHAMPAÑA

Chile

A relatively recent venture, but the best *cuvée* lacks the finesse of the current shipment of Torres Chilean fizz, and does not even stack up against Moët & Chandon's Baron B. made in neighboring Argentina.

CUVÉE MUMM CHAMPAÑA NV BRUT 

With a sweet and slightly amylic aroma, and a better balance of fruit and acidity than either the Nature or Demi-Sec, this just scrapes in.
On purchase $

MUMM NAPA

Napa, California, US

This high-tech operation produced better sparkling wine than Mumm's authentic Champagne in the late 1980s and early 1990s.

MUMM CUVÉE NAPA NV BRUT PRESTIGE 

The basic nonvintage Mumm Cuvée Napa Brut Prestige (known as Cuvée Napa by Mumm Brut on export markets) can sometimes be a bit young, but it seems to have settled down over the last year or two and is back to its simple, fresh, light and easy fruity self.
On purchase $

MUMM CUVÉE NAPA 1991 DVX 88

A single-vineyard sparkler from the Devaux vineyard in Carneros, this has retained an impressive purity of fruit for several years now. Long, rich, and tangy.
Now–1999 $$

MUMM NAPA NV BLANC DE BLANCS 

This is not only the finest quality but also consistently the greatest value *cuvée* in the whole Mumm Napa range, with lovely, creamy fruit. There is a delicious intensity that comes in part from its 30 percent Pinot Gris content, the balance being Chardonnay, of course.
Now–2000 $

MUMM NAPA 1991 WINERY LAKE 

Although it is more intense than any other wine in the Mumm Napa range, Winery Lake does not travel particularly well. Hence, Americans may not enjoy it in other countries. On the other hand, if you have enjoyed it on an export market, you will really love it in California.
Now–1999 $$

MUMM NAPA NV BLANC DE NOIRS 

Labeled Rosé on export markets, this soft, easy, ready-drinking *cuvée* has a more traditional style than Mumm Napa's Sparkling Pinot Noir.
On purchase $

MUMM NAPA SPARKLING PINOT NOIR 

Take a trip on the wild side with this deep-cerise colored fizz. A single-vineyard *cuvée* from the Devaux vineyard in Carneros, this is a true love-or-hate wine, with a wonderful aroma of wild strawberries, and outrageously perfumed Pinot fruit on the palate. It has got to be the ultimate picnic wine.
On purchase $

MUMM SOUTH AFRICA

Tulbagh, South Africa

Made in conjunction with Nicky Krone at Twee Jongegezellen.

MUMM CAP CLASSIQUE NV 85

Fresh, zesty fruit that is long and elegant with a lovely soft mousse of tiny bubbles Knowing Krone's past record, this will develop some mellow complexity, but it too easy to drink now even to bother.
On purchase $

MURÉ

Alsace, France

A great estate, especially for Vendange Tardive, but it has struggled to equal the excellence of the pure Riesling sparkling wine it produced in 1982.

RENÉ MURÉ NV CRÉMANT D'ALSACE BRUT 

Fresh, elegant, fruity style, with a very fine mousse. In a classy Krug-like bottle.
On purchase $

NAUTILUS

Marlborough, New Zealand

Nautilus is owned by the Australian Yalumba group,

NAUTILUS ESTATE NV CUVÉE BRUT MARLBOROUGH 

An overtly fruity style that is not exactly complex but easy and delicious to drink.
On purchase $$

NEDERBURG

Stellenbosch, South Africa

Owned by Stellenbosch Wine Farmers who named this brand after an estate that was renamed Johann Graue in 1972 to honor SWF's first winemaker.

NEDERBURG BLANQUETTE 1993 CAP CLASSIQUE DE CHARDONNAY 

A soft, easy-drinking fizz that had not developed any postdisgorgement aromas when tasted, but scraped through on the fluffy freshness of its fruit.
On purchase $

NEIPPERG

Württemberg, Germany

The Counts of Neipperg have grown vines around their castle for more than 700 years, and made a very positive start with Sekt in 1992.

GRAF VON NEIPPERG 1992 NEIPPERGER SCHLOSSBERG SCHWARZRIESLING SEKT TROCKEN

Just as French vine experts have decided that Meunier is not part of the Pinot family, so the Germans make a pure Meunier that tastes more like Pinot Noir than Pinot Noir! Bottle-fermented.

On purchase $$

NERLEUX

See Domaine de Nerleux

NEUMEYER

Alsace, France

Although I have had a few wines from this producer in Molsheim, none was particularly special, so I was pleasantly surprised to see Neumeyer's name on this *cuvée* when the covers came off.

GÉRARD NEUMEYER, CUVÉE MILLÉSIMÉE 1993 CRÉMANT D'ALSACE BRUT

This has a creamy-malo nose, followed by creamy-rich fruit on the palate, and very good acidity.

Now–2000 $$

NORDHEIM

Württemberg, Germany

This cooperative has 250 members producing some 1,500 cases of Sekt each year. The quality ranges from a chemical-tasting Pinot Blanc to the fourth-best Sekt I tasted this year.

WEINGÄRTNERGENOSSENSCHAFT NORDHEIM 1995 PINOT NOIR SEKT EXTRA BRUT

Really quite sweet for an *extra brut*, but this pure Pinot Noir Sekt has lovely fruit, all cherries and strawberries, with a perfumed aftertaste. Bottle-fermented.

On purchase $$

NORMANS

South Australia, Australia

An underrated producer of still wines, Normans also shows excellent potential for sparkling wines. The basic Brut Cuvée is a blend of Semillon, Chenin Blanc, and Trebbiano.

NORMANS CONQUEST NV BRUT

A nice melange of fruit buoyed up by a lovely cushiony mousse, this is almost a *blanc de noirs* made primarily from Pinot Noir and Grenache, but with five percent of Riesling, which makes for an unusual, but very successful, blend.

On purchase $

NORMANS NV BRUT PINOT NOIR

This is serious stuff, with such a good balance that it has plenty of real Pinot flavor despite the lightweight body, supported by a lovely fluffy mousse.

Now–1999 $

NORTHBROOK SPRINGS

Bishop's Waltham, England, UK

NORTHBROOK SPRINGS 1993 BRUT

This *cuvée* has some flowery finesse on the nose, with rich fruit, correct structure, and a firm mousse of small bubbles. It would be interesting to age this one further, both on and off the yeast.

Now–1999 $

NOSTALGIE

See Beaumont des Crayères

NOTTAGE HILL

See Hardy's

NYETIMBER

West Chiltington, England, UK

The first vintage of Nyetimber was such a success that it was chosen for the Queen's Golden Anniversary,

NYETIMBER 1992 PREMIÈRE CUVÉE BLANC DE BLANCS 

This is one of a rare breed of sparkling wine that needs at least three years on its yeast and, rarer still, an additional two years after disgorgement to slowly develop a mellow, biscuity complexity. At $24 it is the second-most expensive English fizz, but it is far and away the best value for the money. The 1993 Chardonnay-Pinot blend is even better, and I have great hopes for 1994.

1999–2002 $$

NYETIMBER 1993 PREMIÈRE CUVÉE BLANC DE BLANCS 

Not quite the creamy quality of the first vintage, this has a more "English" herbaceous character, but this is uncharted waters, and I will follow its development.

Now–2000 $$

NYETIMBER 1993 

This blend of Chardonnay and Pinot Noir has shown exceptional finesse. If anyone still needs convincing about Nyetimber after its debut vintage, this is the *cuvée* that will do it.

1999–2004 $$

OAK VILLAGE

South Africa

The primary label of an export-only organization called Vinfruco, which is funded by South Africa's largest fruit exporter. Behind the rather commercial name and presentation of Oak Village lurks a serious-quality, brilliant-value sparkling wine.

OAK VILLAGE CUVÉE BRUT NV CAP CLASSIQUE 

I was so surprised by the classic quality and creamy-walnutty richness of this *cuvée* that I had to repeat the tasting.

Now–1999 $

OASIS

Virginia, US

One of the more consistent producers in the state of Virginia.

OASIS BRUT NV VIRGINIA SPARKLING WINE 

The creamy-caramel nose on the Oasis Brut suggests that the malolactic has bee too heavy-handed, and the wine certainl could do with more finesse, but it is a drinkable *cuvée*, eminently drinkable in fact. This is very much in the fizzy Devo toffee mode, but with a little bit more experience of producing sparkling wine, Oasis could be a classy little number.

On purchase $

ODE PANOS

See Spyopoulos

OMNI

See Hardy's

ORLANDO

South Australia, Australia

This French-owned group produces a quarter of Australia's wine production through a number of wineries and brands, including Craigmoor, Morris, and Wyndham Estate.

ORLANDO CARRINGTON FINE CHAMPAGNE NV BRUT 

A firm and flavorful wine with some creamy fruit on nose and palate.

On purchase $

ORLANDO CARRINGTON ROSÉ NV BRUT 

Inexpensive fruity fizz for unthinking, everyday drinking when first released, this *cuvée* quickly picks up a touch of biscuity complexity for those who prefer a more serious style.

On purchase Ⓢ

ORLANDO CARRINGTON 1996 BRUT 

Fresh, easy, vanilla-fruit.

On purchase Ⓢ

ORLANDO TRILOGY NV BRUT 

Elegant fruit aromas follow through onto the palate with plenty of ripe acidity.

On purchase Ⓢ

ORTENBERG

See Schloss Ortenberg

OUDINOT

12 rue Godart-Roger, 51207 Épernay
(326) 54.60.31 FAX (326) 54.78.52

From the same stable as Beaumet (see entry) and Jeanmaire (none submitted), and most of the wines are exactly the same *cuvées*.

OUDINOT NV CUVÉE ROSÉ, BRUT 

Although this pink-colored *cuvée* has an amylic nose, it also has such easy-going, fresh floral fruit that many casual drinkers of Champagne will enjoy it.

On purchase ⓈⓈ

OUDINOT NV CUVÉE BRUT 

More amylic than the Marks & Spencer (UK) own-label shipment, but it has easy-going fruit and a soft mousse.

On purchase ⓈⓈ

OUDINOT 1990 CUVÉE BRUT 

Fresh and flowery, without being amylic, and with very youthful fruit. A good buy for those who want a fruit-driven *cuvée* that does not threaten to turn toasty too quickly in the cellar.

Now–1999 ⓈⓈⓈ

OUDINOT

Loire, France

VEUVE OUDINOT NV TOURAINE BRUT 

Fresh and rich with bright flavors underpinned by high acidity to produce a wine for ready drinking in a lively style.

On purchase Ⓢ

PAILLARD

avenue du Champagne, 51100 Reims
(326) 36.20.22 FAX (326) 36.57.72

The consistency of its elegant Champagnes is likely to make this house the patrimoine of the Paillard family for many generations to come.

BRUNO PAILLARD NV BRUT PREMIÈRE CUVÉE 

Fresh, elegant and satisfying, with a lovely minerally finesse, this is one of the most consistent nonvintage Champagnes on the market.

Now–1999 ⓈⓈ 125F

BRUNO PAILLARD NV BRUT ROSÉ PREMIÈRE CUVÉE 

A *rosé* of great charm and elegance, with delicate red-fruits on the palate and a lovely softness and freshness on the finish.

Now–1999 ⓈⓈ 145F

BRUNO PAILLARD NV BRUT CHARDONNAY RÉSERVE PRIVÉE 

Wonderfully ripe, creamy Chardonnay that is obviously mature, yet with all the freshness that recent disgorgement brings.

Now–2002 ⓈⓈ 160F

BRUNO PAILLARD 1989 BRUT 

This has evolved brilliantly, with oodles of creamy-biscuity richness, and a wonderfully lush, creamy-smooth finish.

Now–2009 ⓈⓈⓈ 170F

PALEINE

See Domaine de la Paleine

PALMER

67 rue Jacquart, 51100 Reims
(326) 07.35.07 FAX (326) 07.45.24

If you judge a cooperative by its reputation with the *négoce* (Champagne houses), which do business with cooperatives every day, then Palmer is one of the very best.

PALMER 1989 BRUT 89

The best vintage Palmer has produced in a long time; rich, expansive, perfumed fruit with amazing freshness for the year.
Now–2005 $$$ 140F

BRUT NV AMAZONE DE PALMER 90

This prestige *cuvée* has deep, penetrating flavor that develops slowly, and is one of the best integrated examples of Chardonnay and Pinot fruit.
Now–2005 $$$ 180F

PANNIER

23 rue Roger Catillon,
02400 Château-Thierry
(23) 69.13.10 FAX (23) 69.18.18

This Aisne cooperative has greatly improved as the proportion of grapes gathered from the Marne has gradually increased in recent years. Pannier has two prestige *cuvées:* Louis Eugène, which is nonvintage and expressive of the house style; and Egérie, which is vintaged and expressive or even an exaggeration of the year in question.

PANNIER NV BRUT TRADITION/SÉLECTION 85

Not recommendable until 1994, Pannier's basic nonvintage has consistently improved since then, and is now really quite rich and satisfying for such a light-structured *cuvée*, with some elegant flowery-finesse on the finish.
On purchase $$ 110F

PANNIER NV BRUT ROSÉ 86

Currently on very good form with attractive cherry Pinot fruit.
On purchase $$ 120F

PANNIER NV LOUIS EUGÈNE 89

Delicate richness of fruit with fine acidity and slow-building biscuitiness on the finish.
Now–2002 $$$ 150F

PANNIER NV LOUIS EUGÈNE ROSÉ 89

Excellent balance of red-fruit richness with biscuity finesse.
Now–2002 $$$ 160F

PANNIER 1990 EGÉRIE 90

The best Egérie yet, with a lovely purity of fruit and a degree of finesse absent from any Pannier wine prior to this date.
Now–2005 $$$ 175F

PARIGOT

Burgundy, France

PARIGOT, CRÉMANT BLANC NV CRÉMANT DE BOURGOGNE BRUT 73

Firm structure, good depth of flavor, and a firm mousse.
Now–2000 $

PARIGOT, CRÉMANT ROSÉ NV CRÉMANT DE BOURGOGNE BRUT 73

A plump, fruity wine that is almost fat and hints of strawberries.
On purchase $

PASSAVANT

See Château de Passavant

PELLETIER

20 rue Jean York, 51700 Passy-Grigny
(326) 52.65.86 FAX (326) 52.65.86

A small family property just downstream from Ste Gemme, where Krug buys some of its best Meunier.

JEAN-MICHEL PELLETIER NV BRUT TRADITION 83

Softer and smoother than the Brut Sélection, with none of the wet-straw characte
On purchase $$ 64F

JEAN-MICHEL PELLETIER 1993 CUVÉE ANAËLLE BRUT 

Extremely rich, smooth, and satisfying. A serious, substantial flavor of some class.

Now–2001 $$$ 90F

PELORUS

Marlborough, New Zealand

Sparkling wine aficionados will not be surprised to learn that "Mad Harry" Osborne of Kristone in California consults here. The 1990 (90 points) and 1992 (91 points) promise to be sensational in the year 2000, but it was the latest release, 1993, that interested me most.

PELORUS 1993 MARLBOROUGH 

The lightest and potentially the best Pelorus vintage so far, this 1993 shows what a strange blessing a cold, rainy harvest can be. The malolactic has just started to dominate the wine, although this will eventually be subsumed by the oakiness, when the two will be transformed into the creamy-toasty complexity that is the hallmark of Pelorus.

Now–2003 $$

PENLEY

South Australia, Australia

Kym Tolley's mother was a Penfolds and his father a Tolley, thus the name Penley. His penchant is for red wines, but he also produces some fizz, made mainly from Pinot Noir, which is almost a forgotten variety in Coonawarra, and some 15 percent Chardonnay.

PENLEY PINOT CHARDONNAY 1991 BRUT 

Sharp and zesty with a touch of malolactic complexity.

Now–1999 $$

PENLEY PINOT CHARDONNAY 1990 BRUT 

The finesse in this *cuvée* puts it into a different class to the 1991 vintage.

Now–1999 $$

PEREJÓN

See Don Perejón

PÉRIGNON

See Moët & Chandon

PERELADA

Ampurdán-Costa Brava, Spain

CASTILLO PERELADA NV CAVA BRUT NATURE RESERVA 

Sweet, easy fruit.

On purchase $

PERRIER

69 avenue de Paris
51016 Chélons-en-Champagne
☎ (326) 68.29.51 FAX (326) 70.57.16

Joseph Perrier is now part of the large Laurent-Perrier group, but the Champagnes are as individual and interesting as ever.

JOSEPH PERRIER NV CUVÉE ROYALE BRUT 

The basic Cuvée Royale Brut is rich, creamy and complex – this is Joseph Perrier on top form.

Now–2000 $$ 120F

JOSEPH PERRIER NV BLANC DE BLANCS, CUVÉE ROYALE BRUT 

Deliciously rich and creamy, the Blanc de Blancs is just starting to pick up biscuity-walnutty complexity.

Now–2002 $$ 132F

JOSEPH PERRIER 1990 CUVÉE ROYALE BRUT 

I have always liked the rich, intense fruit in this vintage, but the first release was spoiled by an oxidative character, which I was glad to see had disappeared from shipments made in early 1998.

(bottle) 2000–2005 $$$

PERRIER-JOUËT

26/28 avenue de Champagne
51200 Épernay
(326) 55.20.53 FAX (326) 54.54.55

This top-quality *grande marque* Champagne owned by Seagram is back on stunning form after a period when it was in threat of being "Mummified" by its sister brand.

PERRIER-JOUËT NV GRAND BRUT

86

The Grand Brut has been equaling its original high standards since early 1997, and the current shipment is fresh and elegant in style, with plenty of fruit and a serious edge to the quality.

Now–2000 $$ 122F

PERRIER-JOUËT NV BLASON DE FRANCE BRUT

The Blason always has more creamy-Chardonnay influence than the Grand Brut. The previous shipment developed faster than it should have done, but this richer, smoother *cuvée* from the current shipment promises to age well.

Now–2002 $$$ 148F

PERRIER-JOUËT NV BLASON DE FRANCE ROSÉ BRUT

Full, yet delicate Pinot flavor, with a soft, velvety finish.

Now–2000 $$$ 162F

PERRIER-JOUËT 1992 BRUT

Lovely and fresh with floral-citrusy notes and a softness of fruit cocooned in crisp acidity, this is one of the most promising 1992s on the market.

1999–2000 $$$

PERRIER-JOUËT 1990 BRUT

90

A deliciously fruity wine that is still available and continues to develop beautiful toasty bottle-aromas.

Now–2000 $$$ 144F

PERRIER-JOUËT 1988 BELLE EPOQUE ROSÉ

Quite fat, toasty, and mature, but a classy vintage with excellent acidity and plenty of life yet.

Now–2005 $$$$ 375F

PERRIER-JOUËT 1986 BELLE EPOQUE ROSÉ

One of the lightest Belle Epoque vintages, but still the class shines through. Currently going very toasty.

Now–2000 $$$$

PERRIER-JOUËT 1985 BELLE EPOQUE ROSÉ

Available from some specialists, this will gradually become indistinguishable from the same vintage of Belle Epoque Brut, as the latter acquires a deeper gold color, while this *cuvée* drops its color to go sunset gold.

Now–2005 $$$$

PERRIER-JOUËT 1995 BELLE EPOQUE BRUT (JEROBOAM)

You might think that $2,000 for a Jeroboam of Belle Epoque is over the top, but this price includes an overnight stay for two at Perrier-Jouët's fabulous Maison Belle Epoque in Épernay, where you will be lavishly entertained. There are just 2,000 individually numbered Jeroboams for the entire world, so order one from your local stockist right away if you are interested. Perrier-Jouët is not disgorging the wine until 1999, and, with such a limited number, advertising has been by word of mouth (until now!). I have not tasted the wine, but the lowest-scoring Belle Epoque vintages in the past 20 or so years have all scored 90 points, so the 1995 should be good too. Mind you, if they filled the Jeroboams with water, they would still be a bargain!

Wait and see $$$$

PERRIER-JOUËT 1990 BELLE EPOQUE BRUT

The vintage has such finesse that it would be all too easy to drink now, but ideally you really should try to keep your hands off it until the millennium.

2000–2008 $$$$ 340F

PERRIER-JOUËT 1988 BELLE EPOQUE BRUT

Still quite widely available in specialty outlets, this vintage can appear to disappoint due to the tightness of the wine, but it's chock-a-block full of extract and comes out with food.

2000–2010 $$$$

PERRIER-JOUËT 1985 BELLE EPOQUE 91

Available in specialty outlets, this vintage has developed a lovely toasty richness, yet remains extraordinarily fresh, with even more extract than the 1988.

Now–2005 $$$$

PETALUMA

South Australia, Australia

Although Bollinger has a financial interest in Petaluma, the famous *grande marque* keeps its distance from any sparkling wines produced outside of Champagne. Croser is entirely Brian Croser's handwork.

CROSER 1994 BRUT 

This vintage seems strangely foursquare if served too cold, but has soft, gentle fatness with nice vanilla-fruit finesse on the finish when not over-chilled.

On purchase $$

PHANTOM

See Saxenburg

PHILIPPONNAT

13 rue du Pont, 51160 Mareuil-sur-Aò
(326) 52.60.43 FAX (326) 52.61.49

In November 1997 Bruno Paillard purchased Philipponnat from the ailing Marie Brizard empire on behalf of the up-and-coming BCC (Boizel Chanoine Champagne) group. The deal included Abel Lepitre, but the jewel in the crown was Clos des Goisses, a single-vineyard Champagne that is on par with the exquisite Salon.

PHILIPPONNAT NV LE REFLET 88

Clos des Goisses grapes have been blended with Chardonnay to make one of the most elegant, ready-drinking non-vintage *cuvées* on the market.

On purchase $$$ 163F

CLOS DES GOISSES 1991 PHILIPPONNAT 

For Clos des Goisses, this has always been very easy to drink when young, with a delicious pineapple-fruit palate that is years away from this Champagne's truly complex potential.

Now–2018 $$$$

CLOS DES GOISSES 1990 PHILIPPONNAT 

Pure acacia aroma and elegant, with intensely flavored fruit on the palate, it is a shame to drink this now, yet very hard to resist.

Now–2030 $$$$

CLOS DES GOISSES 1989 PHILIPPONNAT 

Fat aromas with tight flavors on the palate, this *cuvée* has only recently started to develop richness and complexity.

1999–2020 $$$$

CLOS DES GOISSES 1988 PHILIPPONNAT 

Not fat like the 1989, but very rich indeed, with an aromatic finesse that will one day make a profoundly complex, utterly beguiling mature Champagne.

1999–2025 $$$$ 364F

CLOS DES GOISSES 1986 PHILIPPONNAT 

Not the class of 1985 Clos des Goisses, but great finesse and quality for the year.

Now–2005 $$$$

CLOS DES GOISSES 1985 PHILIPPONNAT 

Classic Clos des Goisses, with a huge, rich, deep flavor and slow-building complexity beginning to form.

2000–2020 $$$$

PIBALEAU

Loire, France

PASCAL PIBALEAU NV BRUT, CRÉMANT DE LOIRE 

Very fresh fruit with a juicy-ripe pear flavor make this a soft-styled apéritif.

On purchase $

PICAMELOT

Burgundy, France

Maison Louis Picamelot has been making sparkling Burgundy since 1926, and this experience is evident in the fact that one of its *cuvées* came equal second in the line-up of Crémant de Bourgogne.

CRÉMANT DE BOURGOGNE, CUVÉE JEANNE THOMAS NV BRUT, LOUIS PICAMELOT 

Toasty-oaky fruit aromas of some finesse, with excellent acidity on the palate.

Now–2000 $

PICAMELOT NV CRÉMANT DE BOURGOGNE BRUT 

An elegant fizz that is full of perfumed fruit that seems to be Pinot Noir, but is different than any other Crémant de Bourgogne in the tasting.

On purchase $

PIPER-HEIDSIECK

See Heidsieck

PISONI

Trentino, Italy

Well-established as one of the best producers of sparkling wine under the Trento DOC.

PISONI BRUT 1992 TRENTO 

Succulent and appealing fruit on the nose becomes much firmer on the palate.

Now–1999 $$

PLANTAGENET

Western Australia, Australia

Named after the shire in which it is situated, Plantagenet was the first to cultivate the Mount Barker area and is its leading winery today, although so far I much prefer its still wines.

PLANTAGENET 1992 BRUT 

This sweet and sour, malty *cuvée* is softer, riper and more accessible than Plantagenet's 1993.

On purchase $

PLATZER

Austria

A small grower in Sud-Osteiermark who produces one of Austria's few interesting sparkling wines.

WEINHOF PLATZER PINOT CUVÉE 

Pure Pinot Blanc with elegant fruit, a firm mouse and well-balanced acidity.

Now–1999 $$

PLOYEZ-JACQUEMART

Ludes, 51500 Rilly-la-Montagne

(326) 61.11.87 FAX (326) 61.12.20

L. d'Harbonville, the prestige *cuvée* from this small, highly respected house, has leaped forward two or three levels of quality as from the 1988 vintage.

L. D'HARBONVILLE 1990 BRUT, PLOYEZ-JACQUEMART

Very rich apricot with high acidity and a tangy finish. It is currently not showing the charm, excitement, or focus of the previous two vintages, but based on the development of those *cuvées* and the undisputed greatness of the year, I must at least reserve judgment.

Wait and see $$$

L. D'HARBONVILLE 1989 BRUT, PLOYEZ-JACQUEMART 

Creamy new oak mingling with beautiful toasty aromas, and excellent acidity.

2000–2005 $$$

L. D'HARBONVILLE 1988 BRUT, PLOYEZ-JACQUEMART 

Intense, high-acid fruit that is as clear as a bell, and destined for lemony-toasty Burgundian-style stardom.

Now–2008 $$$ 235F

POJER & SANDRI

Trentino, Italy

A sparkling wine from a Trentino producer, who makes an excellent range of still wines.

POJER & SANDRI NV CUVÉE '93–'94, EXTRA BRUT

Immaculate presentation and nice, fresh, apricot aromas on the nose, but it lacks the depth and acidity for a top score.

On purchase $

POL ROGER

1 rue Henri Lelarge, 51206 Épernay
(326) 59.58.00 FAX (326) 55.25.70

The "Pol" Star in Champagne's firmament is in stunning form.

WHITE FOIL NV BRUT

The nonvintage is fresh, with supple fruit. It is as clean as a whistle, with a touch of class, and is always perfect for current drinking.

Now–1999 $$

POL ROGER 1990 BRUT

This is already so seductively soft and exquisitely perfumed with such an impeccable balance and cushiony mouse that it is difficult to accept just how much there is in this wine to develop.

Now–2010 $$$ 180F

POL ROGER 1989 BRUT

Like Pol Roger's 1983 and 1992 Brut, the 1989 was not released on all the usual markets, and when exported its distribution was often restricted. In the United Kingdom, for example, the 1989 *cuvée* was exclusively sold by the Oddbins chain. The 1989 was initially very fruity, but like the 1983 it quickly developed a creamy walnutty-biscuity complexity beyond its years.

Now–2005 $$$

POL ROGER 1988 BRUT

The Stevensons' house Champagne – need I say more?

Now–2018 $$$

POL ROGER 1990 BRUT CHARDONNAY

I once said that it is almost perverse that a traditional Pinot-dominated house can produce such a sublime *blanc de blancs* as this *cuvée*, and I have to say now that this is the most sumptuous and creamy vintage yet. This wine lasts a fraction of Pol Roger's classic vintage blend, and although interesting to follow up to 15 years of age, Chardonnay Brut is often at its best when first released, or at least within a year or two.

Now–2002 $$$

POL ROGER 1990 BRUT ROSÉ

A soft, sensual experience, with a panoply of pristine red-fruits on the finish. Pure delight.

Now–2002 $$$

POL ROGER CUVÉE PR 1988 RÉSERVE SPÉCIALE

Richness of fruit in abundance, with class, complexity, and fabulous finesse.

Now–2025 $$$$

POL ROGER CUVÉE SIR WINSTON CHURCHILL 1988 BRUT

Pol Roger has always refused to reveal the composition of this *cuvée*. Most vintages appear to be less Pinot-dominated than the Cuvée PR, even though the opposite would have seemed more fitting. This, however, has a concentrated Pinot character and is so youthful that it would be infanticide to broach just yet.

2003–2030 $$$$

POL ROGER CUVÉE SIR WINSTON CHURCHILL 1985 BRUT

Luscious fruit interwoven with fine acacia floweriness when young, this is now a wine of magnificent richness and finesse.

Now–2025 $$$$

POMMERY

5 Place du Général Gouraud, 51053 Reims
(326) 61.62.63 FAX (326) 61.62.99

Pommery's winemakers have made some of the finest *cuvées* in Champagne when they are allowed to pick according to quality not quantity.

POMMERY NV BRUT ROYAL 80

Simple, fruity, recognizable Pommery style, with a slightly cumbersome finish.
On purchase ⓢⓢ 120F

POMMERY NV BRUT ROYAL APANAGE 89

A huge leap forward for Pommery, with its stricter selection and higher Chardonnay content. Fabulous depth of crisp-mellow flavor, with a lovely slow buildup of fresh yet mature complexity.
Now–2001 ⓢⓢⓢ 150F

POMMERY NV BRUT ROSÉ 

Very pale *blanc de noirs* color, with true *brut* crisp dryness, but very fruity.
Now–2000 ⓢⓢ 160F

POMMERY 1991 BRUT, GRAND CRU 

Firm toasty fruit with a full finish that lacks the finesse of the best Pommery vintages.
Now–1999 ⓢⓢⓢ 160F

POMMERY 1990 BRUT, GRAND CRU 

Very rich and very good, but not in the same class as Pommery's 1989 vintage.
Now–2005 ⓢⓢⓢ

POMMERY 1989 BRUT, GRAND CRU 

Atypically big for Pommery, but has a finesse that many 1989s lack. A great wine.
Now–1999 ⓢⓢⓢ

POMMERY 1988 LOUISE, BRUT 88

Ten years old and not yet together, but the excellent depth and richness guarantee a slow-maturing Champagne of great complexity and finesse.
2000–2006 ⓢⓢⓢⓢ 350F

POMMERY 1989 LOUISE, ROSÉ BRUT 

Classy toasty aromas pervade every molecule of this richly flavored, beautifully balanced *cuvée*. Lovely fruit and acidity.
Now–2002 ⓢⓢⓢⓢ

PONGRÁCZ

See Bergkelder

QUARTET

See Roederer Estate

RAIMAT

See Codorníu

RATZENBERGER

Mittelrhein, Germany.

WEINGUT RATZENBERGER 1993 BACHARACHER KLOSTER FÜRSTENTAL RIESLING SEKT BRUT 74

Really good, crisp style with lots of satisfying depth and length to the fruit.
On purchase ⓢⓢ

WEINGUT RATZENBERGER 1994 BACHARACHER KLOSTER FÜRSTENTAL RIESLING SEKT BRUT 76

Succulent peachy fruit. Bottle-fermented.
On purchase ⓢⓢ

RAVENTÓS I BLANC

Penedès, Spain

Josep Maria left his family's firm, Codorníu, to set up his own house in 1986. The classy presentation stands out among other Cavas.

CAVA GRAN RESERVA PERSONAL 1992 BRUT NATURE, RAVENTÓS I BLANC 

Some malolactic complexity peeping through a richness of fruit that is going biscuity.
Now–1999 ⓢ

CAVA GRAN RESERVA 1993 CAVA BRUT NATURE, RAVENTÓS I BLANC 

Lighter than the Gran Reserva Personal, in a much easier, less complex style, with none of the malolactic aromas showing.
On purchase ⓢ

Raventós Rosell

Penedès, Spain

This offshoot of the Raventós family owns 150 acres of vines and established its own Cava enterprise as recently as 1985.

Joan Raventós Rosell 1994 Cava Brut Nature 

No Joan Raventós wines were submitted this year, but the 1994 tasted last year had lots of fat, delicious fruit to last until now, plus an intriguing blown-wheat aroma.
On purchase $

Rebecca Vineyard

Tasmania, Australia

Joe Chromy recently sold Heemskerk and Jansz to Pipers Brook, but although this included the Rochecombe Vineyard, it did not include the RV brand, which will now be sourced from Rebecca Vineyard. Hopefully, Rebecca is every bit as stunning.

RV Tasmania 1995 Rebecca Vineyard, Heemskerk 

An easy-drinking, fruit driven *cuvée* formerly from the same stable as Jansz, and utterly beguiling it is too, with beautifully bright Pinot fruit and the most succulent of finishes. Seductive stuff!
Now–2000 $

Renaudin

Domaine des Conardins, 51530 Moussy
Tel (326) 54.03.41 Fax (326) 54.31.12

Small, consistently high quality, very expressive Champagnes. The owner, Dominique Tellier, also makes good Kosher Champagne.

R. Renaudin NV Grande Réserve Brut 

A richly flavored *cuvée* with intense fruit and a fresh, biscuity complexity.
Now–2000 $$

R. Renaudin 1987 Brut Rosé 

Not many *rosé* Champagnes benefit from 11 years of aging, but this is now proudly vintaged. An old gold color, this has matured gracefully, with lots of finesse, and is packing a lot of flavor, spreading out beautifully on the finish, like a peacock's tail.
Now–1999 $$$

R. Renaudin 1985 Réserve Spéciale C.D. Brut 

This is still very much a fruit-driven wine, without any sign of complex bottle-aromas, but makes very rich current drinking.
Now–2000 $$$

Ress

Rheingau, Germany

Ress & Compagnie 1991 Spätburgunder Sekt Brut 

Like fruit-flavored candy with bubbles!
On purchase $$

Ress & Compagnie 1994 Riesling Sekt Brut 

A fine structure with a high concentration of fruit. Bottle-fermented.
On purchase $$

Ribeauvillé

Alsace, France

Best known for its Clos du Zahnacker, a classic blend from a region renowned for its pure varietal wines.

Riesling, Crémant d'Alsace NV Brut, Cave Vinicole de Ribeauvillé 

Good Riesling fruit spoiled by a whiff of sulfur, but this will go toasty with time, and the wine has the acidity to take that.
Now–1999 $

Rienth

Württemberg, Germany

Weingut Gerhard Rienth 1995 Fellbacher Goldberg Riesling Sekt Brut

Nice, easy-going, fresh, and fluffy style. Bottle-fermented.

On purchase $$

Robert

25 avenue de la République
51190 Le Mesnil-sur-Oger
(326) 57.52.94 FAX (326) 57.59.22

I was disappointed that only one of the numerous wines submitted survived my blind tastings, as Alain Robert usually makes some of Le Mesnil's greatest grower Champagnes. The 1985 is, however, a wonderful exception.

Alain Robert 1985 Sélection, Blanc de Blancs

Layers of toasty over-ripe peachy fruit, with exquisitely high acidity.

Now–2003 $$$ 163F

(Louis) Roederer

21 Boulevard Lundy, 51053 Reims
(326) 40.42.11 FAX (326) 47.66.51

Roederer's prestige *cuvée,* Cristal, is a license to print money in the US, and the Champagnes produced are of the highest quality.

Louis Roederer NV Brut Premier

The nonvintage Brut Premier is always a good bet, but currently on stunning form. One of the very best nonvintage *cuvées* of the tasting, it even has the same vanilla mid-palate smoothness found in Charles Heidsieck.

Now–2002 $$

Louis Roederer 1990 Brut

Fresh, zesty, creamy-almondy fruit with a very lively mousse. Currently not in the class of Roederer's Blanc de Blancs, but it will gain body, depth, and complexity over the next few years.

2000–2005 $$$

Louis Roederer 1990 Blanc de Blancs Brut

Louis Roederer's best-kept secret, this *cuvée* is the least-known, greatest bargain in the range. Wonderfully rich and succulent with classy, complex, creamy-walnutty fruit.

2000–2005 $$$

Louis Roederer 1991 Rosé Brut

Always very pale with a youthful yet oxidative aromas, this *cuvée* has the acidity to let the palate catch up with the rest of the wine.

1999–2001 $$$

Louis Roederer Cristal 1990 Brut

Full and smooth, and, despite the excellent high acidity, there is already a considerable depth of flavor, with lots of Pinot-rich, biscuity complexity coming through on the finish.

Now–2015 $$$$

Louis Roederer Cristal 1989 Brut

The complexity in this *cuvée* started to emerge in 1996, since when it has shown remarkable finesse for the year.

Now–2010 $$$$

Louis Roederer Cristal 1988 Brut

The richness in this wine is just beginning to swell, but it still needs further aging in order to allow it to develop mellow postdisgorgement bottle-aromas.

2000–2010 $$$$

Louis Roederer Cristal 1985 Brut

95

The 1985 still tastes so young that it appears to be relatively simplistic, but that is, of course, the hallmark of the greatest Cristal *cuvées.*

2000–2015 $$$$

Louis Roederer Cristal 1985 Rosé Brut

The soft, silky, strawberry fruit here is so sublime that this might well turn out to be the best Cristal Rosé since the first and legendary 1974 vintage.

Now–2005 $$$$

Louis Roederer Cristal "2000" 1990 Brut (Methuselah)

A different blend to the 1990 Cristal, and not really Roederer in style. Cristal "2000" has a bit more Chardonnay than the regular Cristal, but the selection of *crus* (Mesnil and Avize) emphasizes this grape, producing a leaner structure with crisp, ripe-green-apple fruit. Evolution in this size of bottle is so slow that I suspect most will be gone long before the *cuvée* is ready. They sell for $2,000, which is more than the cost of eight bottles of the 1990.

2010–2030 $$$$

(Théophile) Roederer

20 rue Andrieux, 51058 Reims
(326) 40.19.00 FAX (326) 47.66.51

The wines are made and stored separately from Louis Roederer's, but while the raw materials determine Théophile Roederer's lower quality and simpler style, the brand benefits from Roederer "know-how" and is an alternative for any Louis customers who are strapped for cash.

Théophile Roederer NV Brut Rosé

Very pale salmon-gold with rare richness for such a light-bodied wine.

Now–2000 $$

Roederer Estate

Mendocino, California, US

The Premier Grand Cru of American sparkling wine, Roederer Estate is owned by the French Champagne house Louis Roederer, which prefers to call the wine Quartet on export.

Roederer Estate NV Brut

Apart from the 1986-based release, this *cuvée* is always so tight, firm, and youthful when first released that it often tastes like green cooking apples, but after two or three years bottle-age, it quietly develops a lovely creamy-biscuity complexity. It is California's greatest sparkling wine.

2000–2003 $$

Roederer Estate NV Brut Rosé

The current *cuvée* has lots of very delicate, soft-fruit flavors.

Now–2000 $$

Roederer Estate L'Ermitage 1991 Brut

Full, yet soft and deliciously fruity wine with lots of youthful complexity.

Now–2001 $$

Roger

See Pol Roger

Rohart

Loire, France

Vouvray, Coeur de Cuvée 1995 Brut, Alain Rohart

Too assertively Chenin for my personal taste, but very good for its type, with a rich finish. Should please Loire purists.

Now–1999 $$

Vouvray, Tàte de Cuvée NV Brut, Alain Rohart

Rich, lively, perfumed fruit.

Now–1999 $

Rolet

Arbois, France

These are the favorite non-Champagne guzzlers of a Dr. Patricia Norman, who is so passionate about the health benefits of drinking wine that she spends more time selling it than practicing medicine.

Rolet NV Crémant du Jura, Brut Rosé

Bruised plums on the nose, with contrasting perfumed fruit on the front to middle palate, and Victoria plums on the finish. All character and no finesse, but who gives a fig, or a plum for that matter?

On purchase $

ROLET NV CRÉMANT DU JURA, BRUT 73

An oxidative bent with no finesse, but the wine is not unpleasant, rather it is strangely chock-full of character.

On purchase $

ROSELL

See Raventos Rosell

ROTARI

Trentino, Italy

ROTARI RISERVA 1993 BRUT, TRENTO 

Fresh and fruity, with good acidity, but unfortunately the fruit peters out shortly after mid-palate, otherwise this would have scored higher.

On purchase $$

ROVELLATS

Penedès, Spain

ROVELLATS CAVA GRAN RESERVA NV BRUT NATURE 

Light, clean, and easy.

On purchase $

ROY

See Tour du Roy

ROYER

120 Grande Rue, 10110 Landreville

(325) 38.52.16 FAX (325) 29.92.26

I was pleased with this *cuvée*, which again emphasizes the potential of Chardonnay in the Aube area, which is closer to Chablis than it is to the rest of Champagne, and has the same soil as Chablis.

ROYER PÈRE NV BLANCS DE BLANCS, CUVÉE PRESTIGE BRUT 

Despite a foamy mousse, this is a jump up from the Cuvée de Réserve, with its rich yet elegant fruit flavor.

Now–1999 $$ 82F

RUGGERI

Italy

Half the wines submitted by this producer passed the test, but the style seems to be either too amylic or too heavily influenced by malolactic, and so the wines lack finesse.

RUGGERI NV CHARDONNAY BRUT 

The nose is restrained, but what shows through is fine and has more finesse than the fresh, fruit on the palate. It has a correct lean structure.

On purchase $

RUGGERI NV PROSECCO DI VALDOBBIADENE EXTRA DRY 

Just as amylic as all the other boring Prosecco, but this has a much greater intensity of flavor.

On purchase $

RUGGERI SUPERIORE DI CARTIZZE NV PROSECCO DI VALDOBBIADENE DRY 

An amylic wine, but with some finesse, much more fruit than other Prosecco and some Muscat-like freshness.

On purchase $

RUHLMANN

Alsace, France

I will always remember the beautiful balance of acidity in this producer's 1988 Crémant d'Alsace.

RUHLMANN 1995 CRÉMANT D'ALSACE BRUT 

A fresh, fat, fruity fizz that needs a little tweaking in its structure and acidity.

On purchase $

RUINART

4 rue des Crayères, 51100 Reims
(326) 85.40.29 FAX (326) 82.88.43

Champagne lovers know Ruinart very well, but in terms of global awareness this continues to be a sleepy little *grande marque* that could easily double its production without harming its reputation for quality. Sales have crept up in recent years.

RUINART "R" NV BRUT 88

As rich and as satisfying as always.
Now–2000 $$

RUINART "R" NV BRUT ROSÉ 87

Recently relaunched in a new bottle-shape with an impressively lighter, fresher, easier-drinking style.
Now–2000 $$

RUINART "R" 1990 BRUT 

A quick developer, but absolutely beguiling, this *cuvée* has lovely toasty aromas and a touch of vanilla to the fruit, with excellent acidity to keep it going.
Now–2002 $$$

RUINART "R" 1992 BRUT 

So young and fruity, but this *cuvée* has a Chablis-like character that will quickly go toasty, so if you do not like those mellowing bottle-aromas, drink this up now.
Now–2002 $$$

DOM RUINART 1990 BLANC DE BLANCS 

It's unusual for Dom Ruinart to be approachable before it enters its toasty stage, but this is already stunning, a lovely, fat, creamy-rich *cuvée*, yet it has not even started to develop the slightest complexity. This could turn out to be on par with the 1979 (94 points).
Now–2008 $$$$

DOM RUINART 1988 BLANC DE BLANCS 

After a somewhat sultry start this *cuvée* has developed into an exotically creamy Champagne that is quite wonderful, yet strangely it is not reminiscent of either Dom Ruinart or 1988!
Now–2008 $$$$

DOM RUINART 1986 BLANC DE BLANCS 

Starting to go really toasty. Not a top Dom Ruinart, but an exceptional 1986.
Now–2008 $$$$

DOM RUINART 1985 BLANC DE BLANCS 

Big, rich, and seductively toasty, yet there is so much undeveloped extract that this vintage still has miles to go.
Now–2010 $$$$

DOM RUINART 1986 ROSÉ 

The 1986 Rosé has lovely red fruit richness now. When mature, this *cuvée* always develops into the quintessence of Pinot Noir, even though it is basically a Dom Ruinart *blanc de blancs* to which 20 percent Pinot Noir vinified as a red wine has been added. It is a really lovely Champagne, but not quite in the same class as the 1981 (94 points).
Now–2005 $$$$

RUSSLER

Rheingau, Germany

WEINGUT FRIEDEL RUSSLER 1995 WALLUFER WALKENBERG RIESLING SEKT BRUT 

Satisfying depth of fresh Riesling fruit for a nondosage wine. Bottle-fermented.
On purchase $$

WEINGUT FRIEDEL RUSSLER 1995 WALLUFER WALKENBERG RIESLING SEKT EXTRA TROCKEN 

Good tangy fruit with a hint of peach. Bottle-fermented.
On purchase $$

STE. MICHELLE

Washington, US

This winery showed great promise for sparkling wine in the late 1970s, but it has struggled ever since to make something decent, let alone anything that is exciting.

DOMAINE STE. MICHELLE NV BRUT 

Better than its Blanc de Blancs, this is more serious in structure, with classic floral aromas and a certain scented complexity to the fruit.

On purchase $$

ST. URBANSHOF

Mosel-Saar-Ruwer, Germany

WEINGUT ST. URBANSHOF 1992 RIESLING SEKT BRUT 

A very soft and gentle expression of Riesling fruit, with some finesse.

On purchase $$

SALINGER

See Seppelt

SALON

Le Mesnil-sur-Oger, 51190 Avize
(326) 57.51.65 FAX (326) 57.79.29

This is the only wine in the world that is not made every year – in nonvintage years the wine will end up either in one of Delamotte's *cuvées* or used by the parent company Laurent-Perrier. Salon is made exclusively from Chardonnay grown in Le Mesnil-sur-Oger from midslope vines over 40 years old, and it is this restricted yield that determines Salon's extraordinary intensity of fruit. The wines need at least 10 years aging, and do not start to interest aficionados until 20 or 30 years old, when they develop a majestic depth and length, with complex aromas and flavors that typically include coconut, macaroons, walnuts, vanilla, and coffee. Only 32 vintages of Salon have ever been produced, and for those who look out for old vintages at auction the very greatest are 1971 (97 points), 1961 (96 points) 1955 (96 points), 1947 (100 points), 1928 (100+ points!).

SALON 1988 

Firm, well structured, and definitely in the muscular mold. Initially, the very pale 1988 had an edge over the 1990, but the latter vintage has since demonstrated its superiority (95 points), although it will be a long time before it is released. This is still, however, a great vintage, with complex, citrusy fruit that is so tight that it will take time – even for Salon – to unfold, but when it does it will be stunning.

2003–2028 $$$$ 420F

SALON 1985 

Very fine, elegant, and pure. An absolute delight now, but capable of maturing gracefully for another 30 years or more.

Now–2025 $$$$

SALON 1983 

It is fascinating to compare this with the 1982, which is a completely different vintage of almost the same age made with the same philosophy. The 1983 was initially firm and very *brut*, with a prune-like character that gave way to a creamy-coconutty, hazelnut-walnut complexity after a spurt of maturation in the mid-1990s. Great intensity, but evolving relatively fast for Salon, and not in the same class as the 1982. Almost impossible to score, but 88 illustrates the difference in quality relative to other Salon vintages.

Now–2013 $$$$ 500F

SALON 1982 

When recently disgorged this vintage is austere, with a mouth-puckering lemony-toastiness, but if given a few years in bottle, it slowly assumes a luscious peachy fruitiness, with toasty-vanilla aromas and a silkiness on the finish, yet heaps of acidity to keep it fresh. Because the disgorgement date makes a vast difference to such a slow-developing Champagne, it should really be indicated on every bottle.

2003–2028 $$$$ 580F

SANDORA

Penedès, Spain

New joint venture between two Champagne groups, Seagram and Vranken-Lafitte.

SANDORA NV CAVA BRUT 

Jot bad, but not special either, and only ıst scrapes in because its 35 percent Chardonnay content provides some ıouthfill, although it is rather soapy and outhful. The balance is Parellada, and his is the worst of all three traditional arieties to blend with Chardonnay on a wo-to-one basis, although the wine hould improve a little in bottle, but only ver a matter of months, not years.

On purchase Ⓢ

SAUMUR

Loire, France

It's hard to believe this cooperative makes as many *cuvées* as it sent me, but not one of the Saumur *cuvées* survived the blind tasting, whereas most of the Crémant de Loire did.

CRÉMANT DE LOIRE BLANC BRUT SPÉCIAL 1994 CAVE DES VIGNERONS DE SAUMUR 

'he only 1994 Loire fizz I could heartily ecommend, this is the year when CVS Crémant de Loire came good, jumping rom 15/85 Chenin/Chardonnay to 0/50. The freshness and finesse stand ut, with a lovely ripe sweetness of fruit n the finish.

Now–1999 Ⓢ

CRÉMANT DE LOIRE, BLANC BRUT SPÉCIAL NV CAVE DES VIGNERONS DE SAUMUR 

)ne of the best Loire sparkling wines I ave tasted, and immeasurably superior o another half-and-half Chenin/Char-lonnay *cuvée* also produced by this ooperative , which just goes to prove hat it is not necessarily the grape arieties or producer that matters, but ather where and how those varieties are rown, and how they are processed.

On purchase Ⓢ

CRÉMANT DE LOIRE, BLANC BRUT SPÉCIAL 1995 CAVE DES VIGNERONS DE SAUMUR 

'he 50 percent Chardonnay gives this Crémant de Loire real mouthfill.

Now–1999 Ⓢ

CRÉMANT DE LOIRE ROSÉ BRUT NV CAVE DES VIGNERONS DE SAUMUR 

A very fresh fizz with lively raspberry fruit, made from Cabernet Franc.

On purchase Ⓢ

CRÉMANT DE LOIRE ROSÉ SEC NV CAVE DES VIGNERONS DE SAUMUR 

This pure Cabernet *rosé* is fat, but fresh, lively and really quite *brut* for a *sec*.

On purchase Ⓢ

MOUSSEUX ROUGE DEMI-SEC NV CAVE DES VIGNERONS DE SAUMUR 

A deep, dark, sweet-raspberry flavored fizz made totally from Cabernet Franc.

Now–2000 Ⓢ

SAVISA

Paarl/Stellenbosch, South Africa

Large Swiss-owned export-oriented company with numerous labels.

JACQUES GERMANIER BRUT NV CAP CLASSIQUE, SONOP 

A sharp, fresh, zingy fizz in an embossed skittle-shaped bottle.

Now–1999 Ⓢ

SAXENBURG

Stellenbosch, South Africa

A rapidly rising star in South Africa's red wine firmament.

LE PHANTOM BRUT NV CAP CLASSIQUE 

High acidity gives the fruit a sharp tang.

Now–2000 Ⓢ

SCHALES

Rheinhessen, Germany

Eiswien as the base for a sparkling wine is a new concept, but there is no doubting the quality of the raw material.

SCHALES SILVANER TROCKEN 1991 PREMIUM SEKT

Amazing botrytis-like aroma, which follows through onto the palate. Just like drinking a fine Auslese with bubbles.

On purchase $$$$

SCHALLER

Alsace, France

Edgard Schaller is better known for his varietal wines, particularly Riesling Grand Cru Mandelberg, but he makes a creditable *crémant.*

SCHALLER, BLANC DE NOIR NV CRÉMANT D'ALSACE BRUT

Firm, crisp fruit and a sturdy structure. It should develop.

Now–1999 $

SCHARFFENBERGER

Mendocino, California, US

Scharffenberger's wines have gained tremendously in elegance and finesse since the early 1990s, particularly the Blanc de Blancs.

SCHARFFENBERGER NV BRUT

Fine, elegant, rich, and smooth, with a lovely creamy-biscuity complexity beginning to build.

On purchase $

SCHARFFENBERGER 1991 BLANC DE BLANCS

Light, soft, and creamy with a silky mousse of minuscule bubbles.

Now–1999 $$

SCHELL

Ahr, Germany

WEINGUT OTGER SCHELL 1993 RECHER HARDTBERG RIESLING SEKT HALBTROCKEN

Sweet, succulent Riesling fruit.

On purchase $$

SCHLOSS

See Hambacher Schloss

SCHLOSS ORTENBERG

Baden, Germany

Established in 1950 as a viticultural school, Schloss Ortenburg currently produces 125 cases of Sekt per year.

WEINGUT SCHLOSS ORTENBERG NV PINOT SEKT BRUT

Extremely ripe and rich, this *cuvée* was marked down because it is not just on the sweet side of *brut,* but so richly sweet as to make a nonsense of the so-called *brut* style. On the other hand, if you are looking for a *brut* that tastes like a Halbtrocken then you might like to look upon this as scoring closer to 80 points. Bottle-fermented.

On purchase $$

SCHLUMBERGER

Loire, France

ROBERT DE SCHLUMBERGER NV TOURAINE BRUT

Although the deep flavor and high acidity of Robert de Schlumberger's nonvintage Touraine Brut would seem to suggest a wine fit for aging, it most definitely is made for ready drinking.

On purchase $

SCHMITGES

Mosel-Saar-Ruwer, Germany

WEINGUT HEINRICH SCHMITGES 1994 ERDENER HERRENBERG RIESLING SEKT BRUT

Crisp, fresh, and focused Riesling fruit. Bottle-fermented.

On purchase $$

SCHRAM

See Schramsberg

SCHRAMSBERG

Napa, California, US

Until Domaine Chandon was set up in 1973, Schramsberg was the only producer of serious quality bottle-fermented sparking wine in the whole of the US. Jamie Davies' aim (formerly shared by his late brother Jack) is to produce rich, complex sparkling wines that are fully mature and expressive of the sun-blessed *terroir* of the Golden State. Much as I respect this decision, I would like to see Schramsberg release much younger wines, particularly on export markets.

SCHRAMSBERG 1991 BLANC DE BLANCS 80

Very fat, and really quite heavy, yet still quite fresh.

On purchase $$

J. SCHRAM 1991 82

Rich and toasty.

On purchase $$

SCHWACH

Alsace, France

BERNARD SCHWACH BRUT RESERVE NV CRÉMANT D'ALSACE 70

This wine scrapes through as an outside bet on how it might develope, based solely on its structure and acidity.

Now–2000 $

SEAVIEW

South Australia, Australia

Part of Southcorp, Seaview's basic range generally has the edge over that of its sister Seppelt brand.

EDWARDS & CHAFFEY 1993 PINOT NOIR CHARDONNAY BRUT, SEAVIEW 

For lovers of toasty fizz only, this *cuvée* has now been at its peak for a couple of years, but it keeps on going thanks to very good acidity.

On purchase $

SEAVIEW ROSÉ NV BRUT 

Creamy strawberry and lavender fruit with a soft mousse.

On purchase $

SEAVIEW PINOT NOIR CHARDONNAY 1994 BRUT 

So smooth and creamy, the richness of fruit in this *cuvée* builds up gently in the mouth to a wonderfully satisfying flavor. This sparkling wine is all about fruit now, but it will become increasingly toasty as the months go by.

Now–2000 $

SEAVIEW PINOT NOIR CHARDONNAY 1993 BRUT 

The big, rich, toasty fruit in this *cuvée* is indicative of how the 1994 will go.

Now–1999 $

SEAVIEW NV BRUT 

Seaview's standard *brut* is fresher, fluffier, and better than the standard *brut* made by its sister Seppelt brand, but, then again, at this end of the market this *cuvée* is also significantly more expensive.

On purchase $

SEAVIEW PINOT NOIR CHARDONNAY 1995 BRUT 

The real richness of fruit to be found in this blend of Chardonnay and Pinot Noir is just beginning to go toasty.

On purchase $

SEAVIEW BLANC DE BLANCS 1995 BRUT 

Unfortunately, there is a touch of oxidativeness already showing on the finish of this wine, which would normally exclude such a *cuvée* from this guide. On the other hand, I cannot bring myself to ignore Seaview's previous track record, which has been excellent, and so I will reserve judgment for now.

Wait and see $

SEDLESCOMBE

Robertsbridge, England, UK

Roy Cook is the winemaker at this proudly organic vineyard.

SEDLESCOMBE ORGANIC 1994 BRUT

The wine was made and estate-bottled at Sedlescombe, but disgorged and dosaged at Chapel Wines in Tenterden. Its fresh garden-herb aroma is unusual, but gives way to rich fruit on the pale. A curiosity.

On purchase $

SEGURA VIUDAS

Penedès, Spain

This is Freixenet's top-performing Cava brand.

RESERVA HEREDAD NV CAVA BRUT, SEGURA VIUDAS

Lots of satisfying fruit-laden flavor that promises to go toasty.

Now–1999 $

SELOSSE

22 rue Ernest Vallée, 51190 Avize

(326) 57.53.56 FAX (326) 57.78.22

Anselme Selosse is fastidious about quality in the vineyard and winery, but there are raw, floral, estery notes in most of the wines. They would benefit from one more year on their sediment, plus another year after disgorgement, before shipping.

JACQUES SELOSSE NV GRAND CRU BLANC DE BLANCS, EXTRA BRUT

Young, flowery Chardonnay. Needs time.

1999–2001 $$$

JACQUES SELOSSE NV GRAND CRU BLANC DE BLANCS BRUT

Vinified in large oak *tonneaux*. It needs time to bring out the richness lurking beneath very young, floral aromas.

1999–2001 $$$

JACQUES SELOSSE NV ORIGINE, GRAND CRU BLANC DE BLANCS BRUT

Vinified in small *barriques*, this is as oaky as expected, although how much the exotic, peachy fruit can be put down to wood, rather than ripeness of fruit, is anyone's guess.

Now–2000 $$$

JACQUES SELOSSE NV GRAND CRU ROSÉ BRUT

Pale apricot color, creamy-oaky aroma, smooth creamy-oaky fruit, still developing.

1999–2001 $$$

JACQUES SELOSSE NV CUVÉE EXQUISE, SEC

Typical Selosse oaky-floral aroma, with extraordinarily tropical fruits and an exotic creamy-fruity sweetness that in purely taste terms is more *demi-sec* than *sec*. An excellent accompaniment to fresh raspberries gratiné.

Now–2000 $$$

JACQUES SELOSSE 1989 GRAND CRU BLANC DE BLANCS BRUT

A well-structured wine that is already rich and fleshy, yet has huge extract, and awaits further development.

2000–2005 $$$

JACQUES SELOSSE 1988 GRAND CRU BLANC DE BLANCS BRUT

Vinified in large oak *tonneaux*. Marked on the finish by the acidity of the 1988 vintage, this is another floral-rich *cuvée* that needs time.

1999–2001 $$$

SENEZ

6 Grande Rue, 10360 Fontette

(326) 29.60.62

CRISTIAN SENEZ 1990 FONTETTE BRUT

A freshly poured glass had an unpleasant plastic aroma, which I could not get past my nose to put inside my body, but this goes away after ten minutes or so, and the palate has a curious coconutty taste.

Wait and see $$$ 120F

CRISTIAN SENEZ 1990 GRANDE RÉSERVE BRUT 

'oo exotic for me, but just saying that vill make some people want to try it.
On purchase ⓈⓈⓈ 120F

CRISTIAN SENEZ 1989 BRUT 

'his wine has an almost woody (not vertly oaky) richness that promises to levelop and could well result in a much igher-scoring wine with time, but this vas the best of the three Senez wines asted, as far as current enjoyability goes.
Now–1999 ⓈⓈⓈ 110F

SEPPELT

Victoria, Australia

There are better sparkling wines than Seppelt's Great Western, but none that offers better value.

SEPPELT GREAT WESTERN NV BRUT 

'his clean, fresh, citrusy-zesty fizz is lefinitely at the bottom end of the Aus-ralian bottle-fermented bubbly market, et consistently makes a decent mouthful, lthough it definitely is not for keeping.
On purchase Ⓢ

SEPPELT 1994 BLANC DE BLANCS BRUT 

'resh, crisp, zesty-lemony fruit with a irm mouse of small bubbles.
Now–2000 Ⓢ

SEPPELT 1992 SPARKLING SHIRAZ 

A heady wine with a big oaky-Shiraz roma, although less oak-dominated than 'alumba's sparkling Cabernet Sauvignon. Bags of fruit and a rich, raisiny complex-ty make this the ideal accompaniment to lmost any dish containing blue cheese.
Now–2000 Ⓢ

SEPPELT GREAT WESTERN NV ROSÉ 

find this easier to drink than Seppelt's ister Seaview Rosé. A nicely structured izz with fine, creamy-rich fruit supported y a firm mousse.
On purchase Ⓢ

SEPPELT 1993 PINOT NOIR CHARDONNAY 

This fat, fresh, and sassy wine is better than the 1991, which was being sold at the same time on some markets.
Now–1999 Ⓢ

SEPPELT 1994 SPARKLING SHIRAZ 

Fresh fruity Shiraz with a touch of oak, this is very much in the same mold as the 1992 vintage.
Now–2000 Ⓢ

SEPPELT 1993 SPARKLING SHIRAZ 

Very fruity style with a nice touch of oak, but not the complexity of the 1992.
Now–2000 Ⓢ

SEPPELT 1985 SHOW SPARKLING SHIRAZ 

This massive, blackcurrant-flavored blockbuster is ripe in every sense of the word, and not for the weak-hearted or indeed anyone other than an out-and-out sparkling Shiraz fanatic.
Now–2000 Ⓢ

SALINGER 1992 BRUT 

The austere, citrusy fruit in this wine is typical of a young Salinger, which needs time to develop finesse.
Now–2001 ⓈⓈ

SALINGER 1991 BRUT 

Fine and very fresh, with fluffy fruit and high acidity balance.
Now–2001 ⓈⓈ

SALINGER 1990 BRUT 

This vintage of Salinger has really quite exceptional finesse for an eight-year-old fizz from Australia.
Now–2001 ⓈⓈ

SERRA

Penedès, Spain

Jaume Serra utilize one of Chile's highest-profile winemakers, Ignacio Recabarren, as consultant.

CRISTALINO NV CAVA BRUT 

Fresh, fruit-driven style.
On purchase Ⓢ

Shadow Creek

See Chandon California

Sieur d'Arques

Limoux, France

Dame d'Arques Tradition NV Blanquette Méthode Ancestrale

This unusual sparkling wine has been made by the ancient Blanquette de Limoux method, which involves no second fermentation, but a continuation of the first. The result should be labeled at least *demi-sec*, perhaps even *doux*, for it is lusciously sweet, with just six percent of alcohol (which is a similar strength to sweet Italian Asti), but it is wonderfully soft with a silky-sweet finish. It is the perfect accompaniment to foie gras. I very much hope that we will see much more *méthode ancestrale* on export markets in the future.

On purchase $

Sieur d'Arques 1991 Crémant de Limoux Brut

This *cuvée* had the most finesse of all the dry Limoux tasted this year. It also had the tiniest bubbles and the most accessible fruit.

On purchase $

Siffert

Alsace, France

It is Siffert's Pinot Noir Coteaux du Haut-Koenigsbourg that usually stands out, but this *crémant* shows some promise.

Siffert NV Crémant d'Alsace Brut

There is a beautiful Riesling aroma in this Crémant d'Alsace, but the fruit is rather fat and the structure, although firm, could be leaner. With more acidity this would have scored higher.

On purchase $

Simonsig

Stellenbosch, South Africa

The first producer of *méthode champenoise* sparkling wine in South Africa, Simonsig has a very large production and cuts its cloth to meet the price. Note that this often means that the more expensive the wine, the better the bargain.

Kaapse Vonkel Brut 1993 Cap Classique, Simonsig

I tasted two totally different versions of this wine within days of each other: one was too oxidative for the age and weight and would not have qualified for entry into this guide; the other had a good, clean fruit-driven style that should pick up some biscuitiness by Christmas 1998 (80 points).

Wait and see $

Kaapse Vonkel Brut 1992 Cap Classique, Simonsig

Classic biscuity aromas, lovely lean structure, fine mousse of tiny bubbles.

Now–2000 $

Sipp Mack

Alsace, France

As Sipp Mack is such a great producer of still Riesling wines, both generic and *grand cru*, I will give this the benefit of the doubt.

Sipp Mack NV Crémant d'Alsace Brut

Strangely fat yet tart fruit here, with fresh, terpene aromas suggesting some Riesling content.

On purchase $

Soldati La Scolca

Gavi, Italy

These wines tend to lean more toward heavy and characterful rather than light and elegant, and could do with more finesse at times.

SOLDATI LA SCOLCA NV BRUT 

Hints of toast and lemon run through the bouquet onto the palate, which is rich and mature, yet firm, with a crisp finish.
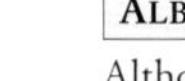
On purchase $

SOLDATI LA SCOLCA NV BRUT, GAVI 

Creamy-malo nose with soft fruit, some peachiness and a creamy-menthol aftertaste. Soft mousse, fine bubbles.
On purchase $

SOLDATI LA SCOLCA NV PAS DOSÈ, GAVI 

Very ripe, fruity aromas with good acidity to highlight the palate.
On purchase $

SOLDATI LA SCOLCA 1986 BRUT MILLESIMATO 

Gets a high score (for Italian sparkling wine) for survival, which is due to its high acidity, and has matured into an exotic, coconutty concoction with apricots and custard on the finish.
On purchase $$

SOLEIL DU MATIN

See Môreson

SOLJANS

Henderson, New Zealand

Until the relatively recent launch of Soljans' classic *brut*-style Legacy, this traditional winery in New Zealand was known only for its sweet, aromatic Vivace Spumante.

SOLJANS ESTATE LEGACY 1995 METHODE TRADITIONNELLE 

This fresh and sprightly fizz is totally fruit-driven.
On purchase $$

SOUNIT

Burgundy, France

CRÉMANT DE BOURGOGNE, CUVÉE CHARDONNAY NV ALBERT SOUNIT 

Although this has a typically amylic aroma, there is some finesse, which could be an indication that this character will dissipate after a while. A dry, light style, with fine acidity.
On purchase $

SOUTIRAN

3 rue des Crayères, 51150 Ambonnay
(326) 57.08.18 FAX (326) 57.81.87

This grower shows good potential, but needs to tame down the oxidative characteristic found in a lot of its sparkling wines.

PATRICK SOUTIRAN NV BRUT ROSÉ, GRAND CRU 

Despite this *cuvée* having a distinctly oxidative style, the fruit is very smooth on the palate, and the mousse has a seductive, cushiony quality
On purchase $$ 88F

PATRICK SOUTIRAN 1992 PRECIEUSE D'ARGENT BRUT, GRAND CRU 

Rich and biscuity, but rather rustic.
On purchase $$$ 109F

SOUTIRAN-PELLETIER

3 rue de Crilly, 51150 Ambonnay
(326) 57.07.87 FAX (326) 57.81.74

Soutiran-Pelletier produces rich and smooth Champagnes that have both complexity and finesse.

A. SOUTIRAN-PELLETIER NV BRUT, GRAND CRU 

Mature and biscuity.
On purchase $$ 81F

A. SOUTIRAN-PELLETIER NV BLANC DE BLANCS CHARDONNAY BRUT, GRAND CRU 

Lovely rich creamy-biscuity fruit on the palate, complexity showing on finish.
Now–2000 $$ 87F

SPECHT

Alsace, France

SPECHT NV CRÉMANT D'ALSACE BRUT 73

This has a rich, succulent fruit, with a cushiony mousse.

On purchase $

SPYOPOULOS

Greece

This fully organic, family-owned winery has just released the best sparkling wine produced in Greece.

ODE PANOS NV BRUT 

Pale, fresh, and clean as a whistle; elegant, creamy fruit of pears and apple. Ode Panos is by far the best Greek sparkling wine available.

On purchase $

STEIN

Nahe, Germany

WEINGUT STEIN 1995 SCHWARZRIESLING WEISSHERBST SEKT BRUT 

A smooth *rosé* of some finesse. *Cuve close.*

On purchase $$

STOEFFLER

Alsace, France

CHARLES STOEFFLER BLANC DE BLANCS 1994 CRÉMANT D'ALSACE BRUT 

Rather sweet, but satisfying, fruity style.

On purchase $

STOFFEL

Alsace, France

STOFFEL NV CRÉMANT D'ALSACE BRUT 

Fresh and fruity with a seductively soft, cushiony mousse, minuscule bubbles, and refreshingly ripe acidity.

On purchase $

STRAUB

Alsace, France

Jos. Straub is best known for his very rich Vendange Tardives under the Domaine de La Tour label,

JOS. STRAUB, CUVÉE JEAN-SÉBASTIEN NV CRÉMANT D'ALSACE BRUT 

Toasty aromas mixed with coffee grounds on the nose, with toasty fruit on the palate, but it needs a leaner structure (without losing ripeness) to score higher.

On purchase $

STUART

See Marie Stuart

SYLVAIN GAUDRON

See Domaine Sylvain Gaudron

SZIGETI

Austria

One of the best dryish Muscat fizzes produced anywhere.

SZIGETI GRÜNER VELTLINER BRUT 

Fresh, simple, but elegant fruit.

On purchase $

SZIGETI MUSKAT OTTONEL EXTRA DRY 

Delicate aromatic fruit on the nose, and with moreish floral-fruity Muscat fruit on the palate.

On purchase $

TAITTINGER

9 Place Saint-Nicaise, 51061 Reims
(326) 85.45.35

Champagne Taittinger is currently a *grande marque* in high gear.

TAITTINGER NV BRUT RÉSERVE. 88

'his light yet luscious *cuvée* has been in ɔp form since early 1997, and the cur-ɛnt shipment has lovely creamy fruit with n elegant balance. Drink the Brut .éserve now while it is young, fresh, and elightfully elegant, or wait a year or two ɔr it to become creamy, biscuity, and 'onderfully complex.
Now–2000 ⓈⓈ 135F

TAITTINGER 1990 BRUT 

'he 1990 Brut is gorgeously fat and reamy, with biscuity fruit.
Now–2002 ⓈⓈⓈ

COMTES DE CHAMPAGNE, BLANC DE BLANCS 1990 BRUT, TAITTINGER 

.bsolutely wonderful now, full of rich, .pe Chardonnay fruit, with a hint of ɔastiness in the background, but this has way to go to fulfill its true potential.
Now–2010 ⓈⓈⓈⓈ

COMTES DE CHAMPAGNE, ROSÉ 1991 BRUT, TAITTINGER 

first tasted this *cuvée* in 1995, when its right cherry fruit flavor was simple and ndeveloped, as all Comtes de Cham-agne are when young, and it still has a 'ay to go before it will lengthen and deep-n into a feast of soft red fruits.
2000–2005 ⓈⓈⓈⓈ

TALTARNI

Victoria, Australia

Dominique Portet reckons the breakthrough in the quality of his sparkling wines came when he began sourcing some of his grapes from Tasmania, which always accounts for at least 20 percent of every blend and is exclusively used for Clover Hill.

TALTARNI CHARDONNAY PINOT NOIR NV BRUT 

A correct lean structure here, tending toward the austere, yet with some generosity of style.
Now–2000 Ⓢ

TALTARNI BRUT TACHE NV CHARDONNAY PINOT NOIR BRUT 

This delightful *rosé* offers a delicious, soft mouthful of fruit, cushioned by a fluffy-fresh mousse, with a nice finesse derived from the balance between the extremes of richness and acidity.
Now–2000 Ⓢ

CLOVER HILL 1994 TASMANIA BRUT 

This has more malty autolysis on the nose than the 1993, but with the same green Chablis-like fruit on palate that has typified other vintages of this Tasmanian *cuvée*. Opinion reserved for another year.
Wait and see ⓈⓈ

TARLANT

51480 Oeuilly
(326) 58.30.60 FAX (326) 58.37.31

A family of vignerons since 1687, the Tarlants' vineyards are spread across five Marne Valley villages, but centered on Oeuilly and Boursault, six milesJ166
west of Épernay. Half the range is classically presented, while the other half is labeled with cheap transparent transfers. Only one wine was submitted this year, but it easily qualified, despite the coconutty aromas (which some people enjoy,

TARLANT NV CUVÉE LOUIS BRUT 

This was so chock-full of coconutty-oak that when the covers came off I was not surprised to discover that it had indeed been fermented in new oak *barriques*, although I was amazed that the oak was Vosges. I have not heard about anyone in Champagne considering to use American oak, but that is what the coconutty character suggests.
Now–1999 ⓈⓈ 136F

TATACHILLA

South Australia, Australia

An old-established winery, Tatachilla has been through many changes in ownership. Recently, Michael Fragos, the senior winemaker, and Daryl Groom, his consultant who has worked in California, have rapidly built up a brilliant reputation for big, rich red wines, and, judging by the wines below, they are clearly quite adept at putting bubbles into bottles as well.

TATACHILLA NV BRUT 

Although soft and creamy, this *cuvée* does have the capacity to age. Very good value.

Now–2000 $

TATACHILLA NV SPARKLING MALBEC 

This highly perfumed *cuvée* has some finesse and is drier than most Australian sparkling reds.

Now–2000 $

TELMONT

1 avenue de Champagne, 51480 Damery

(326) 58.40.33 FAX (326) 58.63.93

Not a consistent range, but always something of interest, and invariably it turns out to be good value.

J. DE TELMONT NV GRANDE RÉSERVE BRUT 

More tutti-frutti than amylic, with a rich fruitiness on the palate.

On purchase $$ 68F

J. DE TELMONT 1990 BLANC DE BLANCS BRUT 

At the moment, this has a strangely perfumed nose with a terpenelike four-square quality on the palate, as if the base wine had been kept as a reserve and bottled later than Spring 1991. I have no idea if that is what happened, but cannot recommend the wine at this stage. However, there is an interesting peachiness that makes me want to follow its evolution; thus judgment is reserved.

Wait and see $$$ 80F

TEMPÉ

Alsace, France

ANDRÉ TEMPÉ NV CRÉMANT D'ALSACE BRUT 

Fresh amylic style, but with more finesse than most, and good acidity.

On purchase $

TENER

See Banfi

THAMES VALLEY VINEYARD

Twyford, England, UK

Owned by Jon Leighton, this is also the home to John Worontschak and The Harvest Group, one of the most progressive contract winemaking companies in the UK.

ASCOT NV BRUT 

Some flowery finesse in this rises above the English wine aromas. There is creamy-vanilla fruit with some fatness yet also finesse on the finish, and a medium-firm mousse of tiny bubbles.

On purchase $

CLOCKTOWER GAMAY NV 

Fine, flowery autolytic aromas with excellent acidity. It certainly tastes younger than the 1992-based blend it is, but if anything this should mean that it will age very gracefully. At the moment, however, it shows elegant fruit neatly underpinned by excellent acidity, which itself is enhanced by a firm mousse of tiny bubbles.

On purchase $

THANISCH

Mosel-Saar-Ruwer, Germany

Currently owned and run by Margaritt Müller-Burggraef, who is the fourth generation of female managers.

WWE. DR. H. THANISCH 1992 RIESLING SEKT BRUT 

.pricoty fruit with some vanilla reaminess. Bottle-fermented.
On purchase $$

THIENOT

14 rue des Moissons, 51100 Reims
(326) 77.50.10 FAX (326) 77.50.19

A high-tech winery just outside Reims.

ALAIN THIENOT NV BRUT 

'ery fresh and fruity.
On purchase $$ 99F

THÜNGERSHEIM

Franken, Germany

WINZERGENOSSENSCHAFT THÜNGERSHEIM NV RÜCKER SCHALK, RÜCKER JESUITENBERG PINOT NOIR SEKT TROCKEN 

legant Pinot fruit. Bottle-fermented.
On purchase $$

TORELLÓ

Penedès, Spain

ALIGUER 1994 CAVA BRUT 

lowery-amylic, but it has some finesse.
On purchase $

AUGUSTÍ TORELLÓ MATA 1994 CAVA BRUT RESERVA 

weet and creamy, but lacks acidity.
On purchase $

KRIPTA BRUT NATURE 1992 GRAN RESERVA CAVA 

'his prestige *cuvée* comes in a replica .oman bottle, which has no flat bottom nd therefore must be kept in an ice-ucket once opened. This vintage is bet-er than the 1991, being cleaner and etter focused, with sweet vanilla fruit on ne palate, but it needs far more acidity.
On purchase $$

TORNAY

2 rue Colbert, 51150 Bouzy
(326) 57.08.58

BERNARD TORNAY NV BRUT CARTE D'OR 

Interesting creamy-fruit on nose, with ripe, exotic, toasty fruit on the palate. Just finishes a bit rustic and could do with a bit of finesse.
Now–1999 $$

TORRES

Chile

Hopefully the current shipment heralds a return to the promise shown by the first *cuvées* of Brut Nature,

MIGUEL TORRES NV BRUT NATURE 

The best Miguel Torres Brut Nature for a very long time, this *cuvée* is light, elegant, and delightful, with a long, deliciously fruity finish.
Now–1999 $

TOUR DU ROY

Bordeaux, France

One of the oldest producers of sparkling wine in Bordeaux.

TOUR DU ROY NV CUVÉE PRESTIGE, CRÉMANT DE BORDEAUX BRUT 

Creamy rich aroma and sweet fruit, with good acidity.
On purchase $

TRIOLET

22 rue des Pressoirs, 51260 Bethon
(326) 80.48.24 FAX (326) 81.16.42

A top Sézannais producer, with complex wines that would be even better if the oxidative character could be toned down.

Marcel Triolet NV Sélection Brut 

The *cuvée* I tasted was pure 1990, with mature, oxidative-biscuity aromas and a sweetness of ripe fruit on the palate. Very rich, creamy fruit on the finish.

On purchase $$

Marcel Triolet NV Brut 

This *cuvée* has a minimum of four years' bottle-age and as much mature, oxidative-biscuitiness as the Brut Sélection, but without the same intensity of fruit.

On purchase $$

Twee Jongegezellen

Tulbagh, South Africa

The presentation might be rather garish, and the wines may be relatively cheap, but Krone Borealis has an established track record for *cuvées* that age extremely well, typically requiring four years to develop a fine, creamy-biscuity complexity.

Krone Borealis Brut 1994 Cap Classique 

A strange high-tone character places a question mark in my mind about this *cuvée,* but it might merely be going through a developmental phase, and if it is like other vintage, it should be drinking nicely by Christmas 1998.

Wait and see $

Krone Borealis Brut 1993 Cap Classique 

Two years ago this was an easy-drinking wine, with deliciously gentle fruit that fell somewhere between the New and Old Worlds in character. Last year it had picked up some biscuity complexity, and now it has lovely toasty aromas. Nicely underpinned by fine acidity, the 1993 is still fresh and has a way to go yet.

Now–2001 $

Krone Borealis Brut 1992 Cap Classique 

The 1992 had a malty-biscuity complexity two years ago, but the biscuitiness was barely perceptible.

1999–2000 $

Krone Borealis Brut 1990 Cap Classique 87

Fresh and breezy fruit with a lovely, mature, creamy-biscuity complexity.

Now–2000 $

Union Champagne

7 rue Pasteur, 51190 Avize
(326) 57.94.22 FAX (326) 57.57.98

Super-cooperative of 1,200 growers, mostly on the Côte des Blancs. Much of its production is sold on to the *négoce* (Champagne houses). Of the remainder, Union Champagne sells about a million bottles under various labels, mainly De Saint Gall, and also Pierre Vaudon and Lechere.

Pierre Vaudon NV Brut, Premier Cru 

A light, buttery-malo aroma, and sweet, easy-drinking, ripe fruit on the palate.

Now-1999 $$

Pierre Vaudon 1990 Brut, Premier Cru 

A lovely creamy-biscuity richness makes this splendid value for money.

Now–2003 $$$

Vallformosa

Penedès, Spain

Vallformosa NV Cava Semi Seco 

Not terribly sweet, but it has plenty of fruit, with a refreshing citrusy flavor.

On purchase $

Varinelles

See Domaine des Varinelles

Vaudon

See Union Champagne

(DE) VENOGE

30 avenue de Champagne, 51204 Epernay
(326) 55.01.01 FAX (326) 54.73.60

Now part of the Remy-Cointreau group and playing a confusingly similar role to Champagne Ferdinand Bonnet. The kitsch Champagne des Princes bottle does not do justice to the quality of the wine inside.

DE VENOGE NV BRUT CORDON BLEU (85)

quaffing fruity style that quickly evelops a creamy richness.

Now–1999 $$

DE VENOGE NV ROSÉ PRINCESSE (83)

'ot so appealing as when it was sold as rémant Rosé, but a light, refreshing yle nonetheless.

On purchase $$ 150F

DE VENOGE 1990 BRUT (90)

ich with creamy-biscuity fruit and lifted y toasty-floral aromas, this is probably e best straight vintage from this house.

Now–2005 $$$ 156F

DE VENOGE CHAMPAGNE DES PRINCES 1990 BRUT 

Jot in the same class as the straight vin-age, but the 1989 and 1985 went through range stages, and this *cuvée* has pro-uced some memorable vintages before.

Wait and see $$$ 290F

VERNIER

See Masachs

VESSELLE

16 rue des Postes, 51150 Bouzy
(326) 57.00.15 FAX (326) 57.09.20

Georges Vesselle is a grower with excellent vineyards and he has always been one of the most intelligent commentators on the industry as a whole.

GEORGES VESSELLE NV BRUT ROSÉ, GRAND CRU (84)

Very pale-apricot color, with lots of Pinot aroma and flavor, but could do with a touch more finesse.

On purchase $$ 103F

GEORGES VESSELLE NV BRUT GRAND CRU (82)

Perfumed Pinot aromas, but the fruit on the palate will lengthen with bottle-age.

Now–1999 $$ 100F

GEORGES VESSELLE 1988 BRUT GRAND CRU 

Lovely toasty aromas overlaying rich Pinot fruit. Brilliant at the table, particularly with simple meat dishes.

Now–1999 $$$

VEUVE CLICQUOT

12 rue du Temple, 51100 Reims
(326) 40.25.42 FAX (326) 40.60.17

Part of the LVMH group, Veuve Clicquot produces Champagne of extraordinary quality for such a large house. Big is truly beautiful here.

VEUVE CLICQUOT NV BRUT 

Why Veuve Clicquot insists on calling this vivid orange-labeled *cuvée* Yellow Label is beyond me, but the quality is not beyond anyone. A very fruity, but serious, certainly not quaffing, style of Champagne that needs two or three years more bottle-age to bring out a wonderful Christmas-cake complexity.

Now–2002 $$ 150F

VEUVE CLICQUOT 1990 BRUT (93)

The difference in freshness and development between this and the 1989 is striking, and it is not as if the grapes in 1989 were riper, as is often suggested. This was much the riper year, with higher alcohol levels even than 1976. There is a long way to go before it switches from fruit-driven mode to a more mellow and complex style. Chardonnay currently dominates, although it represents just a third of the blend, as it does in most Veuve Clicquot vintages.

Now–2020 $$$

VEUVE CLICQUOT 1989 BRUT 90

Full and rich, with creamy-biscuity complexity, and chewy-vanilla fruit that dries off toward the end, then comes back sweet and ripe on the aftertaste.
Now–2009 $$$

VEUVE CLICQUOT 1989 ROSÉ 86

Big, rich, rooty Pinot Noir fruit.
Now–2001 $$$

VEUVE CLICQUOT 1989 RICH RÉSERVE 90

A *demi-sec* of impeccable quality, softer and more luscious than the superb 1988, but with just as much depth and finesse.
Now–2009 $$$

VEUVE CLICQUOT 1990 GRANDE DAME BRUT 95

Beautifully ripe fruit of great finesse. Very young now, it will quickly go toasty, but with lots of life and freshness ahead. Possibly on par with the magnificent 1975.
Now–2020 $$$$

VEUVE CLICQUOT 1989 GRANDE DAME BRUT 94

Fat and sassy fruit with a lovely mellow biscuity richness on the finish.
Now–2010 $$$$ 450F

VEUVE CLICQUOT 1988 GRANDE DAME BRUT ROSÉ 95

A stunning first vintage, this ranks with Laurent-Perrier's 1982 and 1985 Alexandra Rosé as one of the greatest pink Champagnes of all time. Extraordinarily luscious for the vintage, but quite how there can be so much fruit without being at all fat is a mystery. With so much finesse, aging this will be fascinating.
Now–2010 $$$$

VEUVE –

For all other brands beginning with Veuve, see under main name

VIGNERONS DE –

See under main name

VILLA –

See under main name

VILLIERA

Paarl, South Africa

Owned by the Grier family, who used to employ Champenois Jean-Louis Denois as consultant.

VILLIERA TRADITION BRUT ROSÉ NV CAP CLASSIQUE 71

Soft, perfumed aromas, full, fattish fruit, lifted by a soft mousse of small bubbles.
On purchase $

VILLIERA TRADITION CARTE ROUGE BRUT NV CAP CLASSIQUE 82

Classic *méthode champenoise* creamy-rich fruit, mellowed by nicely understated malolactic. This *cuvée* includes Pinotage and Chenin Blanc.
Now–2000 $

VILLIERA TRADITION PREMIERE CUVÉE 1990 CAP CLASSIQUE 80

There is no autolytic finesse to be found, but this *cuvée* is recompensed by its lovely peachy fruit.
On purchase $

VILMART

4 rue de la République
51500 Rilly-la-Montagne
(326) 03.40.01 FAX (326) 03.46.57

The greatest grower Champagne continues to excel.

VILMART NV GRANDE RÉSERVE BRUT 85

A good value, fresh, and fruity style.
On purchase $$

VILMART NV BLANC DE BLANCS BRUT 86

The yummiest, glugiest, creamiest fruit-driven *cuvée* in the range.
On purchase $$

VILMART NV GRANDE CELLIER BRUT 87

:lassic structure with fine fruit and a .ow-building biscuitiness, this is where ıe complexity and true aging potential ı the Vilmart range begins.

Now-2003 $$ 90F

VILMART 1991 GRANDE CELLIER D'OR BRUT 

.lthough not quite the same quality as 'ilmart's Coeur de Cuvée, Grand Cellier 'Or is more classic and, relative to most intage Champagnes, offers extraordinary alue for the money.

Now–2005 $$$

VILMART 1990 GRANDE CELLIER D'OR BRUT 

.n exquisite depth of fruit with brilliant cidity and deep, mellow biscuity-complex romas continuing to build. Buy it in ıagnums, drink one at the millennium, nd keep the rest for five years or more.

Now–2010 $$$ 100F

VILMART 1991 COEUR DE CUVÉE 

:oeur de Cuvée means "heart of the *uvée,*" and that is literally what this is: rom every 2,000 liters of *vin de cuvée* 'ilmart plucks out the best 800 liters and inifies it in small *barriques* of new oak. 'hey got a bit carried away with this intage, which was far too oaky when ırst released. It would have benefited rom 10 years' yeast contact to absorb as ıuch of the oakiness as possible. This is .evertheless the best 1991 I have tasted, nd more postdisgorgement aging should ury the more obvious oaky traits.

2000–2010 $$$$ 186F

VILMART 1990 COEUR DE CUVÉE 99

)ne of the three greatest Champagnes nade in the last 25 years, this *cuvée* has a abulous, rich, creamy-brioche nose. Its ruit is incredibly luscious because the uge ripe acidity has been skillfully alanced by a generous dosage.

Now–2015 $$$$

VILMART 1989 COEUR DE CUVÉE 

'his has lost the heavy oxidative character hat spoiled the wine when first released, nd its true finesse is now in full bloom.

Now–2006 $$$$

VILMART 1990 CUVÉE DU NOUVEAU MONDE IIIE MILLÉNIUM BRUT 

The new oak in this special *cuvée* is so dominant that it tastes like an Australian Chardonnay with bubbles, and having now tasted it five times I am convinced that the oakiness is increasing. It is so far off the wall for Champagne, and the base wine so unlike anything else in the Vilmart range, that I must reserve judgment for a few years.

Wait and see $$$$ 175F

VITTEAUT-ALBERTI

Burgundy, France

L. VITTEAUT-ALBERTI, BLANC DE BLANCS NV BRUT, CRÉMANT DE BOURGOGNE 

You can taste the selection in this lovely fruit-driven wine, which is not too *brut* and has a silky-soft mousse.

On purchase $

VIUDAS

See Segura Viudas

VRANKEN

42 avenue de Champagne, 51200 Epernay

(326) 53.33.20 FAX (326) 51.87.07

This group includes Charles Lafitte, René Lallement, Demoiselle, Sacotte, Charbaut, Barancourt, and the recently acquired Heidsieck & Co Monopole.

DEMOISELLE NV BRUT 

This used to be amylic, but the current *cuvée* is lovely and fresh, with fruit and charm, and not a hint of peardrops. Much preferred to the Demoiselle 1990.

On purchase $$

CHARLES LAFITTE 1990 BRUT 

A surprisingly rich, biscuity Champagne of some quality for this secondary brand.

On purchase $$$

WACHTENBURG

Pfalz, Germany

WACHTENBURG 1995 WACHENHEIMER BISCHOFSGARTEN PINOT NOIR BLANC DE NOIRS 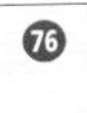

Very moreish strawberry fruit that suggests an exaggeration of Pinot Noir.

On purchase $$

WEINGARTNER –, WEINGUT –, WEINHOF –

For brands prefixed with any of these words (Ger. cooperative/wine estate), see under main name

WESTHALTEN

Alsace, France

CUVÉE MARÉCHAL LEFEBVRE, WESTHALTEN NV CRÉMANT D'ALSACE BRUT 

Light and fruity now, but will go toasty.

Now–1999 $

HEIM IMPÉRIAL D'ALSACE NV CRÉMANT D'ALSACE BRUT 

Once a producer in its own right, Heim is now just a label belonging Westhalten. This fizzy Chablis-style *crémant* could develop, but I am not certain.

Wait and see $

WICKHAM

Shedfield, England, UK

Surprisingly good, classic *brut*-style wine from the Kerner grape.

WICKHAM PREMIÈRE CUVÉE 1993 BRUT 

The classic flowery finesse of autolysis on the nose, plus some class and a serious hint of vanilla-complexity of fruit to finish.

Now–1999 $$

WILHELMSHOF

Pfalz, Germany

WILHELMSHOF 1995 SPÄTBURGUNDER BLANC DE NOIRS SEKT BRUT 

An impeccable balance of succulent fruit and sherbety ripe acidity. Bottle-fermented.

On purchase $$

WINZERVEREIN –

For brands prefixed by this (Ger. cooperative), see under main name

WINZERSEKT

Rheinhessen, Germany

This cooperative is dedicated to the production of Sekt.

WINZERSEKT 1994 PINOT NOIR ROSÉ SEKT EXTRA SEKT TROCKEN 

Finely structured fruit with nice acidity and a soft, cushiony mousse. A food wine. Bottle-fermented.

On purchase $$

WOLFBERGER

Alsace, France

Brand name of the Eguisheim cooperative, the largest producer in Alsace.

WOLFBERGER RIESLING NV CRÉMANT D'ALSACE BRUT 

Terpeney Riesling aroma follows onto the palate, with nice honeyed richness, but finishes a bit too soft.

On purchase $

WOLFBERGER ROSÉ NV CRÉMANT D'ALSACE BRUT 

Nice cherry-Pinot aromas, with soft fruit lifted by the effervescence on the palate, but needs more acidity for a higher score

On purchase $

WOLFBERGER, BLANC DE NOIRS NV CRÉMANT D'ALSACE BRUT 

This scrapes in because even though the sample I received was corked, the sweet, ripe fruit was evident.

On purchase $

WOLFBERGER, CHARDONNAY NV CRÉMANT D'ALSACE, EXTRA BRUT 

Not much Chardonnay character, unless you stretch the apricot fruit to the peachy richness of New World Chardonnay, and bring it back to Alsace. It could also do with some finesse, but it is better than many other Crémant d'Alsace.

On purchase $

WOLFBERGER, PRESTIGE NV CRÉMANT D'ALSACE 

This *cuvée* still has the best balance of all Wolfberger sparkling wines, the fruitiness and lovely ripe acidity benefiting from a certain amount of Riesling in the blend.

Now–1999 $

WOLFBERGER, TOKAY PINOT GRIS NV CRÉMANT D'ALSACE BRUT 

Despite a need to tweak the structure to a leaner bent, this pure varietal fizz is quite interesting, and promises to develop well.

Now–1999 $

WOOLDINGS

Whitchurch, England, UK

Owner-winemaker Charles Cunningham is so serious about perfecting sparkling wine that he organizes field trips to Champagne for himself and other English fizz producers.

WOOLDINGS 1994 BRUT 72

Creamy-rich and tangy, like the 1992. Still needs a touch more finesse, but a resounding success compared to the 1993.

Now–1999 $$

WYNDHAM ESTATE

New South Wales, Australia

WYNDHAM CUVÉE 1995 BRUT 

Trying to be broad and complex, and halfway getting there, but needs more acidity for a higher score.

On purchase $

XENIUS

See COVIDES

YALDARA

South Australia, Australia

These bubblies are firmly aimed at the budget end of the market.

YALDARA NV BRUT 

The fruit is too exotic for a *brut*-style fizz, but if the wine is thoroughly chilled, it reduces the exotic effect.

On purchase $

YALDARA NV BRUT 

Fresh, soft, raspberry fizz.

On purchase $

YALUMBA

South Australia, Australia

Best known for its simple fruity fizz under the Angas Brut and Angas Rosé labels, Yalumba also produces bottle-fermented sparkling wines under its eponymous brand, and it owns Nautilus in New Zealand.

ANGAS NV BRUT 

The new shipment appears to be a sea-change in style, even hinting of Chardonnay on the nose, although this is just one of 14 grapes used. Very fresh and fattish, with an exotic tropical fruit finish.

On purchase $

YALUMBA CUVÉE ONE PINOT NOIR CHARDONNAY NV BRUT 

There are lovely biscuity aromas on the nose, but this *cuvée* needs time to build a balancing, mellow richness on the palate.

1999-2000 $

YALUMBA D 1994 BRUT 

I liked the tight, austere flavors and lean fruit structure, all of which promised to open up very slowly into something special, but there was too much sulfur for it to receive a definite score.

Wait and see $$

YALUMBA CUVÉE TWO PRESTIGE NV CABERNET SAUVIGNON 

Deep, dark, and according to its back label, "mischievous," this fizzy red wine has a minty Cabernet flavor, with big, oaky overtones.

Now–1999 $

YARRABANK

Victoria, Australia

A recent joint venture between Champagne Veuve Devaux and Yering Station with input from Devaux's winemaker, Claude Thibaut.

YARRABANK 1993 CUVÉE NO 1 BRUT 

There is plenty of acidity to keep the tangy-rich fruit in this wine extremely fresh and lively.

Now–2000 $$

YARRA BURN

See Hardy's

YELLOWGLEN

Victoria, Australia

This operation, owned by Mildara-Blass, is where Claude Thibaut gained experience before working at Iron Horse in California.

YELLOWGLEN NV BRUT PINOT NOIR CHARDONNAY 

Lovely ripe fruit framed in a nicely lean structure and underpinned by fine acidity with a touch of fatness for good mouthfill.

On purchase $

YELLOWGLEN 1995 BRUT 

An early drinking vintage *cuvée* with fine, elegant fruit supported by a nicely structured mousse of tiny bubbles.

On purchase $

ZÄHRINGER

Baden, Germany

A member of Ecovin, a body that adheres to biodynamic wine production.

ZÄHRINGER 1992 VIERLIG PINOT BLANC SEKT BRUT 

This wine comes in a tall Rhine bottle with a very classy, understated label. Some botrytis (noble rot) and quite sweet fruit for a *brut*. Very soft mousse.

ZÄHRINGER 1990 ECOVIN SPÄTBURGUNDER ROT SEKT BRUT 

This deep, dark red fizz is Germany's answer to Sparkling Shiraz!

ZAMUNER

Veneto, Italy

ZAMUNER 1992 ROSÉ BRUT, SPUMANTE TRADIZIONALE 

Fresh, peppery fruit going to cappuccino, with a zesty, uplifting finish.

Now–1999 $$

ZAMUNER 1991 EXTRA BRUT, SPUMANTE CLASSICO 

First time I have ever found peanuts on any sparkling wine, but it has good acidity.

On purchase $$

ZARDETTO

Italy

ZARDETTO NV PROSECCO DI CONEGLIANO BRUT 

Scrapes in as a fresh, light and fruity fizz for those who don't like their *brut* too dry.

On purchase $

Glossary

A glossary of common technical and tasting terms used to describe Champagnes and sparkling wines.

Abbreviations: (Fr.) French (Ger.) German (It.) Italian (Sp.) Spanish.

Accessible Easy to drink.
Acidic Some people confuse this term with bitter. Think of lemon juice as acidic, lemon peel as bitter. The right acidity is vital for sparkling wine.
Aftertaste The flavor and aroma left in the mouth after the wine has been swallowed.
Ages gracefully A wine that retains finesse as it matures.
Aggressive The opposite of soft and smooth.
Amylic The peardrop, banana, or bubblegum aromas of amyl or isoamyl acetate, lots of which can be produced if the first fermentation is conducted at a low temperature. An amylic preponderance is not ideal for classic sparkling wine as it overshadows the subtle aromas of autolysis, and may prevent the development of postdisgorgement bottle-aromas. *See also Autolysis, Bottle-aromas.*
AOC (Fr.) Appellation d'Origine Contrôlée, the top rung of the French wine quality system. Champagne is unique in that it does not have to indicate that it is an AOC wine on the label, because the name Champagne is considered sufficient guarantee.
Appellation Literally a "name," this usually refers to an official geographical-based designation for a wine.
Aroma Some people use the word aroma for grape-derived fragrance, and bouquet for more winey odors, especially when developed in bottle; however, the two are synonymous in this book.
Aromatic grape varieties Grapes such as the Gewürztraminer, Muscat, and Riesling overwhelm the subtle effects of autolysis and are thus too aromatic for classic *brut* sparkling wines, yet this character often makes them ideal for sweet styles of sparkling wine.
Assemblage (Fr.) The blending of base wines that creates the final *cuvée*.
Asti (It.) A town in Northern Italy that gives its name to a fine sweet sparkling wine.
Atmosphere A measurement of atmospheric pressure. One atmosphere is 15 lbs per square inch (psi). A sparkling wine can be anything up to six atmospheres, or 90 lbs psi. This decreases when the bottle is chilled for serving. A fully sparkling wine of six atmospheres will be just 2.5 atmospheres at 44° F / 6° C.
Austere A wine that lacks fruit.
Autolysis The breakdown of yeast cells after the second fermentation that creates the inimitable "champagny" character.
Autolytic The smell of a freshly disgorged *brut*-style fizz. This is not "yeasty" but has an acacia-like flowery finesse.
Balance A harmonious relationship between acids, alcohol, fruit, tannin (only in some red sparkling wines), and other natural elements.
Balthazar Large bottle equivalent to 16 normal-sized 75 cl bottles.
Barrel-fermented Some houses, e.g., Krug, ferment in old, well-used oak barrels. A few others, e.g., Selosse and Vilmart, use new oak, a fashion picked up by a number of New World producers, e.g., Pelorus and Kristone.
Barrique (Fr.) Literally means "barrel," but generically used in English-speaking countries for any small oak cask. Often denotes the use of new oak.
Base wines Fully fermented dry wines that, when blended together, form the basis of a sparkling wine *cuvée.*
Biscuity A desirable aspect of bouquet found particularly in a well-matured Pinot Noir-dominated Champagne. Some top-quality Chardonnay-dominated wines can also acquire a creamy-biscuitness.
Bitterness Either an unpleasant aspect of a poorly made wine or an expected characteristic of undeveloped, concentrated flavors that should, with maturity, become rich and delicious. *See also Acidic.*
Blanc de Blancs (Fr.) A white wine made from white grapes.
Blanc de Noirs (Fr.) A white wine made from black grapes.
Blind, blind tasting An objective tasting where the identity of wines is unknown until the taster has made notes and given scores. All competitive tastings are blind.
Blowsy Overblown and exaggerated.
Blush wine Synonym of *rosé.*
BOB Buyer's Own Brand, under which many retailers and restaurants sell wine.
Body The extract of fruit and alcoholic strength together give an impression of weight in the mouth.
Bottle-age The length of time a wine spends in bottle before it is consumed. A wine that has good bottle-age is one that has sufficient time to mature properly. Bottle-aging has a mellowing effect.
Bottle-aromas Mellowing aromas created after disgorgement.
Bottle-fermented I use this without discrimination for any sparkling wine that has undergone a second fermentation in bottle, but when seen on a label, it invariably means the wine has been made by the transfer method.
Bouquet *See Aroma.*
Breed The finesse of a wine based on the intrinsic qualities of grape and *terroir* (growing environment) combined with the irrefutable skill and experience of a great winemaker.
Brut (Fr.) Dry. Literally means "raw" or "bone dry," but in practice there is always some sweetness in a sparkling wine.
Buttery Normally caused by diacetyl, which the food industry uses to make margarine taste more like butter. It is fine in still Chardonnays, but the taste detracts from the finesse of sparkling wines.
Caramel An extreme version of buttery.
Cava (Sp.) The generic appellation for *méthode champenoise* wines produced in various delimited areas of Spain, mostly in the Penedès region near Barcelona.
Cave, caves (Fr.) Literally cellar, cellars.
Champagne (Fr.) Specifically a sparkling wine produced in the delimited area of Champagne in Northern France.
"Champagne," "Champaña" The appellation for sparkling wine made in Champagne is protected within the EU but is sometimes used loosely elsewhere, especially in the

US, where it is legal to sell domestically produced "champagne." It is also exploited by the Champenois themselves, who call their South American products Champaña.

Champenois (Fr.) The people of Champagne.

Chardonnay One of the greatest sparkling wine grapes for the classic *brut* style.

Charmat (Fr.) *See Cuve close.*

Chef de caves (Fr.) Literally the "cellar manager," but can also mean the winemaker.

Courtier en vins (Fr.) A wine broker who acts as a go-between for growers and producers.

Crayères (Fr.) Chalk-pits in Northern France dug out in Gallo-Roman times.

Creamy Creaminess is most apparent in Chardonnay-based sparkling wines. The sensation, picked up at the back of the throat, is believed to be a combination of the finesse of the mousse (created by the most minuscule of bubbles and their slow release) and a subtle malolactic influence.

Creamy-biscuity *See Biscuity.*

Creamy-caramel malo A lesser, more acceptable version of caramel.

Crémant (Fr.) A sparkling wine with a gentler mousse than normal.

Cru (Fr.) Literally a "growth," *cru* normally refers to a vineyard site, although in Champagne it is a term used for an entire village.

Cushiony A beautifully soft, ultrafine sensation caused by the minuscule bubbles of a first-rate mousse.

Cuve close (Fr.) A method invented by Eugène Charmat of producing sparkling wine through a second fermentation in a sealed vat or tank. Synonymous with Charmat method or tank method.

Cuvée (Fr.) Originally the wine of one *cuve* or vat, this now refers to a precise blend or specific product, which may be blended from several vats.

Débourbage (Fr.) The settling process that removes bits of skin, pips, and so on from the freshly pressed grape juice.

Dégorgement (Fr.) *See Disgorgement.*

Demi-sec (Fr.) Literally "semi-dry," but actually meaning semisweet to sweet.

Disgorgement The removal of sediment after the second fermentation.

DOC/DOCG (It.) Denominazione di Origine Controllata/e Garantita. Italian wine quality system based on grape variety and origin. "Garantita" denotes an extra rung of quality.

Dosage (Fr.) The amount of sugar solution added to a sparkling wine after disgorgement.

Doux (Fr.) Literally "sweet," actually very sweet.

Dry straw *See Straw.*

Easy-drinking Probably not a complex wine, but it slips down easily.

English aroma A very fresh herbaceous character.

Explosive A sparkling wine can be literally explosive in the bottle, which is due to defects on the inner surface, or "explosive" in the mouth, which is due to the wine. The latter is often because too much carbonic gas is free (not bound to the wine), although why this sometimes occurs is not fully understood.

Extra-brut Drier than *brut*, possibly no dosage.

Extra-sec (Fr.) Literally "extra-dry," but usually merely dry to medium dry.

Fat Full in body and extract.

Fixed sulfur Sulfur is added to wine primarily as a preservative to prevent oxidation. Most of the sulfur molecules fix onto other molecules in the wine, especially the oxygen molecules. Sometimes they combine disastrously with other molecules, creating bad smells. However, the toasty bottle-aroma adored by most Champagne aficionados is also possibly a by-product of fixed sulfur. *See also Free sulfur.*

Flowery Floral aromas are found in young sparkling wines and are the precursors to the fuller, deeper, fruitier aromas of maturity. Specific acacia aromas are found in recently disgorged wines of any age.

Foudre (Fr.) A large wooden cask or vat.

Foxy The highly perfumed character of certain indigenous American grapes. It can be sickly sweet and cloying to other nations' palates.

Free sulfur The acrid odor of free sulfur – smelling like a recently extinguished match – will go away with time in bottle, or a swirl of the glass. *See also Fixed sulfur, Sulfur.*

Frizzante (It.) Semisparkling or slightly fizzy: the equivalent of *pétillant*.

Frizzantino (It.) Very lightly sparkling: the same as *perlant*.

Fruity Although wine is made from grapes, it will not have a fruity flavor unless the grapes have the correct combination of ripeness and acidity. Simple fruity fizz is fine if it is inexpensive, but fruit alone is insufficient for a classic sparkling wine.

Full Usually refers to body, e.g., full-bodied. But a wine can be light in body yet full in flavor.

Fully fermented A wine that is allowed to complete its natural course of fermentation and so yield a totally dry wine.

Fully sparkling A wine with a pressure of 5–6 atmospheres.

Grande marque (Fr.) Literally a great or famous brand.

Herbaceous A green-leaf or white-currant characteristic that is usually associated with under-ripeness, particularly with aromatic grape varieties.

Jeroboam Large bottle equivalent to four normal-sized 75 cl bottles.

Lees The sediment that accumulates in a vat or bottle during fermentation.

Light A qualification of body.

Liqueur d'expédition (Fr.) Solution of sugar and wine added to a sparkling wine after disgorgement.

Liqueur de tirage (Fr.) The bottling liqueur – made of wine, yeast, and sugar – that induces the mousse.

Magnum Large bottle equivalent to two normal-sized 75 cl bottles, the ideal volume for ageing Champagne.

Malolactic/Malo A biochemical process that turns the hard malic acid of unripe grapes into soft lactic acid and carbonic gas.

Méthode champenoise (Fr.) The process developed by the Champenois that converts a fully fermented still wine into a sparkling wine through the induction of a second fermentation in the same bottle in which it is sold *(see pp10–11)*.

Methuselah Large bottle equivalent to eight normal-sized 75 cl bottles.
Mono-cru Champagne made from a single *cru*.
Mousse The thousands of fine bubbles in a sparkling wine.
Mousseux (Fr.) Sparkling, foaming, etc.
Nebuchadnezzar Large bottle equivalent to 20 normal-sized 75 cl bottles.
Négociant (Fr.) Commonly used to describe large wine-producing companies.
Nondosage (Fr.) A sparkling wine that has received no dosage of *liqueur de tirage*.
Nonvintage (NV) In theory a blend of at least two different years, but many producers, particularly in Champagne, grade their *cuvées* on selection, often selling a pure vintage *sans année* (without year).
Oaky The aromatic quality picked up from new oak, usually consisting of the creamy-vanilla aroma of vanillin, a natural oak aldehyde and also the principal aromatic component in vanilla pods.
Organic A generic term for wines that are produced with the minimum amount of sulfur, from grapes grown without chemical fertilizers, pesticides, or herbicides.
Oxidation, oxidized From the moment grapes are pressed or crushed, oxidation sets in. It is an unavoidable part of fermentation and essential to the maturation process: "oxidative" denotes a certain maturity. To say a wine is "oxidized," however, means that it has been subjected to too much oxidation and has an unwanted sherrylike character.
Oxidative A wine that openly demonstrates the character of maturation on the nose or palate. The longer it takes to appear in a wine, the more finesse the wine will have.
Peppery A somewhat incongruous taste associated with sparkling wine. If detected as just a flicker in a young blend, it can add to the wine's future complexity, but be wary of a dominant pepperiness.
Perlant (Fr.) Lightly sparkling.
Perlwein (Ger.) Cheap, semi-sparkling wine made by carbonating a still wine.
Pétillance, pétillant (Fr.) A wine with enough carbonic gas to create a light sparkle.
Pinot Noir (Fr.) Black grape variety used in Champagne.
Récoltant-manipulant (Fr.) A grower who produces Champagne exclusively from his or her own vineyards.
Rehoboam Large bottle equivalent to six normal-sized 75 cl bottles.
Remuage (Fr.) The process whereby the sediment is encouraged down to the neck of the bottle in preparation for disgorgement.
Reserve wines Older wines added to a nonvintage blend to create a sense of maturity.
Rich, richness A balanced wealth of fruit and depth on the palate and finish.
Rooty Usually refers to a certain rooty richness found in Pinot Noir. Not vegetal, which is a negative term.
Rosado (Sp.) Pink.
Rosé (Fr.) Pink.
Saignée (Fr.) The process of drawing off surplus liquid from the press or vat in order to produce a *rosé* wine from the free-run juice. In cooler wine regions, the remaining mass of grape pulp may be used to make a darker red wine than would normally be possible because of a greater ratio of solids to liquid.
Salmanazar Large bottle equivalent to 12 normal-sized 75 cl bottles.
Sassy Used to describe fruit in a wine that is lively, jaunty, breezy, etc.
Sboccatura (It.) Disgorged.
Sec (Fr.) Literally "dry", but effectively medium to medium-sweet.
Sekt (Ger.) Sparkling wine produced in Germany, usually by the *cuve close* method.
Soft An attractive smoothness caused when fruit has the upperhand over acidity. This is very desirable, but a wine that is too soft will lack acidity.
Solera (Sp.) System of continually refreshing an established blend with a small amount of new wine.
Sprightly fruitiness A positive outcome of ultra-fruitiness accentuated by volatile acidity. The term is used in this book instead of "VA fruitiness."
Spumante (It.) Literally just "sparkling," but refers to a fully sparkling wine. *See also Fully sparkling.*
Straw Strawlike aromas often blight sparkling wines. Sometimes the aroma is reminiscent of dry straw, other times wet straw, sometimes it is simply strawlike. The aroma possibly comes from the yeast, or rotten grapes, or the reaction of yeast on rotten grapes.
Structure The structure of a wine is based on the balance of its solids (tannin, acidity, sugar, and extract or density of fruit flavor) with the alcohol, and how positively the form feels in the mouth.
Sulfur, SO_2 A preservative used primarily to prevent oxidation. *See also Fixed sulfur, Free sulfur.*
Tank method Another term for *cuve close.*
Terpene A terpene character may indicate Riesling in the blend but is more likely to be due to the base wine being kept unduly long in tank.
Toasty The slow-developing bottle-induced aroma associated with Chardonnay.
Transfer method Decanting under pressure from one bottle to another, not the ideal of *méthode champenoise*
VA Volatile acidity.
VA fruitiness Ultrafruitiness accentuated by volatile acidity. This can be a positive factor, but volatile acidity has such negative connotations that I have used "sprightly fruitiness" instead.
Vanilla *See Oaky.*
Vin de cuvée (Fr.) Made only from the first and therefore the best pressing.
Vin de garde (Fr.) Wine that is capable of great improvement if left to age.
Vin de taille Made from the second pressing.
Vintage The harvest or wine of a single year.
Volatile acidity This has a sweet vinegary aroma and if too obvious may be deemed a fault. But a certain amount of volatile acidity is essential for fruitiness, and high levels can sometimes be a positive factor. *See also Sprightly fruitiness, VA fruitiness.*
Wet straw *See Straw.*

US and Canadian Vineyards

A listing of major vineyards producing sparkling wine in the US and Canada.

US Vineyards

The following list focuses on producers of traditional method sparkling wines in the United States, but includes some producers of transfer and bulk process sparkling wines.

California dominates production, with some 80 percent of the total. It also has a large majority of the traditional method specialists operating on a national or international scale. All California sparkling wines listed here are made by the traditional method; most vintners use the traditional varieties of Champagne: Chardonnay and Pinot Noir. Sparkling wine specialists in the states of Oregon, New Mexico, and Washington largely follow suit but on much more limited scales.

New York is another important producing state with a focus on wines from *Vitis vinifera*. However, some New York wineries use French-American hybrid grapes or native American grapes. In the South and Midwest, French-American and native American varieties dominate, with only a few specialists in these regions working with *Vitis vinifera* varieties.

These wineries specialize in sparkling wine for a national or international market.

* These wineries specialize in sparkling wine but sell only in a local or regional market.

All others produce sparkling wine as a sideline to their main business, which is usually still wine.

ARIZONA

Kokopelli Winery
Rt. 1, Box 961
Willcox, AZ 95643
☎ 520-384-3800
FAX 520-384-5205

Sonoita Vineyard, Ltd.
Canelo Rd.,
3 miles south of Elgin
Tucson, AZ 95718
☎ 520-455-5893

R.W. Webb Winery, Inc.
P. O. Box 669
13605 E. Benson Hwy.
(Frontage Rd.)
Vail, AZ 85641
☎ 520-762-5777
FAX 520-762-5898

ARKANSAS

Post Familie Winery
Rt. 1, Box 1
Altus, AR 72821
☎ 501-468-2741
FAX 501-468-2740

Wiederkehr Winery
Rt. 1, Box 14
Altus, AR 72821
☎ 501-468-2611
FAX 501-468-4791

CALIFORNIA

Acacia
2750 Las Amigas Road
Napa, CA 94559
☎ 707-226-9991
FAX 707-226-1685

 # S. Anderson
1473 Yountville Crossroad
Yountville CA 94599
☎ 707-944-8642
FAX 707-944-8020
Brands: S. Anderson, Tivoli
Products: S. Anderson vintage Napa Valley Brut, vintage Napa Valley Blanc de Noirs; vintage Napa Valley Rose, Tivoli Napa Valley Brut

Beaulieu Vineyard
P. O. Box 219
Rutherford, CA 94573
☎ 707-967-5200
FAX 707-963-5920

Benziger Family Winery
1883 London Ranch Road
Glen Ellen, CA 95442
☎ 707-935-3000
FAX 707-935-3016

 # Codorniu Napa
1345 Henry Road
Napa, CA 94559
☎ 707-224-1672
Product: nonvintage Carneros Brut (luxury cuvee in process)

Culbertson
See: Thornton Winery

 # Domaine Carneros
P. O. Box 5420
Napa, CA 94581
☎ 707-257-0101
FAX 707-257-3020
Products: vintage Carneros Brut, vintage Carneros Blanc de Blancs, vintage Carneros Brut Rose

 # Domaine Chandon
One California Drive
Yountville, CA 94599
☎ 707-944-8844
Brands: Chandon (American market), Shadow Creek (export market)
Products: nonvintage Napa Valley Brut, nonvintage Carneros Blanc de Noirs, nonvintage Napa Valley Reserve, nonvintage Napa Valley etoile, nonvintage Napa Valley etoile Rose, nonvintage Napa Valley Fleur de Vigne

Domaine Montreaux
See: Monticello Vineyards

 # Gloria Ferrer
P. O. Box 1427
Sonoma, CA 95476
☎ 707-996-7256
FAX 707-996-0720
Brand: Gloria Ferrer
Products: nonvintage Sonoma County Brut, nonvintage Sonoma County Blanc de Noirs, vintage vintage Sonoma County Royal Cuvee, vintage Carneros Cuvee, vintage Carneros Cuvee – Late Disgorged, nonvintage Sonoma County Rose

Filsinger
39050 De Portola Road
Temcula, CA 92592
☎ 909-676-4594

homas Fogarty
)37 Alpine Road
ortola, CA 94028
650-851-6777
650-851-5840

. & J. Gallo-Sonoma
)0 Yosemite Blvd.
odesto, CA 95354
209-579-3111
rand: Indigo Hills

Handley Cellars
O. Box 66
hilo, CA 95466
707-895-3876
707-895 2603
oduct: vintage Anderson Valley
rut, vintage Anderson Valley
lanc de Blancs, vintage
nderson valley Brut Rose

ndigo Hills
ee E. & J. Gallo-Sonoma

Iron Horse
786 Ross Station Road
ebastopol, CA 95472
707-887-1507
707-887-1337
roducts: vintage Sonoma-Green
alley Brut, vintage Sonoma-
reen Valley Wedding Cuvee,
ntage Sonoma-Green Valley
es Vrais Amis, vintage Sonoma-
reen Valley Brut Rose

epson
)400 S. Highway 101
kiah, CA 95482
707-468-8936
(no listing)

J Wine Co.
O. Box 6009
1447 Old Redwood Hwy.
ealdsburg, CA 94558
707-431-5410
OT OPEN TO THE PUBLIC
707-431-5400
707-431-5207
rand: J
roduct: vintage Sonoma
ounty Brut, Russian River

endall-Jackson
irway Court
anta Rosa, CA 95403
707-579-3040
7079-579-3128
rand: Kristone

F. Korbel & Bros.
3250 River Road
uerneville, CA 95482
707-887-2294
707-869-2981

Products: nonvintage California Brut, nonvintage California Naturel, nonvintage California Blanc de Blancs, nonvintage California Blanc de Noirs, nonvintage California Chardonnay Champagne, nonvintage California Rose

Kristone
See: Kendall-Jackson

Mirassou Vineyards
3000 Aborn Road
San Jose, CA 95135
408-274-4000
408-270-5881

Robert Mondavi
P. O. Box 106
Oakville, CA 94562
707-226-1395
707-224-5251

Monticello Vineyards
4242 Big Ranch Road
Napa, CA 94558
707-253-2802
707-253-1019
Brand: Domaine Montreaux

 # Mumm Napa Valley
P. O. Drawer 500
Rutherford, CA 94573
707-942-3400
707-942-3469
Products: nonvintage Napa Valley Brut Prestige, nonvintage Napa Valley Blanc de Blancs, nonvintage Napa Valley Blanc de Noirs, vintage Brut 'Winery Lake' Cuvee, vintage Napa Valley Brut Reserve (phasing out), vintage Napa Valley DVX (luxury cuvee), nonvintage Napa Valley Brut Rose

Navarro
P.O. Box 47
5601 Hwy. 128
Philo, CA 95466
707-895-3686
707-895-3647

 # Roederer Estate
383 Fourth Street, Suite 400
Oakland, CA 94607
tel 510-286-2000
fax 510-286-2010
Products: nonvintage Anderson Valley Brut, nonvintage Anderson Valley Brut Rose, vintage Anderson Valley l'Ermitage (luxury cuvee)

Rutherford Benchmarks
P. O. Box 460
Rutherford, CA 95473
800-706-9463
707-963-3593
Brand: Van der Kamp

 # Scharffenberger Cellars
P. O. Box 365
8501 Hwy. 128
Philo, CA 95466
707-895-2065
707-895-2758
Products: nonvintage Mendocino Brut, nonvintage Mendocino Blanc de Blancs, nonvintage Mendocino Rose, nonvintage Mendocino Cremant
N.B. This winery is now using the Pacific Echo label exclusively, but still referring to the winery as Scharffenberger.

 # Schramsberg
1400 Schramsberg Road
Calistoga, CA 94515
707-942-4558
707-942-5943
Brands: Schramsberg, J. Schram, Mirabelle
Products: Schramsberg vintage Napa Valley Brut, vintage Napa Valley Blanc de Blancs, vintage Napa Valley Blanc de Noirs, vintage Napa Valley Reserve, vintage Napa Valley Rose Cuvee de Pinot, vintage Napa Valley Cremant, J. Schram vintage Napa Valley Brut (in effect the luxury cuvee), Mirabelle California Brut

Schug Carneros Estate
602 Bonneau Road
Sonoma, CA 95476
707-939-9363
707-939-9364

Sebastiani Vineyards
P. O. Box AA
Sonoma, CA 95476
707-938-5532.
(no listing)

Thornton Winery
P. O. Box 9008
32575 Rancho California Rd.
Temecula, CA 92589
909-699-.0099
909-699-5536
Brand: Culbertson

Van der Kamp
See: Rutherford Benchmarks

Wente Vineyards
5565 Tesla Road
Livermore, CA 94550
☎ 510-456-2300
FAX 510-447-2972

Windsor Vineyards
P. O. Box 368, Windsor, CA 95492
11455 Old Redwood Rd.
Healdsburg, CA 95448
☎ 707-433-6511
FAX 707-433-8635

COLORADO

The Vineland Corp.
3553 E Road
Palisade, CO 81526
☎ 970-464-7921
FAX 970-464-0574
Brands: Colorado Cellars, Rocky Mountain Vineyards, Colorado Mountain Vineyards

CONNECTICUT

Haight Vineyard
29 Chestnut Hill Road
Litchfield, CT 06759
☎ 860-567-4045

Hopkins Vineyard
Hopkins Road
New Preston, CT 06777
☎ 860-868-7954
FAX 860-868-1768

GEORGIA

Georgia Wines, Inc.
447 High Point Dr.
Chickamauga, GA 30707
☎ 706-937-2177
FAX 706-931-2851

HAWAII

Tedeschi Vineyard, Limited
P. O. Box 953 Ulupalakua
Maui, HI 96970
☎ 808-878-1266
FAX 808-876-0127
Brand: Maui Brut

IDAHO

Camas Winery
110 S. Main St., Moscow, ID 83843
☎ 208-882-0214
FAX 208-882-0214
Brands: Camas Winery, Life Force

*** Cocolalla Winery**
14550 E. Bunco Road
Athol, ID 83801
☎ 208-683-2473
Brand: Cocolalla-in-the-Selkirks

Ste. Chapelle Winery
19348 Lowell, Caldwell, ID 83605
☎ 208-459-7222
FAX 208-459-9783

Weston
16316 Orchard Ave.
Caldwell, ID 83605
☎ 208-459-2631
Brands: Weston, Idaho Vineyards

ILLINOIS

Galena Cellars
P. O. Box 207
515 S. Main St.
Galena, IL 61036
☎ 815-777-3330
FAX 815-777-3335
Brands: Galena Cellars, Lawlor Family

Thompson Winery Co.
P. O. Box 127
Monee, IL 60449
☎ 708-534-8050
FAX 708-534-8587
Brand: Pere Marquette

INDIANA

Oliver Wine Co.
8024 N. State Road 37
Bloomington, IN 47408
☎ 812-876-5800
FAX 812-876-9309
Brands: Oliver, Camelot

KENTUCKY

Premium Brands Inc.
P. O. Box 785
Bardstown, KY 40004
☎ 502-348-0081
Brand: Voltiere

MAINE

Bartlett Maine Estate
R.R. #1, Box 598
Gouldsboro, ME 04607
☎ 207-546-2408
FAX 207-546-2554

MARYLAND

Boordy Vineyards
12820 Long Green Pike
Hydes, MD 21082
☎ 410-592-5015
FAX 410-592-5385

MASSACHUSETTS

Chicama Vineyards
Stoney Hill Road
West Tisbury, MA 02575
☎ 508-693-0309
FAX 508-693-5628
Brand: SeaMist Sparkling Wine

Westport Rivers Vineyards & Winery
417 Hixbridge Road
Westport, MA 02790
☎ 508-636-3423
FAX 508-636-4133

MICHIGAN

Chateau Chantal
15900 Rue de Vin
Traverse City, MI 49686
☎ 616-223-4110
FAX 616-223-4110

Chateau Grand Traverse
12239 Center Road
Traverse City, MI 49686
☎ 616-223-7355
FAX 616-223-4105
Brands: Chateau Grand Traverse, O'Keefe Cellars, Old Mission Winery

Fenn Valley Vineyards
6130 122d Ave.
Fennville, MI 49408
☎ 616-561-2396
FAX 616-561-2973

Good Harbor Vineyards
34 South Manitou Trail
Lake Lee Lanau, MI
☎ 616-256-7165
FAX 616-256-7378

L. Mawby Vineyards & Winery
4519 S. Elm Valley Road
Suttons Bay, MI 49682
☎ 616-271-3522

*** Sharon Mills Winery**
5701 Sharon Hollow Road
Manchester, MI 48158
☎ 313-428-9160

St. Julien Wine Company
P. O. Box 127
716 Kalamazoo St.
Paw Paw, MI 49079
☎ 616-657-5568
FAX 616-657-5743

Tabor Hill
185 Mt. Tabor Hill Rd.
Buchanan, MI 49107
☎ 616-422-1161
FAX 616-422-2787
Brand: Grand Mark

Warner Vineyards
P. O. Box 269
706 Kalamazoo St.
Paw Paw, MI 49079
☎ 616-657-3165
FAX 616-657-4154

MINNESOTA

J. Bird Wines
36337 Polk St.
Stanchfield, MN 55080
☎ 612-689-0237

MISSOURI

Augusta Winery
P. O. Box 8
5601 High St.
Augusta, MO 63332
☎ 314-228-4301
FAX 314-228-4683
Brands: Augusta Winery, Cedar Ridge, Anthony Winery

Hermannhof
P. O. Box 271
330 E. First St.
Hermann, MO 65041
☎ 573-486-5959
FAX 573-486-3415

Montelle
P. O. Box 147
Hwy. 99
Augusta, MO 63332
☎ 314-228-4464
FAX 314-228-4799

St. James
540 Sidney St.
St. James, MO 65559
☎ 573-265-7912
FAX 573-265-6200

***Winery of the Little Hills**
501 S. Main St.
St. Charles, MO 63301
☎ 314-946-9339

NEW JERSEY

Alba Vineyard
269 Rt. 627
Milford, NY 08848
☎ 908-995-7800
FAX 908-995-7155

Amalthea Cellars
267-A Hayes Mill Rd
Atco, NJ 08004
☎ 609-768-8585

Amwell Valley Vineyard
80 Old York Road
Ringoes, NJ 08551
☎ 908-788-5852
FAX 908-788-1030

Kings Road Vineyard
Box 360, Rt. 579
Asbury, NJ 08802
☎ 908-479-6611
FAX 908-479-1366

Tamuzza Vineyards
P. O. Box 247
Hope, NJ 07844
☎ 908-459-5878
FAX 908-459-5560
Brand: Domaine St. Gregory

Tomasello Winery
225 White Horse Pike
Hammonton, NJ 08037
☎ 609-561-0567
FAX 609-561-8617

NEW MEXICO

Elephant Butte
P. O. Box 1606
Truth or Consequences, NM 87901
☎ 888-857-9463 (toll-free)
FAX 505-894-9156
Brand: Mont Jallon
Products: Brut, Blanc de Noirs, Blanc de Blancs.

Gruet
8400 Pan-American Freeway NE
Albuquerque, NM 87113
☎ 505-821-0055
FAX 505-821-0066
Products: Brut, Blanc de Blancs

New Mexico Wineries
P. O. Box 1180
Deming, NM 88031
☎ 505-546-9324
FAX 505-546-7905
Brand: D. H. Lescombes

San Felipe
2011 Mountain Rd.
Albuquerque, NM 87104
☎ 505-843-8171
FAX 505-843-8107

NEW YORK

Anthony Road
1225 Anthony Road
Penn Yan, NY 14527
☎ 315-536-2182
FAX 315-536-5851

Benmarl
P. O. Box 549
Marlboro, NY 12542
☎ 9149-236-4265
FAX 914-236-7270
Brand: Cuvee du Vigneron

Bully Hill
8843 Greyton H. Taylor Memorial Drive
Hammondsport, NY 14840
☎ 607-868-3610
FAX 607-868-3205

Canandaigua Wine Co. Inc.
116 Buffalo St.
Canandaigua, NY 14424
☎ 716-394-7900
FAX 716-394-6017
Brand: Great Western

*** Chateau Frank**
9683 Middle Road
Hammondsport, NY 14840
☎ 607-868-4885

Clinton Vineyards
Schultzville Road
Clinton Corners, NY 12514
☎ 914-266-5372
FAX 212-421-1670

Four Chimneys Farm Winery
211 Hall Road
Himrod, NY 14842
☎ 607-243-7502
FAX 607-243-8156
Brand: Coronation

 # Glenora
5435 Route 14
Dundee, NY 14837
tel 607-243-5511
fax 607-243-5514
Products: vintage Brut, vintage Blanc de Blancs

Hazlitt
P. O. Box 53, Hector, NY 14841
☎ 607-546-9463
FAX 607-546-5712

Hosmer
6999 Rt. 89
Orid, NY 14521
☎ 607-869-3393
FAX 607-869-9409

Jamesport Vineyards
P. O. Box 842
Main Road
Jamesport, NY 11947
☎ 516-9722-5256
FAX 516-722-5256

Knapp Vineyards
2770 County Road 128
Romulus, NY 14541
☎ 607-869-9271
FAX 607-869-3212

Lamoreaux Landing Wine Cellars
9224 Rt. 414
Lodi, NY 14860
☎ 607-582-6011
FAX 607-582-6010

Lenz Winery
Main Road
Peconic, NY 11958
☎ 516-734-6010
FAX 516-734-6069

Lucas Vineyards
3862 County Road 150
Interlaken, NY 14847
☎ 607-532-4825
FAX 607-532-8580

Pindar
Rt. 25, Main Road, Box 332
Peconic, NY 11958
☎ 516-734-6200
FAX 516-734-6205

Regent Champagne Cellars
200 Blue Point Road
Highland, NY 12528
☎ 914-691-7296
FAX 914-691-7298

Sagpond Vineyards
P. O .Box 1768
Bridgehampton, NY 11932
☎ 516-537-5106
FAX 516-537-5107
Brand: La Ferme Martin

Swedish Hill Vineyards
4565 Rt. 414
Romulus, NY 14541
☎ 315-549-8326
FAX 315-549-8477

Wagner Vineyards
9322 Rt. 414, Lodi, NY 14860
☎ 607-582-6450
FAX 607-582-6446

Herman J. Wiemer Vineyard
P. O. Box 38, Rt. 14
Dundee, NY 14837
☎ 607-243-7971
FAX 607-243-7983

Woodbury Vineyards
3230 S. Roberts Rd.
Fredonia, NY 14063
☎ 716-679-9463
FAX 716-679-9464

NORTH CAROLINA

Biltmore Estate
One North Park Square
Asheville, NC 28801
☎ 704-274-6280
FAX 704-274-6282
Brand: Chateau Biltmore

Duplin Wine Cellars
P. O. Box 756
Rose Hill, NC 28458
☎ 910-289-3888
FAX 910-289-3094

N.C. Waldensian
1530–19th St. S.W.
Hickory, NC 28602
☎ 704-327-3867
FAX 704-327-8279

OHIO

Chalet Debonne
7743 Doty Rd.
Madison, OH 44057
☎ 216-466-3485
FAX 216-466-6753

Firelands Wine Co.
917 Bardshar Rd.
Sandusky, OH 44870
☎ 419-625-5474
FAX 419-625-4887

Klingshirn
33050 Webber Rd.
Avon Lake, OH 44012
☎ 216-933-6666
FAX 216-933-7896

Lonz
Middle Bass Island
Middle Bass, OH 43446
☎ 419-285-5411

Markko Winery
4500 S. Ridge Rd.
Conneaut, OH 44030
☎ 216-593-3197
FAX 216-599-7022
Brand: Excelsior

Moyer Vineyards
3859 US Rt. 52
Manchester, OH 45144
☎ 937-549-2957

Valley Vineyards
2276 E. US R. 22
Morrow, OH 45152
☎ 513-899-2485
FAX 513-899-9022

OREGON

 # Argyle
(Dundee Wine Co.)
P. O. Box 280
691 Hwy. 9W
Dundee, OR 97115
☎ 503-538-8520
FAX 503-538-2055

Chateau Benoit
6580 N.E. Mineral Springs Rd.
Carlton, OR 97111
☎ 503-864-2991
FAX 503-864-2203

Cooper Mountain Vineyard
9480 S.W. Grabhorn
Beaverton, OR 97007
☎ 503-649-0027
FAX 503-649-0702

Duck Pond Cellars
P. O. Box 429
Dundee, OR 97115
☎ 503-538-3199
FAX 503-538-3190
Brand: Arterberry

Edgefield
2126 S.W. Halsey
Troutdale, OR 97060
☎ 503-665-2992
FAX 503-661-1968

Eola Hills
501 S. Pacific Hwy. 99 W.
Rickreall, OR 97371
☎ 503-623-2405
FAX 503-623-0350

Flynn Vineyards
2200 W. Pacific Hwy.
Rickreall, OR 97371
☎ 503-623-8683
FAX 503-623-0908

Laurel Ridge
P. O. Box 456
46350 N.W. David Hill Rd.
Forest Grove, OR 97116
☎ 503-359-5436
FAX 503-359-0366

LaVelle Vineyards
89697 Sheffler Rd.
Elmira, OR 97437
☎ 541-935-9406
FAX 541-935-7202

Orchard Heights
6057 Orchard Heights Rd. N.W.
Salem, OR 97304
☎ 503-391-7308
FAX 503.391-7308

Rex Hill
30835 N. Hwy. 99 W.
Newberg, OR 97132
☎ 503-538-0666
FAX 503-538-1409

St. Innocent
1360 Tandem Ave. N.E.
Salem, OR 97303
☎ 503-378-1526
FAX 503-378-1041

PENNSYLVANIA

The Chaddsford Winery
632 Baltimore Pike
Chadds Ford, PA 19317
☎ 610-388-6221
FAX 610-388-0360

Conneaut Cellars
P. O. Box 5072, Rt. 322
Conneaut Lake, PA 16316
☎ 814-382-3999
FAX 814-382-6151

Mazza Vineyards
11815 East Lake Rd.
North East, PA 16428
☎ 814-725-8695
FAX 814-725-3948

Penn Shore Vineyards
10225 East Lake Rd.
North East, PA 16428
☎ 814-725-8688

TEXAS

Cap Rock
Rt. 6, Box 713K
Lubbock, TX 79423
☎ 806-863-2704
FAX 806-863-2712

Delaney Vineyards & Winery
2000 Champagne Blvd.
Grapevine, TX 76051
☎ 817-481-5668
FAX 817-251-8119

La Buena Vida (Smith Estates)
650 Vineyard Ln.
Springtown, TX 76802
☎ 817-481-9463
FAX 817-421-3635

Llano Estacado
P. O. Box 3487,
Lubbock, TX 79452
☎ 806-745-2258
FAX 806-748-1674

Hill Country Cellars
P. O. Box 26146
Austin, TX 78755
☎ 512-259-2000
FAX 512-259-2092
Brand: Moyer

VIRGINIA

Barboursville
P. O. Box 136, 17655 Winery Rd.
Barboursville VA 22923
☎ 540-832-3824
FAX 540-832-7522

Ingleside Plantation Vineyards
P. O. Box 1038, Rt. 638
Oak Grove, VA 22443
☎ 804-224-8687
FAX 804-224-8573

Oasis Vineyard
14141 Hume Rd.
Hume, VA 22639
☎ 540-635-7627
FAX 540-635-4563

Prince Michel Vineyards
HCR 4, Box 77, Leon, VA 22725
☎ 540-547-3707
FAX 540-547-3088

WASHINGTON

Arbor Crest
4705 N. Fruithill Rd.
Spokane, WA 99207
☎ 509-927-9463
FAX 509-927-0574

Blackwood Canyon
53258 N. Sunset Dr. N.E.
Benton City, WA 99320
☎ 509-588-6249
FAX 509-588-5195

Covey Run
1500 Vintage Rd.
Zillah, WA 98953
☎ 509-829-6235
FAX 509-829-6895

*** Domaine Whittlesey Mark**
5318-22d Ave. N.W.
Seattle, WA 98117
☎ 425-451-9525

 # Domaine Ste. Michelle
P. O. Box 1976
14111 NE 145th St.
Woodinville, WA 98072
☎ 509-875-2061
FAX 509-875-2568
Products: nonvintage Columbia Valley Brut, nonvintage Columbia Valley Blanc de Noirs

Horizon's Edge
4530 E. Zillah Dr.
Zillah, WA 98953
☎ 509-829-6401

Mont Elise
Box 28, Bingen, WA 98605
☎ 509-493-3001

*** Mountain Dome**
E. 16315 Temple Rd.
Spokane, WA 99207
☎ 509-928-2788
FAX 509-922-8078

Preston
502 E. Vineyard Dr.
Pasco, WA 99301
☎ 509-545-1990
FAX 509-545-1098

Tagaris
P. O. Box 5433
Pasco, WA 99301
☎ 509-547-3590
FAX 509-547-8264

Willow Crest
55002 N. Gap Rd.
Prosser, WA 99350
☎ 509-786-7999

WISCONSIN

*** Bountiful Harvest**
16008 Pine Tree Rd.
Highland, WI 53543
☎ 608-592-5254

Cedar Creek
N. 70 W. 6340 Bridge Rd.
Cedarburg, WI 53012
☎ 414-377-8020
FAX 414-375-9428

Wollersheim
P. O. Box 87, Hwy. 188
Prairie du Sac, WI 53578
☎ 608-643-6515
FAX 608-643-8149

Canadian Vineyards

Provincial appellations, such as Ontario, use 100 percent Canadian-grown grapes, a minimum of 85 percent from the province indicated. Specific appellations, such as Okanagan Valley, are 100 percent from the province named, a minimum of 85 percent from the area named.

Estate bottled wines and wines designated by vineyard names are 100 percent from grapes owned or controlled by the winery or vineyard indicated.

BRITISH COLUMBIA

Andres Wines Ltd. (BC)
2120 Vintner St.
Port Moody, BC V3H 1WB
☎ 604-937-3411
FAX 604-937-5487

Calona Wines Ltd.
1125 Richter St.
Kelowna, BC V1Y 2K6
☎ 250-762-3332
FAX 250-762-2999

Le Comte Estate Winery
RR1, Box 498
Okanagan Falls, BC V0H 1RO
☎ 604-497-8267
FAX 604-497-8073

Okanagan Cellars
N Hwy 97, Box 1650
Oliver, BC V0H 1T0
☎ 604-498-4981
FAX 604-498-6505

Sumac Ridge Estate Winery
P. O. Box 307
Summerland, BC V0H 1Z0
☎ 604-494-0451
FAX 604-494-3456

Summerhill Estate Winery
RR4, 4870 Chute Lake Rd.
Keiowna, BC V1Y 7R3
☎ 604-764-8000
FAX 604-764-3456

NEW BRUNSWICK

Vincor International
P. O. Box 150
Scoudouc, NB E0A 1N0
☎ 902-453-0070
FAX 902-532-4445

NOVA SCOTIA

Andres Wines (Atlantic)
P. O. Box 724, Truro, NS B2N 5E8
☎ 902-895-2874
FAX 902-893-4976

Sainte Famille Wines Ltd
RR2, Dudley Park Ln.
Falmouth, NS B0P 1L0
☎ 902-798-8311
FAX 902-798-9418

ONTARIO

Andres Wines Ltd.
Q.E.W. & Kelson Rd., P. O. Box 10550, Winona, ONT L8E 5S4
☎ 905-643-4131
FAX 905-643-4944

Chateau des Charmes Wines
1025 York Rd., P. O. Box 280
St. David's, ONT L0S 1P0
☎ 905-262-4219
FAX 905-262-5548

Colio Wines of Canada
1 Colio Dr., Box 372
Harrow, ONT N0R 1G0
☎ 519-738-2241
FAX 519-738-3070

Hillebrand Estates Winery
RR2, Hwy. 55, Niagara-on-the-Lake, ONT L0S 1J0
☎ 905-468-3201
FAX 905-468-4789

Inniskillin Wines
RR1, Niagara Parkway, Niagara-on-the-Lake, ONT L0S 1J0
☎ 905-468-2187
FAX 905-468-5355

Jackson-Triggs Vintners
4887 Dorchester Rd.
Niagara Falls, ONT L2E 6N8
☎ 905-358-7141
FAX 905-358-7750

Magnotta Winery Estates
110 Cidermill Ave.
Vaughn, ONT L4K 4L9
☎ 905-738-9463
FAX 905-738-5551

Pelee Island Winery
455 Hwy. 18 E
Kingsville, ONT N9Y 2K5
☎ 519-733-6551
FAX 519-733-6553

Vincor International, Inc.
6611 Edwards Blvd.
Mississauga, ONT L5T 2H8
☎ 905-564-6900
FAX 905-564-6909

Vinoteca Winery
61 Caster Ave.
Woodbridge, ONT L4L 5Z2
☎ 905-856-5700
FAX 905-856-8208

QUEBEC

Celliers Du Monde, Inc.
50 Rue De la Barre-Bur 110
Longueuil, QUE J4K 5G2
☎ 514-878-3050
FAX 514-651-5453

Dumont Vins & Spiritueux
175 Marieville Rd.
Rougemont, QUE J0L 1M0
☎ 514-861-2404
FAX 514-469-4879

Les Vins Andres du Quebec Ltee.
3755 Rue Picard
St. Hyacinthe, QUE J2S 1H3
☎ 514-773-7468
FAX 514-773-0789

Paul Masson & Cie Ltee.
2101 Trans-Canada Hwy.
Dorral, QUE H9P 1J1
☎ 514-683-2200
FAX 514-683-3494

Verger Du Minot
376 Covey-Hill
Hemmingford, QUE J0L 1H0
☎ 514-247-3111
FAX 514-247-2684

Vignoble De L'Orpailleur
1086 RT 202
Dunham QUE J0E 1M0
☎ 514-295-2763
FAX 514-295-3112

Vignoble des Pins
136 Grand Sabrevois
Sabrevois, QUE J0J 2G0
☎ 514-347-1073
FAX 514-347-1073

Vincor International, Inc.
175 Chemin marieville Rd.
Rougemont, QUE J0L 1M0
☎ 514-469-3104
FAX 514-469-2175

Tasting Notes

Blank forms for recording your own observations about individual Champagnes and sparkling wines.

How to Use the Tasting Notes

These blank forms are intended for readers who want to record their own observations about Champagnes and sparkling wines. They are based on the author's personal tasting notebook. It is surprising how even dedicated professionals can neglect to record the most essential information about a wine, such as whether it is white or *rosé*, and dry or sweet, let alone such details as the level of acidity and depth of color. This might seem too obvious to record at the time, yet there are so many wines that could, by name alone, be one of several different styles. Formulated specifically for sparkling wine, the forms allow you to record the most important elements of taste and quality by checking or circling boxes.

Sweetness, Depth of Color, and Body
An objective assessment should be made of these factors. Limpidity is assumed to be good; if not, the wine is faulty.

Nose, Palate, and Finish
These boxes are for purely hedonistic judgment. This kind of evaluation should stand even if the wine is not true to type.

Score
An overall score out of 100 *(see p67)* can be awarded to rank the wine easily against others.

Wine name:
Price: Available from:
Wine type: White ☐ Rosé ☐ Red ☐

Score

Sweetness	Depth of color	Body	Nose	Palate	Finish
			Faulty	*Faulty*	*Faulty*
Extremely dry	*Watery*	*Very light*	*Below par*	*Below par*	*Below par*
Dry	*Light*	*Light*	*Average*	*Average*	*Average*
Medium dry	*Light–medium*	*Light–medium*	*Fair*	*Fair*	*Fair*
Medium sweet	*Medium–full*	*Medium–full*	*Very good*	*Very good*	*Very good*
Sweet	*Full*	*Full*	*Excellent*	*Excellent*	*Excellent*
Intensely sweet	*Opaque*	*Massive*	*Great*	*Great*	*Great*

Mousse	Acidity	Evolution
Firm	*Too much*	*Peak*
Soft	*Balanced*	*Can keep*
Bubbles	*Not enough*	*Lay down*
Tiny		
Medium		
Coarse		

Status: *Great classic or great gulping*

Comments:

Status
This follows from the "Great" option under Nose, Palate, and Finish. Sometimes a wine can be so stunning that it warrants the accolade of "Great," yet might simply be a "gulping" wine, rather than a classic.

Mousse
The degree of effervescence and bubble size should be indicated.

Acidity and Evolution
The Acidity and Evolution boxes are quick alternatives to putting more details under *Comments*.

Comments
Keep these short. The fewer fruits, flowers, spices, nuts, etc., used in a description, the clearer your picture of that wine when you consult the notes later.

Wine name:

Price: Available from:

Wine type: *White* ☐ *Rosé* ☐ *Red* ☐

Score

Sweetness	Depth of color	Body	Nose	Palate	Finish
			Faulty	*Faulty*	*Faulty*
Extremely dry	*Watery*	*Very light*	*Below par*	*Below par*	*Below par*
Dry	*Light*	*Light*	*Average*	*Average*	*Average*
Medium dry	*Light–medium*	*Light–medium*	*Fair*	*Fair*	*Fair*
Medium sweet	*Medium–full*	*Medium–full*	*Very good*	*Very good*	*Very good*
Sweet	*Full*	*Full*	*Excellent*	*Excellent*	*Excellent*
Intensely sweet	*Opaque*	*Massive*	*Great*	*Great*	*Great*

Status	*Great classic or great gulping*

Mousse	Acidity	Evolution
Firm	*Too much*	*Peak*
Soft	*Balanced*	*Can keep*
Bubbles	*Not enough*	*Lay down*
Tiny		
Medium		
Coarse		

Comments:

Wine name:

Price: Available from:

Wine type: *White* ☐ *Rosé* ☐ *Red* ☐

Score

Sweetness	Depth of color	Body	Nose	Palate	Finish
			Faulty	*Faulty*	*Faulty*
Extremely dry	*Watery*	*Very light*	*Below par*	*Below par*	*Below par*
Dry	*Light*	*Light*	*Average*	*Average*	*Average*
Medium dry	*Light–medium*	*Light–medium*	*Fair*	*Fair*	*Fair*
Medium sweet	*Medium–full*	*Medium–full*	*Very good*	*Very good*	*Very good*
Sweet	*Full*	*Full*	*Excellent*	*Excellent*	*Excellent*
Intensely sweet	*Opaque*	*Massive*	*Great*	*Great*	*Great*

Status	*Great classic or great gulping*

Mousse	Acidity	Evolution
Firm	*Too much*	*Peak*
Soft	*Balanced*	*Can keep*
Bubbles	*Not enough*	*Lay down*
Tiny		
Medium		
Coarse		

Comments:

Wine name:

Price: Available from:

Wine type: White ☐ Rosé ☐ Red ☐

Score

Sweetness	Depth of color	Body	Nose	Palate	Finish
			Faulty	Faulty	Faulty
Extremely dry	Watery	Very light	Below par	Below par	Below par
Dry	Light	Light	Average	Average	Average
Medium dry	Light–medium	Light–medium	Fair	Fair	Fair
Medium sweet	Medium–full	Medium–full	Very good	Very good	Very good
Sweet	Full	Full	Excellent	Excellent	Excellent
Intensely sweet	Opaque	Massive	Great	Great	Great

Mousse	Acidity	Evolution
Firm	Too much	Peak
Soft	Balanced	Can keep
Bubbles	Not enough	Lay down
Tiny		
Medium		
Coarse		

Status	Great classic or great gulping

Comments:

Wine name:

Price: Available from:

Wine type: White ☐ Rosé ☐ Red ☐

Score

Sweetness	Depth of color	Body	Nose	Palate	Finish
			Faulty	Faulty	Faulty
Extremely dry	Watery	Very light	Below par	Below par	Below par
Dry	Light	Light	Average	Average	Average
Medium dry	Light–medium	Light–medium	Fair	Fair	Fair
Medium sweet	Medium–full	Medium–full	Very good	Very good	Very good
Sweet	Full	Full	Excellent	Excellent	Excellent
Intensely sweet	Opaque	Massive	Great	Great	Great

Mousse	Acidity	Evolution
Firm	Too much	Peak
Soft	Balanced	Can keep
Bubbles	Not enough	Lay down
Tiny		
Medium		
Coarse		

Status	Great classic or great gulping

Comments:

Wine name:

Price: Available from:

Wine type: *White* ☐ *Rosé* ☐ *Red* ☐

Score

Sweetness	Depth of color	Body	Nose	Palate	Finish
			Faulty	*Faulty*	*Faulty*
Extremely dry	*Watery*	*Very light*	*Below par*	*Below par*	*Below par*
Dry	*Light*	*Light*	*Average*	*Average*	*Average*
Medium dry	*Light–medium*	*Light–medium*	*Fair*	*Fair*	*Fair*
Medium sweet	*Medium–full*	*Medium–full*	*Very good*	*Very good*	*Very good*
Sweet	*Full*	*Full*	*Excellent*	*Excellent*	*Excellent*
Intensely sweet	*Opaque*	*Massive*	*Great*	*Great*	*Great*

Status	*Great classic or great gulping*

Mousse	Acidity	Evolution
Firm	*Too much*	*Peak*
Soft	*Balanced*	*Can keep*
Bubbles	*Not enough*	*Lay down*
Tiny		
Medium		
Coarse		

Comments:

Wine name:

Price: Available from:

Wine type: *White* ☐ *Rosé* ☐ *Red* ☐

Score

Sweetness	Depth of color	Body	Nose	Palate	Finish
			Faulty	*Faulty*	*Faulty*
Extremely dry	*Watery*	*Very light*	*Below par*	*Below par*	*Below par*
Dry	*Light*	*Light*	*Average*	*Average*	*Average*
Medium dry	*Light–medium*	*Light–medium*	*Fair*	*Fair*	*Fair*
Medium sweet	*Medium–full*	*Medium–full*	*Very good*	*Very good*	*Very good*
Sweet	*Full*	*Full*	*Excellent*	*Excellent*	*Excellent*
Intensely sweet	*Opaque*	*Massive*	*Great*	*Great*	*Great*

Status	*Great classic or great gulping*

Mousse	Acidity	Evolution
Firm	*Too much*	*Peak*
Soft	*Balanced*	*Can keep*
Bubbles	*Not enough*	*Lay down*
Tiny		
Medium		
Coarse		

Comments:

Author's Acknowledgments

I am as pleased as Punch to work with Dorling Kindersley on any book, as this publisher is second to none when it comes to design, illustration, presentation, and marketing, but I am particularly grateful to Christopher Davis, whose personal enthusiasm for this guide steamrollered it through the normally lengthy acceptance phase that every author has to face.

On the editorial side, my first thanks must go to Rosalyn Thiro, who was on my case daily. From personal knowledge I am only too well aware that, until now, most annual guides have had to skimp on design, forsake color, and be printed on low-grade paper, which leaves me eternally indebted to Anthony Limerick, whose artistic talents have made this book a wine guide any author would be proud of. Also at Dorling Kindersley I must thank Vivien Crump and David Lamb.

My gratitude cannot be properly expressed to the hundreds of producers who at great expense sent me samples from all four corners of the wine world, but I hope they all realize how appreciative I am, even those whose wines failed to pass muster (perhaps a new vintage or a different *cuvée* may qualify in a future edition). I am also greatly obliged to the following, who either organized a large centralized tasting or arranged for an industry-wide shipment of samples to my tasting facility: Maureen Ashley MW (for freelance services on behalf of Italian producers); Luis Avides Moreira (Wines of Portugal); Nelly Blau Picard (UPECB, Burgundy); Daniel Brennan (formerly of Wines from Spain); Stéphane Chaboud (Syndicat des Vignerons de Saint Péray); Tina Cody (Wines of South Africa); Maria do Cé Hespanha (Wines of Portugal); Nicole Dufour (CIVAS, Anjou-Saumur); Mme Faure (Syndicat de Die); Roger Fisher (T&CVA for English and Welsh sparkling wines); Dieter Greiner (Deutsches Weininstitut); Rosemary Hall (Wines of Austria); Sarah Hately (Westbury Blake for Wines of Canada); Graham Hines (Wines from Spain); Jane Hunt MW (formerly Wines of South Africa); Tony Keys (formerly of Australian Wine Bureau); Jon Leighton (Thames Valley Vineyards for English and Welsh sparkling wines); Georgina McDermott (Syndicat des Maisons de Saumur); Lisa McGovern (New Zealand Wine Guild); Steffen Maus (The German Wine Information Service); Françoise Peretti (Champagne Information Bureau); Hazel Murphy and Georgie Beach (Australian Wine Bureau); Emma Roberts (SOPEXA, France); Olivier Sohler (SPCA, Alsace); James S. Trezise (New York Wine & Grape Foundation); Barbara Tysome (German Wine Information Service); Michelle Vernoux (SVR Bordeaux); Emma Wellings (formerly Westbury Blake for Wines of Canada); and Victoria Williams (Wines of Chile).

I must also thank those from individual estates who coordinated the collection, information, and samples from other producers, including Colin Cameron (Caxton Tower for Dragon Seal, China); Rémy Gauthier (Varichon & Clerc, Seysell); Jeff Grier (Villiera Estate, South Africa); Jane Hunter (Hunter's Wines, New Zealand); and Alex and Claire Taylor (Canto Perlic, Gaillac); and, last but not least, Jeff Porter of Evenlode Press, who provided invaluable logistics support.

My sincere apologies for any omissions.

DK Publishing, Inc. Acknowledgments
Barbara Minton, Joan Nixon, Robert Thompson

Picture Researchers
Brigitte Arora, Ellen Root

Special Photography and Design
Andy Crawford, Steve Gorton, Neil Lukas, Dave Pugh

Special thanks to Bernard Higton for the initial design.

Dorling Kindersley would like to thank the following companies for providing items to be photographed: **Codorníu, Matthias Deis, Freiherr zu Knyphausen, Nyetimber, Screwpull International, Vilmart, Winzersekt Sprendlingen**

Picture Credits
t – top; tl – top left; tlc – top left center; tc – top center; trc – top right center; tr – top right; cla – center left above; ca – center above; cra – center right above; cl – center left; c – center; cr – center right; clb – center left below; cb – center below; crb – center right below; bl – bottom left; b – bottom; bc – bottom center; bcl – bottom center left; br – bottom right; bra – bottom right above; brb – bottom right below; d – detail

Allsport: Adrian Murrell 56t; **Bellavista**: 48b; **Guido Berlucchi**: 49t, 50b; **Billecart-Salmon:** 22t; **Bollinger**: 11t, 23t/c/b; **Bouvet-Ladubay**: 39b; **Ca'del Bosco**: 51t; **CBI**, London: 11crb; **Cephas**: Andy Christodolo 2–3; Kevin Judd 59t; Alain Proust 61t, 62t; Mick Rock 13t, 16t, 24t, 27c, 35t, 36br, 37t, 44t, 47b, 55b; **Codorníu**: 41tr/cl, 43b; **Corbis**: W. Wayne Lockwood, M. D. 12t; **Culver Pictures**: 52t; **Deutsches Weininstitut**: 46t; **DIAF**, Paris: Jean-Daniel Sudres 1 (insert), 4t, 19t; Daniel Thierry 6t; **E.T. Archive**: 8t, 54t; **Mary Evans Picture Library**: 8b, 9cr/br, 45t, 46c, 47t; **Ferrari**: Joachim Falco 5c; 48t, 51b; **Freixenet**: 40t, 42b, 43t, 40–41b; **Hulton-Getty**: 9t; **Gosset**: 21b, 24bl; **Gramona**: 42t; **Charles Heidsieck**: 17, 25cr; De Visu 25t; **Seppelt/Image Library, State Library of New South Wales**: 58b; **Jackson Estate**: 59b; **Jacquesson & Fils**: 26t/b; **Kobal Collection**: 52c; **Krug**: 14t, 27t; **Laurent-Perrier**: 28t; **Moët & Chandon**: 16c, 20b, 29b; **Pol Roger**: 31t/c/b; **Janet Price**: 12b, 32b; **Retrograph Archive**, London: Martin Breese 16b, 29t; **Louis Roederer**: 9bl; Jean-Claude Rouzaud 30t; Michel Jolyot 30b; **Root Stock**, Ludwigsburg: Hendrik Holler 4–5b, 36bl, 38b, 44b, 52–53b, 54b, 56b, 61b, 62b; **Ruinart**: 18c; *Champagne Ruinart, Rheims*, Alphonse Mucha @ ADAGP, Paris and DACS, London 1998 32r; **Salon**: 33b; **Scope**: Bernard Galeron 50t; Michel Guillard 22b; Eric Quentin 20t; **Southcorp Wines Europe**: 57bl; **SOPEXA (UK)**: 39T; **Topham Picturepoint**: Ulf Berglund 60t; **Veuve Clicquot Ponsardin**: 5t, 11cra/b, 34t/b; **Villiera Estate**: 63t/b; **Vilmart & Ciel**: 35b; **Visual Arts Library**: Collection Kharbine-Tapabor 9cl, 18b, 21t, 10, 33t, 55t; **John Wyand**: 64t; **Yalumba**: 57br, 58t

Back Jacket: **Cephas:** Mick Rock top left; StockFood bottom; **The Image Bank:** David de Lossy top right